DEAR
FRANCESCA

from the family of

VALVONA & CROLLA ®

19 Elm Row, Edinburgh EH7 4AA
Tel: +44 (0)131 556 6066
Fax: +44 (0)131 556 1668

www.valvonacrolla.com
shop online and mail order

DEAR
FRANCESCA

An Italian Journey of
Recipes Recounted with Love

MARY
CONTINI

EBURY
PRESS

Ali nostri nonni, un' abbraccio d'amore

Cesido behind the counter of his shop in Cockenzie

First published in Great Britain in 2002
This paperback edition first published in 2003

7 9 10 8 6

Text and photographs © Mary Contini 2002

Special photography © Mitch Jenkins 2002

Mary Contini has asserted her right to be identified as the author of this work under the Copyright, Designs and Patents Act 1988.

First published by Ebury Press

Random House, 20 Vauxhall Bridge Road, London SW1V 2SA

Random House Australia (Pty) Limited
20 Alfred Street, Milsons Point, Sydney, New South Wales 2061, Australia
Random House New Zealand Limited
18 Poland Road, Glenfield, Auckland 10, New Zealand
Random House (Pty) Limited
Isle of Houghton, Corner of Boundary Road & Carse O'Gowrie,
Houghton 2198, South Africa
The Random House Group Limited Reg. No. 954009

www.randomhouse.co.uk

A CIP catalogue record for this book is available from the British Library.

Salsiccia Fonteluna®, Big Phil® and Fior' Fiore® extra virgin olive oil are registered trademarks.

Editor: Susan Fleming
Special photography of author: Mitch Jenkins

Map: Katy Hepburn

ISBN 9780091892357 (from January 2007)
ISBN 009189235X

Papers used by Ebury Press are natural, recyclable products made from wood grown in sustainable forests.

Printed and bound in Great Britain by Cox and Wyman

CONTENTS

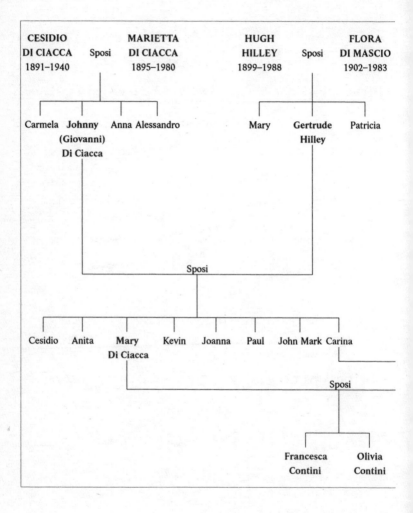

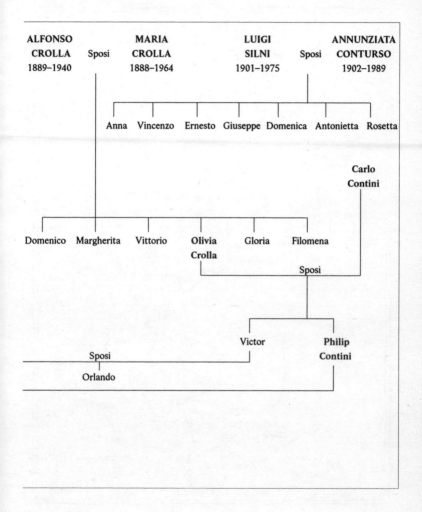

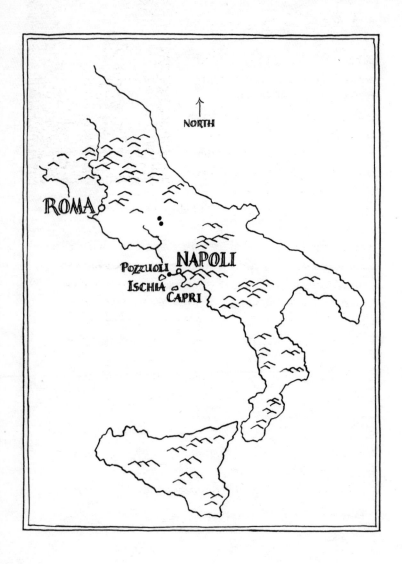

NORTH

ROMA

Pozzuoli

NAPOLI

Ischia

Capri

Dear Francesca

When I was young I felt I had no heritage. Our family had no roots. As the daughter of an Italian immigrant living in a small Scottish community, I was different from my friends. As a child you felt the same. When asked at the tender age of six if you were Italian or Scottish you said with huge insight, 'I feel Italian when I'm in Scotland and Scottish when I'm in Italy.'

The truth is, Francesca, you have truly honourable roots. Your great-grandparents emigrated from poverty and squalor and worked hard and long to give you a better future. I have no material things left from them to give you. No furniture, jewellery or paintings handed down from generation to generation. They came to Scotland with no more than they could carry.

What they have left you is an instinct to live healthily and eat well and, most precious of all, a strong respect for God, family and your neighbour.

So, dear Francesca, here in these pages is that heritage of your family that was handed down to me by word of mouth, with humour and love.

Treasure it; it's more precious than jewels.

all my love
Mummy

Lett 5   presso Orazio Cervi   Lac 7

Picinisco

Prov. di Caserta

16 Dec. 1919

Dear Rosalind

Rome being vile, we came on here. It is a bit staggeringly primitive. You cross a great stony river bed, then an icy river on a plank, then climb unfootable paths, while the ass struggles behind with your luggage. The house contains a rather cave-like kitchen downstairs — the other rooms are a wine-press and a wine-storing place + corn bin: upstairs are three bedrooms, and a semi-barn for maize-cobs: beds + bare floor. There is one tea-spoon — one saucer — two cups — one plate — two glasses — *the whole supply of crockery.* Everything must be cooked gipsy-fashion in the chimney over a wood fire. The chickens wander in, the ass is tied to the doorpost + makes his droppings on the doorstep, + brays his head off. The natives are "in costume" — brigands with skin sandals and white-swathed strapped legs, women in sort of swiss bodices + white shirts with full, full sleeves — very handsome — speaking a perfectly unintelligible dialect + no Italian — The village 2 miles away, a sheer scramble — no road whatever — The Market at Atena, 5 miles away — perfectly wonderful to look at, costume + colour — there you buy your weeks provision. We went yesterday.

The straps go no higher: these swathed pieces are the front of the foot.

Letter from D.H. Lawrence written from Picinisco to Rosalind Baynes, dated 16th December 1919

I CIACCA, PICINISCO, ITALY 1910–1920

Francesca, my grandmother, Marietta Di Ciacca was a cousin of Orazio Cervi, and my father, Johnny (Giovanni) Di Ciacca, was born on 23 December 1919, the very same week Lawrence wrote that letter.

Marietta's family lived in a huddle of farm hovels, I Ciacca, a stone's throw from the house in Picinisco that D. H. Lawrence visited. Picinisco is 725 metres above sea level, high in the Abruzzi mountains, south of Rome. As in many remote villages the population had been isolated for centuries. The uncontaminated genetic line had left an unusual inheritance. The features of some of the people bore a strong resemblance to their Roman ancestors. Their employment prospects were stamped on their faces. By the end of the nineteenth century, Picinisco had gained a reputation as a source of handsome boys to work as artists' models. Their features were perfect for the fashion of the time, the painting and sculpture of Roman Christians. Famous artists like Holman Hunt used boys from Picinisco as models. Other artists from Paris and London made the arduous journey up into the mountains to engage the youngsters for the same reason. By the turn of the century there were more than a hundred working in Britain. For the first time there was hope for the villagers of improving their lot. An opportunity to make some money, unheard of, where for centuries bartering had been the only form of exchange. Their families could now buy land, pay for medical bills or finance education.

Marietta had actually been born in London, in 1895. The poverty and hardship Lawrence describes so vividly had already driven her father to look for a better life, first in Paris and then in London. Tragically, her mother had died when Marietta was still very young, and her father had had to return to Italy with his family. In the eyes of the villagers, Marietta was a sophisticated young girl, having grown up in the capital of Britain. Most likely she had come from even more poverty and hardship in the slums of Clerkenwell's Little Italy, but to those who had never been further than the local market in Atina, she had a coloured past. She had been on a ship. She could write. She could speak English, albeit with a Cockney accent!

She loved Italy with a passion, but was stifled by the strictness of the old life. She was bound by the strict moral code of the community. She wasn't allowed out alone in public places. She had to keep her head covered and had to conform to her father's wishes. On the farm she tended the goats, acted as mother to her brothers and sisters, cooked and kept house. She wore peasant dress, long rough woollen skirts and a long-sleeved modest white blouse covered by a strapped bodice. Her black apron reached down to her feet. Like all the women she wore no undergarments, impractical considering there was no plumbing or toilets. She wore traditional coarse leather sandals, 'le ciocie', strapped to her feet with thongs criss-crossed up her leg.

The family was poor, living from harvest to harvest. The children around her were scruffy ragamuffins, grubby to say the least. There was no bath: just a tub laboriously filled with water that had been heated on the fire once a week. They wore rough clothes and ran barefoot. There was no money for shoes.

Alessandro was Marietta's eight-year-old nephew. When it was time to make his first Holy Communion, he was sent down the mountain to get his first 'ciocie'. He had some pecorino cheese with him, wrapped in vine leaves and muslin and tied with string. He could use this to barter for his sandals at the market. Having set off at dawn, he was expected home in the early evening. Night fell and there was no sign of the boy. Where was he? What in heaven's name had happened? In the culture of uncertainty that comes with living in such remote parts, the worst was suspected. Marietta and all the family were terrified. What if he had been stolen by bandits, or worse still, attacked by the wolves

Marietta aged about twenty-one

or wild boar that roamed the hills? With torches of sticks to light the darkened path, Marietta's father and his brothers set out to search. There was no sign of the boy. They called and cried out but to no avail. In the morning they searched again and after another anxious night they suspected the worst had happened. He must be dead.

But the next day Alessandro appeared. Exhausted and hungry, he was strangely excited, unaware of the concerns of his family. He had walked home wearing his new, first-ever pair of 'le ciocie'. He was so proud to be like his older brothers and cousins, no longer barefoot. He was so desperate to wear them and to be regarded as grown up, the poor lad hadn't realised that the string that tied them together on the stall had first to be cut. Not discouraged, he had taken two whole days to walk home the five miles up the mountain, with steps no longer than the length of the string between his sandals. At night he slept under bushes, his wonderful new sandals clasped to his heart.

Marietta was nineteen. She wanted to grow up too. She wanted a husband and family of her own. She wanted to return to London and start her own life. Custom dictated that she should wait until her father found her a husband. He needed her on the farm and was in no hurry. Marietta had other ideas, though. A fiercely independent girl, she had already set her cap. Cesidio Di Ciacca, her cousin, had fought in the Boer War and returned to his village as a hero. Tempted to find a better life, he had already tried his fortunes in Scotland working in an ice-cream shop in Edinburgh. He was a gentle, handsome lad of twenty-three, with a straight Roman nose and sleepy green eyes. He had a calm sweet nature whereas Marietta was fiery and headstrong. It would be a good match.

The only time she was alone was when she took the goats up the mountainside to sweet pastures. 'I used to secretly meet Cesidio behind a bush when I was tending the goats,' she told me. 'We were so much in love.' She said all they did was whisper and cuddle and plan for their future. Perhaps they held hands or stole a fleeting kiss. Cesidio pledged himself to Marietta and they decided to marry and start a new life away from the suffocating restrictions of their families.

Village etiquette was strict. Cesidio had to ask her father, cap in hand, for permission to marry. Until then they weren't allowed to be alone or to walk out without a chaperone. When they danced the 'tarantella' or the 'ballarella' at a fiesta, they had to hold a handkerchief between them so that even their hands never touched.

On her wedding morning, as was tradition, the bride was dressed in clean white linen from top to toe by the local seamstress. She was then presented to her future mother-in-law, who checked that her son was 'getting a good woman'. (The next morning Marietta would be expected to take her linen to her mother-in-law to prove that the marriage had been consummated – and that she had been a virgin!) To signify her public approval of the bride, the mother-in-law pinned a gift of gold on to Marietta's linen and then helped finish dressing her, piling her hair high and adorning it with beautiful combs and a white lace headscarf.

Marietta walked from her house up the dirt track to the church in Picinisco followed by her father, her brothers and all her family. The children ran laughing and screaming around the wedding procession, jumping to catch the sugar confetti that were scattered from side to side. Cesidio escorted her into the church holding an embroidered handkerchief between them. After the ceremony both families, the priests and all the villagers joined in a wonderful feast.

In the evening the bride and groom made their way back to her father's house, followed by the revellers. Following tradition, at the door, Cesidio pulled Marietta away. He made his declaration to the crowd. 'You're no longer your father's daughter. Now you are my wife.'

With a roar of approval, the clapping crowd cheered, 'Viva gli sposi!'

Rhythmic hand-clapping and louder and louder shouting encouraged Cesidio to take her hand. The crowd's cry in unison, 'Baci! Baci! Baci!' gave permission for the first public kiss. What an emotional moment for the innocent couple . . .

Cesidio took Marietta to her new home, probably his father's house. He led her to their bedroom, followed by the crowd. The large high family bed was all decked out with the linen and bedcovers that Marietta's mother had collected for her when she was a little girl. On the beautiful hand-sewn cover was scattered confetti, sugared almonds. Custom dictates that the guests must now enter the bedroom and leave a gift of money for the new couple. To show face, 'bella figura', the gifts must be substantial, each man giving more than the other, to prove his wealth and to display his power within the community. All in all Cesidio and Marietta did very well and collected a good deal of lire to help them fulfil their dreams for their future.

Within four years they would have left their remote mountain village for good.

FONTITUNE, ITALY 1910–1920

Francesca, your dad's grandparents, Alfonso and Maria Crolla, had an even more austere existence. Where Picinisco had access to the market at Atina, a five-mile walk away, they lived a further 275 metres higher up the mountain. Fontitune was a hamlet of barely a couple of dozen houses perched on the side of the mountain, shadowed by Monte Meta. There was no road, only a dirt-track winding up the mountain, passable only with donkey and cart. It had a population of about a hundred, almost all with the same Crolla surname. Their dialect was different from the villagers further down the mountain, derived directly from Roman Latin.

The Crollas were self-sufficient. They farmed sheep and grew crops on the little land that they had. Vines were grown precariously on the side of the mountain, their roots reaching deep into the sparse earth. In the autumn, the grapes were harvested and piled into large round wooden tubs. The women climbed in and pressed the grapes, their skirts daringly pulled up above their knees, their feet and ankles stained by the juices. The wine produced was garnet red, fruity and tart, leaving purple stains on the mouths of those who tasted it. It was bottled into odd bottles and flagons, stored for the year ahead.

Tomatoes would be harvested, rinsed and dried in the sun before being simmered in a large pot over the fire and stored in empty beer or wine bottles. These would be used to make sauces in the winter months. Wheat grew with great difficulty on the dry hillside. Any crop was ground and stored, coarse and

Fontitune, c. 1890

un-husked in dark sacks. More successful was corn, an easier crop to grow since Roman times. It was once known as 'Roman wheat'. This was ground into polenta, the basic carbohydrate of the diet. Bread and pasta would probably have been made with polenta flour.

In November the olives from their few ancient trees were collected by hand. Old nets or pieces of cloth were draped under the branches to collect any that dropped to the ground. Nothing was wasted. They were then taken to a communal press down in Picinisco to be ground between huge granite stone wheels, producing a rich, grassy green, sweet olive oil. The leaves and pulp left over from the pressing were used as fertiliser, the olive stones dried and used as fuel in the winter.

The families' main produce was pecorino cheese, made from their sheep's spring milk. It was moulded into rush baskets and laid on slats, turned and checked, maturing as the season progressed. The whey left behind was mixed with the rennet collected from a sheep's stomach so that the solid proteins would set to make fresh ricotta. Both these cheeses were in high demand from the villagers down the mountain and had a reputation as the best as far afield as Naples and Rome.

The houses were built one stacked against the other, most no more than a single room. There was no running water, no sink or toilet. Any water had to be collected from a well in the piazza, which gave abundant, icy-cold spring water all year round. There was no electricity, no light at night. No gas, no heat in the winter. No telephone, no post office, no shops. The only means of communication was word of mouth. There was no policeman or taxman! The most powerful source of authority was the priest from Picinisco.

Wood was collected and stored against the sides of the hovels, ready for the winter freeze when some of the few animals they owned were brought inside to provide heat for the family. One large high bed was pushed against the wall. The thick mattress was stuffed with dried corn sheaves, rustling, spiky and coarse.

Alfonso, Maria, their first child Domenico, and his parents all slept together, huddled in the bed to keep warm in the freezing nights. (Domenico was ill as a baby, suffering from pneumonia.) In the sweltering heat of the summer they chose to sleep outside, desperate for a breath of air or whisper of a breeze to relieve the suffocating heat. The large, coarse wooden table with a few rough chairs was the focal point of the family's single room. A fire against one wall held one large pot, swinging precariously, filled with thick, warming winter soup, or bubbling with golden yellow polenta. 'Sugo' or sauce was made with tomato and pork sausage. Delicious smells lingered and mixed with the stench of the animals.

Bread was baked once a week. Huge solid loaves, made with a mixture of coarsely ground polenta and wheat, were leavened without yeast or salt. They were baked in a communal oven and eaten as a staple with every meal. When the bread became stale and hardened, olive oil was drizzled on it. More often it was simply splashed with water to soften it before adding it to soups or stews. The family ate twice a day, good hearty food. Nothing was wasted. Everything had a use.

During the winter, Maria and the other women rarely left the hamlet. Occasionally they would go down the mountain to barter meagre supplies, visit the church or exchange gossip with the Piciniscani, but in all they were a private people, suspicious of outsiders.

After the desolate winter, spring on the mountain was glorious. The sun, bright, clear and delicious, warmed the soul and lifted the spirits. Spring herbs and flowers were abundant. The sweet aromatic smelling herbs, 'odore fresce', filled the air: jasmine, camomile, oregano, rosemary and thyme. Maria collected the herbs and leaves to use in her salads, to dry for flavouring and preserving her food, and to use as remedies.

Now, the families moved down to the coast, to Formia, Mondragone and Gaeta. The sheep, goats, women and children were packed up on to donkeys and rickety carts, and they all set out for a four- to five-day trek. There the shepherds camped and grazed the sheep on the salty wild herbs of the marshy coastline. They lambed the sheep and milked them, making fresh ricotta in rough utensils on fires made of broken sticks. The women poured the warm rich cream cheese into cone-shaped wicker baskets, and carried them on the donkeys or on trays around their necks into the towns. The children ran barefoot alongside, calling to the locals of their arrival. The women of the town would lower baskets out of their windows and trade the ricotta for provisions.

No doubt the families returned in the late spring with baccalà (salted cod) and salted anchovies, flour and sugar, coffee, nails and hardware. Cheroot cigars, salt and 'scopa' playing cards were purchased at the 'tabaccaio'.

The summers were swelteringly hot. Water had to be carried from the well, sweet, delicious and ice-cold. The land was thin, dry and unyielding, but there was enough food: tomatoes, zucchini, peperone, corn and wheat. Figs could be picked abundantly from gnarled trees, eaten warm from the sun, oozing with sweet juice. Trees planted precariously on the mountainside produced peaches, pears, plums and apricots, and bulbous golden-yellow lemons were picked from the tree, so sweet they could be eaten raw.

There was still a lot of work to do but the tremendous heat made the pace of life slow. Hot afternoons were spent resting in the shade, and the cool, long evenings were spent sitting outside until late, drinking wine, smoking a cheroot and talking. The men, with their only jacket pulled over their working clothes and their hats perched comfortably on the backs of their heads, playing scopa and complaining about their wives. They probably played those haunting tunes Lawrence talks of on their 'zampogne' (bagpipes) and sang ancient songs.

On the wall, long skirts pulled to one side, children nestling on their laps, the women talked. 'Cosa hai mangiato?' 'What have you had to eat?' They would discuss the flavour of each dish, argue about the best way to cook something, and congratulate and admire the woman who was regarded as expert in making the particular dish being discussed. Everyone knew that Giovanni didn't like too much onion, Alfonso preferred polenta and little Bambino had a passion for gnocchi.

There was food, but the life was desperately hard. It hadn't improved for generations. The mountains were remote and dangerous. As their families increased there was no more land to give to their children. Things were surely better elsewhere. Things wouldn't improve here. They had to get out!

Alfonso had fought in the Boer War and had seen and heard talk of the opportunities 'all'estero', 'abroad'. Alfonso's father had already tried his hand in London, selling ice-cream in the streets, not unlike selling ricotta in the streets of Mondragone. He'd had some success but had come home. Alfonso and his brothers now decided it was their turn to leave the family and to look for better opportunities. They would try Edinburgh or Glasgow. You could get the boat to America.

Strong, strapping, handsome lads, used to harsh mountain life, they were fit and hardy. They had no transport and very little money for fares, but walking to them was natural. They walked down the mountain. They walked to the coast and then along the Appian Way to Rome, following the route of the Roman soldiers who may have been their ancestors. They walked northwards, past Genoa, through France and to Calais. They may have played their shepherd's pipes, taken odd jobs in return for bed and bread, or hitched lifts on passing carts when they could.

They met cousins or friends from Picinisco in London, took rest and shelter and walked on. They probably met up with more compatriots who had settled in Manchester. They stopped, rested and walked on. They walked over the Borders. They walked to Edinburgh.

EDINBURGH, SCOTLAND 1910–1934

Since as early as 1860 there had been Italians in Edinburgh. By the 1900s, there was a fledgling immigrant Italian community. They congregated on Sundays at St Patrick's Church in the Cowgate for Mass, and afterwards sat under the leafy elm trees in the Grassmarket, reminiscent of the piazzas they had left in Italy. Many of them were from Atina or Picinisco and knew Alfonso and his brothers. They exchanged news, found them rooms and offered them work. Alfonso's first job was with relations in an ice-cream shop in Leith.

Alfonso, right, and his brother Emidio, c.1914

Alfonso wrote to Maria. His news was eagerly awaited. Maria got the priest to read the letter for her as she couldn't read or write. Although Alfonso had experienced much hardship, confusion and fear, he didn't tell her. He told her instead of his longings, his longing to see her again, his longing to hold his son in his arms, his hope that she would come soon. He prayed that they would all soon be safely together.

He included two ten shilling notes, folded neatly between the purple silver paper of Cadbury's chocolate bars, most of his savings.

The letters kept coming. The money in the purple silver paper increased until Maria had enough to set out with Domenico to join Alfonso in their new life.

They worked hard and prospered. They set up an ice-cream shop in Easter Road. There was plenty of work. They needed help. Alfonso encouraged others from Fontitune to join them. He then sent for his brother-in-law who followed the same path and set off for Scotland. He travelled by train up from London, looking out for his station, 'Edimburgo. Edimburgo. Edimburgo'. In rhythm with the train he repeated the words so that he wouldn't forget. He didn't speak English. He couldn't write. 'Edimburgo. Edimburgo. Edimburgo.' The train pulled in at Waverley Station and stopped. He was confused. This wasn't 'Edimburgo'. As the train started to pull out of the station, back the way it had come, he realised his mistake. He had missed his stop.

With all the bravado of a young adventurer, he was not daunted. Refusing to return to London, he waited until the train slowed down. His few belongings were wrapped in a sheet and tied with a belt. He grabbed it, threw it from the train and jumped, rolling down the embankment, tumbling into Scotland. Luckily he didn't hurt himself. He picked himself up and looked around. To the left he saw the distinctive mound of Arthur's Seat. To the north he saw the glistening blue Firth of Forth with the majestic Forth Rail Bridge in the distance. It was beautiful. Scotland was beautiful. His spirits lifted. His heart sang. He started to walk down towards the coast. He tripped and began to run. He came to a hedge and dirt-track and heading down the hill, he ended up in Cockenzie, a lovely old fishing village. It was somehow familiar. It reminded him of the villages on the coast in Italy. This would do him. With the help of the brothers in

Edinburgh, he rented a shop already owned by an Italian, Mary Coppola, and set up business in Cockenzie.

In I Ciacca, Marietta heard about the Crolla brothers' success. She longed to return to Britain to try to improve her life. She talked with Cesidio and encouraged him to try again. He shouldn't worry. She would wait in Italy with the children until he sent for her. She would be all right.

Cesidio had some money saved up from their wedding so he made his way to Cassino and took the train to Paris. From Calais he took the ferry across the Channel and arrived in Newhaven. He made his way to the ice-cream shop now belonging to another of Alfonso's brothers, 'Crolla Newhaven'. After a warm welcome and dinner with Maria, Alfonso arranged for Cesidio to get work in partnership with his brother-in-law in Cockenzie. Cesidio lived in a single room at the back of the small shop. This room became his home with just enough space for a bed, a chair and a little stove. He hung his clothes to dry above his bed. Not used to the damp weather, he was surprised at how long they took to dry. The room had a warm, damp smell that was not unpleasant.

He worked all hours learning the skills of making ice-cream and fish and chips, and making every effort to understand the distinctive Cockenzie dialect. Just like the village he had left, this was a small, close hard-working community and gradually he gained their trust. Behind the counter of his shop, proudly dressed in clean white overalls, he became their friend. They couldn't pronounce his unusual name, and as was their wont, gave him a nickname. By 1923, Cesidio was called 'Sis' and was so confident of his new home and new friends he wrote to tell Marietta to come.

Anxious but thrilled and excited, she set off with their two children, Carmela and the three-year-old Giovanni, my father. She packed a parcel of bread, salami and cheese and wrapped it

24

in a cloth. She wore her only set of 'good clothes', long skirts with her traditional red petticoats worn on saints' days and feasts. The rest of her belongings were tied in a cloth bundle, strapped with string and carried on her head. She already spoke English and Cesidio had sent her enough money for the train. After a four-day journey, alone with her small children, she arrived in Waverley Station, exhausted and penniless. A guard on duty took pity on this odd-looking, dishevelled girl with crying, grubby children. He kindly gave her enough money to get a bus down the coast to Portobello. From there she started to walk.

A villager making his way home was intrigued by an exotic-looking, dark-skinned girl with a cloth parcel balanced precariously on her head.  Her long full skirts swayed evocatively as she walked, a shocking glimpse of red petticoats showing from time to time. She had a baby strapped to her chest and held an exhausted young girl tightly by the hand, dragging her along as they went. He knew 'Sis's' wife was on her way. This must be her. He stopped and gave her a lift on the back of his cart down to Cockenzie.

Cesidio had been so worried. He was so

Marietta, Carmela and the baby, Giovanni, (Johnny) just before leaving for Scotland, c. 1920 relieved to see them arrive safe and well. He held her close, kissing her hard on the lips and squeezing her until the baby started to cry and little Carmela pushed him away. With joy and excitement he proudly showed them their new home: the room with the bed at the back of the ice-cream shop.

With her beloved Cesidio, Marietta would stay anywhere. She made a vow to God that she would settle here, work hard and make a better life for her children. One day she would go back to Picinisco, but never in poverty again.

The two men worked together in the shop for a few years. Before long, both families became too big for the cramped space they had. One family would have to find another property. They decided to toss a coin to see who would choose.

Cesidio won. He decided to stay. He took over the rent of the shop and the room at the back and proudly painted his name – C. Di Ciacca – above the door.

The Di Ciacca and Crolla families kept in touch and supported each other. They tried to keep their Italian traditions alive: faith in God, honesty, friendship and hard work. Maria visited Marietta with her young children. They kept their rich varied store of traditional Italian recipes. At home they had always grown their own food. Now, for the first time, they had to buy it. They bought olive oil, pasta and tins of tomatoes from a wholesaler of Italian produce based in St John's Hill, not far from the Grassmarket. Ralph Valvona had come from Atina and established his business as early as the 1860s importing Italian provisions for the fledgling Italian community in Scotland.

The women soon realised that Scotland had a wealth of its own wonderful ingredients: beef, hill lamb and game. Cockenzie had a fishing fleet and Marietta bought fish for her shop and her family straight from the fishermen as they landed the catch. They had milk delivered from the local farm to make ice-cream. They still made ricotta. There was plenty of flour for making bread and pasta. They found greens and salads, unlike their own, but still good. They got welcome parcels of sausages and pecorino across from Italy, and gradually settled into cooking in a new environment.

The style of cooking didn't change. They cooked only those dishes that they had the ingredients for. They gradually learned how to cook local dishes, but preferred their familiar Italian flavours. Because of their poverty they had by necessity kept their cooking simple. They had had no refrigeration and understood the importance of hygiene. They depended on cooking quickly and easily so that they had fresh food every day. They knew that the tastiest food is made in the simplest way, with the best ingredients. They never used recipes or scales, but relied on taste to adjust the flavourings. Even cakes and pastries were made without scales, if anything using a cup as a measuring tool.

Both women were instinctive mothers, making every effort to feed their families to the best of their ability. They made treats and spoiled everyone with their favourite dishes, always feeding themselves last, happy their children and husbands were contented.

Francesca, I wonder if our modern ways are better? I sometimes wonder even with all our modern conveniences there is even more pressure on working mothers these days? I hope you still have time to enjoy cooking good fresh, simple food for yourself and your family. Maybe the simplicity of these recipes will help.

HOW TO EAT WELL

'Così si mangia bene.'
'This is how to eat well.'

Cesidio behind the counter of his shop in Cockenzie

Francesca, before you learn to cook, learn to shop.

I make sure I buy my meat, poultry and fish from the best butchers and fishmongers. Alternatively I enjoy shopping in the farmers' markets that are, thankfully, having great success around the country. Use all your instincts when shopping for food. A good shopkeeper will be happy to give you information about the source of the food, the best way to cook it, or the best cut for the dish you want to make.

I rarely decide a menu before shopping for food, but prefer to choose my meat or fish depending on what looks particularly fresh or good. The fashion of pre-packaging food has decreased our shopping skills. Make shopping for food all part of the fun. I really enjoy the whole experience of shopping in small specialist shops. They have the expertise and experience to provide the best ingredients and are more often than not dedicated food lovers who are happy to give advice and help.

Good fruit and vegetables have to be searched out. Again, I usually buy in local shops, though I find some of the super-markets have good fruit and vegetable sections. I try to pay atten-tion to country of origin, choosing locally grown or – so I'm biased – Italian-grown produce where possible.

Shop for fresh food at least twice a week. For simplicity, rely on pasta, cheese and salad or soups and grills through the week. At the weekends, we are more likely to eat more, but the all-day Sunday lunches with everyone around the table are sadly a thing of the past.

Of course we all have to shop in supermarkets as well. It is inevitable. When you do, use different skills. They tend to place products in the best positions to encourage the shopper to buy them. Stand back and take time to see what else is on offer. These days there are good raw ingredients nestling on the shelves. I always check the sell-by date: the freshest products will be at the back of the shelves, the older ones at the front. Choose the freshest. Pay attention to the country of origin. It's a good clue to the quality of the produce. Unfortunately, the more carefully produced raw ingredients do cost more. On the other hand, if you look at the price you pay for ready-made food, then cooking with good ingredients can be just as economical.

Once the shopping is done, my cooking style is simple and fast. I flavour most foods simply with extra virgin olive oil, garlic and fresh herbs, relying on Maldon salt and pepper to lift the flavour. I don't make puddings very much any more, preferring to eat fresh fruit or some really good cheese.

And what about the washing-up? The dishwasher is always on. Packing the dishwasher is not such a chore . . . though I do think it shouldn't be the cook's job!

MY PALATE OF INGREDIENTS

Anchovies
ACCIUGHE

I use anchovies as a flavour enhancer. Use those that have been preserved either in salt or under oil. Whichever you use, buy the best quality you can find. The salted ones have to be rinsed, the skin scraped off and the bones pulled away. Anchovies preserved in oil are ready to use.

A fillet or two of anchovy melted into olive oil will act as a subtle but effective foil for the flavours in the dish. Used with moderation they will not leave any hint of fishiness.

Salted anchovies are an ancient form of flavouring that is just as effective today. The Romans used an ingredient called 'garum' which was basically anchovies preserved in salt. The liquid thrown off was used as well, described unappetisingly by Pliny the Elder as 'the liquid from rotten fish'.

Butter
BURRO

Butter is wonderful. Good butter is even better. Find a butter you like the flavour of. I choose unsalted because the flavour is sweeter. Farmhouse butters are exceptional, fuller flavoured and dense. If you can find it, do try Italian butter. It is creamy in flavour, very distinctive and wonderful to cook with.

I don't use margarine or olive oil spreads. Even though the adverts will tell you otherwise, neither do Italian grandmothers, though they have been known to chase young boys! For me, the healthy option is to use limited amounts of natural butter in cooking. Low-fat spreads may have fewer calories but they are also most likely stacked with other unwanted ingredients that counteract any benefit.

Buy or bake really good chewy bread and don't put butter or spreads on the table. We don't put dishes of oil on the table either. The bread just needs all the lovely juices wiped from your plate to moisten it.

Extra Virgin Olive Oil
OLIO EXTRA VIRGINE DI OLIVA

There is a lot of confusion associated with olive oil. 'Cold-pressed' extra virgin olive oil is still made today by the same traditional methods used by my grandparents. The olives are sorted, then simply pressed between two huge stone wheels to squeeze out the oils and the juices. Just as fresh fruit juices do not have the same taste and quality, so cold-pressed oils do not all taste the same.

The best oils come from well-tended olive groves, some many hundreds of years old. The olives are carefully harvested by hand, a laborious and exhausting job. (Bruising or mechanical harvesting affects the quality of the oil.) Any stones, leaves or twigs are removed and as soon after harvest as possible the olives are pressed between the gigantic stones. (Modern methods use stainless-steel hydraulic presses to squeeze the olives.) This is a natural process carried out at ambient temperature, hence 'cold pressed'. The mixture of oil and water that is collected is spun and separated in a centrifuge, the water being siphoned off and used as fertiliser.

To class the oil as extra virgin it must have a low acidity of 0.5–1 per cent. The lower the acidity, the better the keeping qualities of the oil. (The extra virgin label does not necessarily signify that the oil was naturally cold pressed. Modern methods of production can use chemicals to reduce acidity and qualify the oil as extra virgin.) The oil lasts in a cool, dark cupboard for twelve to eighteen months after pressing. Its flavour depends on the type of olives that were used and the area they were grown in. The flavour of the oil will also change and mellow as it ages, just like good wine, and can have a price ticket to match.

Estate extra virgin olive oil is more expensive because of the labour intensiveness of the production. A good estate will prune the olive trees well so that the olives are fullest in flavour but obviously this limits production. If you buy single-estate oil, choose one that has the season it was harvested on the label.

Generally, Tuscan oils are big flavoured, hot and peppery. When they are first harvested they produce a distinctive fiery bite at the back of the throat that mellows with age. Abruzzan and Puglian oils are sweeter and gentler, but still very fruity. Ligurian oils are extremely light and elegant and are delicious with salads and for making pesto. Sicilian oil is very aromatic, and is extremely good.

Remember, oil goes rancid and should be kept in a cool dark place, so don't buy fancy bottles to display on your kitchen shelf.

At the other end of the spectrum you find mass-produced extra virgin olive oils, olive oil and the new 'light' olive oils. These have very probably been chemically purified to produce a product that is consistent from year to year, reliable and cheap enough for the mass market. They may use a mixture of olives from different farms and regions of Italy, or even imported from other countries.

I like to use single-estate cold-pressed extra virgin olive oil for salads and drizzling on grilled foods and soups. For most of my cooking I use Puglian extra virgin olive oil, Fior' Fiore. It's fruity, flavoursome and gentle.

Francesca, don't get hung up about olive oil. My advice is to invest in the best of both worlds. Use commercial branded extra virgin oil for cooking and if you can afford it, choose a single-estate cold-pressed extra virgin olive oil for salads, grilled foods and for dressing antipasto. It really transforms the flavour of food.

'Light' olive oil (i.e. commercial, neutral-flavoured olive oil), vegetable oil or corn oil is good for mayonnaise or deep-frying. Almond, hazelnut and peanut oils can all be quite delicious, but I don't use them enough to merit buying a bottle. If you do buy them, use them within a few months of opening, as they easily become rancid.

Fonteluna Sausage
SALSICCIA FONTELUNA

Francesca, in the winter, our ancestors relied on stored and preserved food for their survival. The abundance of the warm months of spring, summer and autumn would come to an end, and life could only continue if enough food and fuel had been laid aside.

Each family, except the very poorest, kept a pig. It was looked after, well fed and fattened with windfall fruit, corn and scraps. The children collected nuts and wild herbs to feed it, encouraged to spoil it like a pet. In the autumn the pet was slaughtered. Prosciutto and salame were prepared and hung on the rafters to dry. Nothing was wasted. Off-cuts of the pig were ground with lean meat and mixed with fat then seasoned with salt, peppercorns and spices. The flavoured meat was pushed into the casings made from the gut of the pig and twisted to make 'salsiccie', sausages. They were hung in the main room of the house, drying in the gentle heat of the first autumn evening fires in the hearth. Some were buried into jars of pure white creamy lardo, which had been rendered from the fat of the pig. The sausage was used in soups and sauces, pizza and 'pastone', pies. It was eaten raw, cured by its drying, sliced thin and chewed with chunks of bread.

Naturally, once they had emigrated, the women wanted to keep the tradition of cooking with the sausage alive. At first they had it sent across from Fontitune by their parents who still lived there. In Fontitune, the pattern of life hadn't changed, so now that there were fewer mouths to feed and with the little money being sent across from Scotland, it was no hardship to send 'salsiccie' and pecorino cheese to their children abroad.

Today, Salsiccia Fonteluna is made especially for Valvona & Crolla, Ltd, to the same recipe from all those years ago. You can substitute dried Calabrese sausage or salsiccia Napoletana, but both are flavoured with more chilli and are much spicier. Alternatively, use cubes of smoked pancetta, Italian streaky bacon.

Salt
SALE

It's not so long ago that salt in southern Italy had to be purchased in the 'sali e tabacchi', salt and tobacco shops, stored on high shelves with the cigarettes. Since ancient times it has always been respected as an essential flavouring and preservative for food.

A diet high in processed foods, crisps and snacks contains a dangerously high level of hidden salt – one of the reasons for the shocking statistics of high blood pressure in our modern culture. Unfortunately, ready-made convenience foods usually rely on extra salt to replace flavour that is lost in the processing.

I nearly always cook with fresh ingredients. I use salt as a natural flavour enhancer for my food, and prefer Maldon sea salt. Its texture is flaky and crystallised so you can add it by hand, sprinkled into food to taste. It's clean and flavoursome with no metallic or brassy aftertaste. Maldon sea salt is entirely natural and contains no added chemicals or preservatives.

Halen Môn sea salt from Anglesey is also delicious. There are other lovely salts from France and Italy, each with their own level of saltiness. In general, you need to use less sea salt than table salt. I do use normal table salt for salting pasta water and boiling potatoes and vegetables.

Pepper
PEPE

I don't automatically add pepper to my food. I often use peper-oncino or dried chilli to add heat instead. When I do use pepper for a spicy, pungent heat and flavour, I use Parameswaran's Special Wynad Pepper. I always use it freshly ground or coarsely crushed.

This beautifully flavoured pepper is grown on the plateau in the Kerala mountains of India. The pepper grown here is the finest in India. Unlike other commercial peppers, 'Para' allows the berries to ripen on the pepper vines as long as possible, until they achieve a reddish colour. Between January and March, with great effort, they are harvested by hand to prevent damage to the delicate berries. It can take up to four or five pickings to harvest one vine. The berries are then laid out on mats and dried in the sun.

The result is a pepper berry with a full and complex flavour. Where mass-produced black pepper can have a hot taste with a metallic aftertaste, Wynad pepper gives a warm, complex heat with a background of spicy flavours like cinnamon and clove. Used in cooking it lifts and enhances flavour rather than simply adding heat.

Para also prepares white peppercorns. The ripe berries are harvested by hand and soaked in water for seven to nine days, then the outer skin is removed completely. This results in a sharper, less subtle flavour than the black pepper, but provides just as much heat. I use white pepper in white sauces and soups to add a background heat. It transforms simple buttered boiled cabbage. Black pepper can always be used if you don't have white.

Wynad pepper is harvested and sold every year while much commercial pepper may be mixed from many years' crops. It has no artificial chemicals or preservatives used in its production.

Dried Red Chilli
PEPERONCINO

Just like my nonna always did, buy some fresh, red, hot chilli peppers, string them together like a daisy chain and hang them up to dry in the kitchen. They become fiery hot and pungent as they dry and a small amount can be used to add heat and spice to sauces, stews or soups. Smaller chillies usually have a hotter flavour. The seeds can be especially hot so just knock them out by shaking the chilli before using it. (Remember not to touch your eyes or lips after touching chillies.) You can buy ready-dried red chillies, but they tend to be very dry and old and can be punishingly hot.

Sometimes, I use fresh green chilli to give a bright, clean heat to dishes, especially if I'm using it with green fresh coriander.

Parmesan Cheese
PARMIGIANO REGGIANO

Parmigiano Reggiano has been made from unpasteurised cow's milk, produced under strict legislation, in the Emilia-Romagna region of Italy for thousands of years. Some records of production go back to the twelfth century. The cows are only fed on grass and hay.

Parmigiano Reggiano has a distinctive stamp on its rind, which indicates the actual farm where the milk was produced, and the date the cheese was made. It performs its magic best when it is bought fresh, in good condition and is at least eighteen months old. I always buy Parmigiano freshly cut from its 20 kg wheel.

Store the cheese at the bottom of the fridge wrapped in some foil or greaseproof paper. To get the best flavour from the cheese always grate it freshly. The moist, soft, juicy crumbs will make your mouth water and activate your taste-buds. Because the cheese is washed in a salt bath it is fairly salty. This, with its high incidence of natural flavour, magically transforms the flavours of food to which it is added.

Pre-packaged, ready-grated or pre-shaved Parmigiano is inferior in flavour and invariably more expensive than freshly cut cheese. Never wasting anything, Marietta and Maria always scrubbed the rind of the cheese and added it to soups to give an added flavour and a soft, chewy chunk of cheese to eat with the soup.

Don't forget to enjoy Parmigiano Reggiano as a table cheese. When it is freshly cut and in good condition eat it with ripe pears and rich red wine.

Marietta and Cesidio harvesting grapes and corn in Picinisco

Sheeps' Milk Cheese
PECORINO

Our grandparents from Picinisco were shepherds. They made pecorino from their sheep's milk in the spring to preserve and use as supplies through the winter. The women also made ricotta from the whey left over from the cheese-making process. They naturally used pecorino in all their cooking, and didn't use Parmigiano Reggiano (the cows' milk cheese made in the north of Italy) until they came to Scotland.

There are many types of pecorino available. Pecorino romano is typical of the area around Rome, Lazio. It is mature, sharp and fairly salty, making it ideal for grating. It is rarely eaten as a table cheese. Today it is often made in Sardinia. Pecorino pienza is made in the spring and is best eaten young, fresh and creamily sweet. It is perfect eaten with fresh fruit. Traditionally it was rubbed with the sheep's blood to give it a distinctive red skin, an ancient marketing tool! Today, in our hygienic times, it is rubbed with tomato paste. Most readily available is pecorino sardo from Sardinia. It is good eaten when young but is also matured for three to four months and used as a grating cheese. These days it is usually sold with a distinctive yellow, ridged wax covering. Slightly sweet, salty and sharp, it is a cheaper alternative to Parmigiano.

As a child I remember my nonna getting parcels of young, fresh pecorino from Italy. It came wrapped in layers of muslin, tied with string and in a brown paper parcel, sealed with red wax. The paper was oily and stained, and the smell of maturing cheese that had travelled several days unrefrigerated was over-powering. From time to time the cheese, once opened, revealed swarming maggots in the centre. Nonna regarded this as a bonus – 'the goodness of the cheese'. No amount of education on her granddaughters' part would convince her otherwise.

Made from 100 per cent sheeps' milk, pecorino is a useful

alternative to Parmigiano for those with cows' milk intolerance. Fresh pecorino melts into luxurious lazy ribbons when grated over pasta. We called it 'stringy' cheese.

Stock and Cubes
BRODO E DADI

I rarely use stock in soups or stews, letting the ingredients themselves produce the flavour needed. I really believe that you can't make a really perfect risotto without the body and flavour that comes from a good home-made stock.

If anything, I'm a chicken stock or broth addict, and will make a litre or so once a week. It's a really simple process and as it freezes well I always have some on hand (see page 90). I rarely make any other stock, though a 'ham end', soaked overnight to get rid of any salt, and simmered in a couple of litres of water with a small onion, a carrot and a stick of celery, makes a lovely ham-flavoured stock for soups or tomato risotto (see page 181).

Remember that if you use hot water instead of stock in soups you will need to add more salt than you expect to replace the salt in stock and in stock cubes. I'm not a stock-cube snob but I do prefer not to rely on them. Marigold stock granules are made without artificial ingredients, and are very good, but I tend to use Knorr or Starr chicken stock cubes! Many Italians will crumble a little secretly into their cooking if they don't have some concentrated chicken stock to hand.

It's worth trying some of the commercial fresh stocks found in supermarkets.

To tell you the truth, Francesca, your favourite chicken soup when you were small was nothing more than alphabet pastina in a broth of chicken stock cube with chopped fresh parsley! Don't tell Nonna!

SOFFRITTO

This is the fundamental flavour base for many soups and stews in our cooking. It refers to the flavour and texture created by slowly sautéing finely chopped onions in extra virgin olive oil or butter until they are soft and translucent. Sometimes chopped shallots, celery or carrots are used. Their flavours are gently teased and captured to make the foundation of the dish. There is no great skill required, just patience. Patience to chop the ingredients finely enough, and patience to let them cook very slowly and not let them burn.

Once this flavour base is prepared, the rest of the cooking is usually very straightforward and easy. Don't try to hasten the process by adding salt. This will simply release water and stew the onions instead of sautéing them. The salt will also highlight the flavour of the onion later on in the dish, a bit unpleasant. A soffritto should be a gentle background blend of flavour.

Garlic
AGLIO

If you avoid garlic because you hate the smell on your breath after eating it, it's most likely that the garlic you are using is old, or you are simply using too much. As garlic ages it gets more pungent and becomes an overpowering bully! Many recipes call for too much garlic. Contrary to popular belief, garlic is used sparingly in Italy, with the exception of Naples, where they do nothing sparingly!

We haven't cottoned on in this country yet, but garlic is also a seasonal product. Fresh young garlic comes into season at the end of March. The bulbs are soft and pale and difficult to peel, the outer casing hardly formed. The flavour is sweet yet still pungent, and absolutely delicious roasted. As the garlic matures the cloves become more distinctive and familiar, and the flavour more intense.

Use garlic with restraint. The more pressed or crushed garlic is, the more it releases its essential oils, making its flavour even more pungent and overpowering. I tend to slice it into slivers to release some of its flavour rather than chop it finely. The flavour of garlic also changes subtly depending on how you cook it. If you allow it to brown, its flavour becomes slightly sharp and acidic. It is used like this particularly in Puglia, in the south of Italy, to give a very distinctive flavour. Garlic sautéed with freshly chopped parsley, as with the mussels on page 112, gives an entirely different characteristic, gentle and unassuming. The parsley, which is the herb to chew if you are going out kissing after eating garlic, acts to sweeten and takes away its smell.

If you buy tresses of garlic, keep them in a cool dark place otherwise they will sprout and spoil. I tend to buy a little garlic as I need it, but always have some in the kitchen. Later on in the summer the huge purple French, Roscoff and Brittany garlic comes on to the market. This has a strident, couldn't-care-less flavour and is brilliant for fast grilling and roasting summer foods.

Just one thing, Francesca, don't buy a garlic press, powdered garlic or garlic granules . . . please!

Onions and Shallots
CIPOLLE E SCALOGNE

I use onions to add flavour and texture to slow-cooked sauces and stews. Choose sweet onions or shallots. Spanish or French onions are particularly good. Red onions are sweeter and can look very appealing. Shallots have a more subtle flavour.

So that onions and shallots melt down and disappear into the sauce, always chop them very finely. This applies especially when preparing onions for the base of sugo or risotto. They should be indiscernible in the finished dish. By the way, don't prepare onions for use the next day. They take on a tarnished intense flavour reminiscent of hamburger stalls.

If you like onions in salads but don't want the lingering effects on the breath, slice them thinly and soak them in two or three changes of cold water for half an hour or so. This leaves their flavour sweet and mild while keeping a nice crispy texture.

If you are tempted to buy a string of onions, remember they'll sprout and spoil if you hang them in the light. Buy them to use, not just for decoration.

The Herb Garden
ERBE

Little plastic containers of fresh herbs are expensive and not practical for the home cook. There are better supplies of herbs than in the past, but at the same time it is still much easier and far more economical to grow them at home.

If you have a garden, all manner of herbs will grow easily. I tend to plant most of my herbs in terracotta pots near the kitchen door, just so that I can pop out and take what I need come rain or shine. If you don't have a garden, window-boxes are very successful.

Of the hardy, woody herbs I keep thyme, sage, bay and rose-mary. They all grow easily, look very pretty and are a treat to use as the fancy takes me without checking the fridge to see if there is a mouldy pack of them in the vegetable drawer. They look after themselves, spasmodic culinary pruning keeps them in check and considering the cost of a plastic pack, pay for themselves within weeks.

Fresh oregano is a bit flabby, woolly and insipid. It looks very nice to grow and if you take a bunch just before it flowers in June or July and hang it up in the kitchen, drying it for a

week or two, its flavour magically intensifies. You can then store it for six months or so in a sealed jar. This 'freshly dried' oregano has an intense perfume and flavour and is perfect for pizza, tomatoes and Greek lamb dishes. You can find good dried oregano in bunches from Spanish or Italian suppliers. Commercial dried oregano in spice jars can often be overpowering and stale. (Be brave. Throw out all those spices and herbs that have been lurking on the spice rack for years.)

Johnny with an old aunt in Picinisco, c.1930

Chives look lovely in the early summer with their purple pompom flowers, again a lovely plant to grow. I use them in potato salads and in omelettes.

Of the annual herbs, basil is king in my book. It grows very easily from seed every year or you can buy a plant from a plant nursery. Up here in Scotland we have to keep basil indoors, such is the inconsistency of our summer! It does have a fatal attraction for white fly in the late summer so keep it away from other houseplants.

Every autumn some nuns in Liguria send freshly dried basil in a beautiful muslin bag to my aunt. The large crumpled leaves are aromatic and beautifully flavoured, ideal for the winter. If you have grown very sweet aromatic basil, try drying some at home. Hang up a bunch of leaves upside down in a warm place. When they are completely dry keep them in an airtight container for the winter. Fresh basil is imported from Israel in the winter and is widely available.

I use so much flat-leaf parsley I can never grow enough, and have to supplement my stock from the fruit shop. Curly-leaf parsley is just as good for stock and stews if that's all you can get, but flat-leaf is more delicate for salads and dressing vegetables.

Rocket, 'rughetta', is a wild herb with an intense spicy, peppery flavour. It grows like a weed. Nowadays it is also culti-vated, when it is referred to as 'rucola' and is invariably less peppery. It is also called 'arugula' in America. Shop-bought rocket can be ridiculously expensive and usually lacks the bite of wild rocket. Sow it from seed into a patch of earth and you will have peppery, spicy leaves within a few weeks. Recently we have gone overboard with this herb. I first tasted it twenty years ago when Renzo, my cousin, took me up Monte Meta, the mountain above Picinisco, to look for wild herbs and to get fresh ricotta from the shepherds. He showed us true wild rocket which has very narrow leaves and is extremely peppery and hot. The cultivated wild rocket that is available here is not as pungent or as appealing but is still very good. I prefer the taste of spring and summer rocket. In the late autumn and winter it is probably forced and can be bland and flabby. If you cook with rocket use it at the very last minute, just to warm it through. Its flavour disappears with heat.

Fresh coriander is the herb that gives my palate a jolt. Lazily, I tend to cook with my Mediterranean palate, and fresh coriander isn't a herb we have traditionally used. Oddly, we do use coriander seeds for preserving and flavouring pork and curing meats, but not as a herb in its fresh state. Adding a few leaves to a salad snaps me out of complacency, and added to broth with green chilli transforms the flavours wonderfully. Use coriander with grilled fish and to make spicy salsas. It marries well with lemon and fresh green chilli.

Tinned Tomatoes
POMODORI IN SCATOLA

In winter, I rely on Neapolitan San Marzano tinned plum tomatoes. San Marzano tomatoes are long and plump with a bright red colour. They should nestle in a thick juice. These tomatoes are grown in abundance on the rich alluvial soil around Naples and Campania. They are very sweet and juicy and are perfect for sauces. Good tinned tomatoes make a great difference to the taste of any sugo. I prefer Cirio, Vitale or Lupa. Once you find a brand you like, it's wise to stick to it.

Some tinned tomatoes have added herbs or garlic. I don't use these, preferring to add flavourings to suit my own taste. I don't use tomato purée, and use passata, ready-sieved tomatoes, only in soup.

The patron saint of Naples is San Gennaro. A relic of the saint's blood is kept in a jewel-encrusted vial in Naples Cathedral. On the first Sunday in May and on his feast day, 19 September, thousands of Neapolitans throng the cathedral. The cardinal holds up the vial to the crowds to show the miracle of the lique-faction of the blood. Above the cheers of the crowd, screams and cries are heard imploring the saint for miracles and to cure the sick. As the blood liquefies, an audible sigh of relief sweeps through the crowd as good luck for the year ahead is assured. (Many believe that this 'miracle' will also ensure a good season for the Napoli football team!) Not to let a marketing opportunity pass, a Neapolitan firm sells tinned tomatoes evocatively named 'Il Miracolo di San Gennaro'. They are so good it is a miracle!

(Francesca, not far from the cathedral is a church dedicated to Santa Patrizia. She was a defiled virgin martyr of the seventeenth century who has been given the elevated position of patron saint of expectant mothers. Her blood is kept in a similar vial to that of San Gennaro. It liquefies every Tuesday at 11 o'clock! There is no crowd to acclaim the saint. Not much fuss is made of Santa Patrizia's busy schedule. Even if you're a saint, you still have to play second fiddle to men in Naples!)

Fresh Tomatoes
POMODORI FRESCHI

Thankfully, compared to a few years ago, there is a far better selection of fresh tomatoes available now. I have to confess real prejudice here. I have rarely tasted any tomatoes that beat those grown in the south of Italy. Tomatoes are native to South America, which suggests they need plenty of sunshine. The Italians grow different styles of tomatoes for different uses and for different seasons.

The most famous are the San Marzano plum tomatoes grown mostly for the canned market. If you can get a hold of these fresh in the summer they make beautiful tomato sugo (see page 157). I've tasted cherry plum tomatoes grown just under the crater of Vesuvius, still covered in black smoky dust. Their flavour was extreme, almost like a concentrated tomato soaked in ash. Fabulous!

Ripe tomatoes harvested on the stem can have a lovely flavour, but not always. Like all fresh produce on sale, some will look better than they taste. If they are sweet, they make a lovely summer soup. Cook them on the stems and sieve them after to extract the most flavour. Remember basil is the perfect partner to tomatoes, but mint is very refreshing as well.

Pachino cherry tomatoes are grown in the winter months in Sicily, where the warm African breezes keep the frosts away. They are very intense and sweet and a real treat in the winter, when anything remotely reminding me of sunnier times lifts my spirits. They are fabulous roasted or simply squashed into extra virgin olive oil to make a fresh sugo. There are many varieties of cherry tomatoes around these days. Buy the sweetest you can find. Be aware that the seeds of cherry tomatoes can sometimes be bitter when cooked. I sometimes de-seed them just by squashing them in my hands and separating out some of the seeds.

In late winter and early spring the Sardinians grow an intriguing Camone tomato that is particularly good eaten raw in salads. It defies instinct as it is best eaten while still partly green. It has the advantage of being sweet but with a thick, crunchy skin, which marries perfectly with Sardinian pecorino and extra virgin olive oil. They also grow Nerino plum tomatoes in the summer. These have a similar flavour and are eaten in salads with a simple dressing of extra virgin olive oil, Maldon salt and freshly dried oregano. The nearest thing to be found here are those sweet home-grown tomatoes that dedicated gardeners grow in their greenhouses all over the country. Make friends with a dedicated gardener!

All I can say is trust your taste-buds. Choose the tomatoes that have good flavour when you can find them. Make a note of their name and enjoy!

Intensify the flavour of tomatoes with salt, fresh basil and extra virgin olive oil. Cherry tomatoes doused in oil and roasted at a high temperature take on a far more intense flavour, which can then be used for pizza or with pasta.

Lemons
LIMONI

Freshly squeezed lemon juice is a magical ingredient. Its natural acidity complements and lifts the flavour of any fatty foods. It transforms the flavour of grilled steak, pork, fish and lamb. It lifts the taste of salad and acts as a natural flavour enhancer in desserts, ices and cream-based sauces.

Remember that most lemons have a coating of wax on them to preserve them. This should be washed off with soapy water and rinsed before use, especially if you are using the rind. Choose organic or unwaxed lemons if you can. I often warm lemons before use to get the most juice out of them.

The best lemons I've ever tasted are Amalfi lemons from the south of Italy – large, often the size of your hand, and deliciously sweet and juicy. They are sometimes served as a salad, dressed, believe it or not, with extra virgin olive oil and lemon juice!

Wine Vinegar
ACETO DI VINO

Until the recent invasion of balsamic vinegar, we always used red or white wine vinegars in our salads. The flavour is acidic and can be a bit sharp, but it is very useful for preserving and works very well with warm food to cut any oiliness or fattiness. It is used in some dishes to produce a specific regional flavour. In the south of Italy most cooks have never heard of balsamic vinegar and use only standard mass-produced red and white wine vinegars.

Traditional Balsamic Vinegar
ACETO BALSAMICO TRADIZIONALE DI MODENA

Traditional balsamic vinegar from Modena is not the splash-it-all-over product that has elbowed out any other vinegar from our kitchen cupboards over the last few years. Aceto balsamico tradizionale is a unique product that has been produced in Modena by the same method in very limited quantities for hundreds of years. The small numbers of families who are legally allowed to produce it, and who form part of the 'Consorzio', rightly regard it as an heirloom and proudly protect and legislate its production. It is made exclusively from crushed Trebbiano grapes whose unfermented musts are condensed by heating and are aged over a period of a minimum of ten years. Every year, the liquid is mixed with a small amount of new season's must and then decanted through a series of barrels of different woods – oak, cherry, chestnut, mulberry and ash. The ageing vinegar absorbs a subtle hint of each, building up complex flavour.

This practice rewards the patient farmer with a thick, syrupy, sweet and sour, incredible liquid, a few drops of which can transform the flavour of food. It is sold in designated bottles of 50 cl (500 ml), each of which is sealed with red wax and stamped with the consortium's legal stamp. Every bottle of balsamic vinegar is numbered and recorded. It can cost up to £40 for a small bottle, and is one of the most delicious taste experiences in the world.

If you are lucky enough to have some, use it sparingly. A few drops only drizzled over grilled meat or fish is nothing short of sublime. Add a teaspoon to risotto or strawberries, or add a dessertspoon to home-made vanilla ice-cream.

Balsamic Vinegar
ACETO BALSAMICO

Where aceto balsamico tradizionale is the 'parfum' of vinegars, the splash-it-all-over commercial balsamic vinegar that crops up in recipes is the 'eau de toilette'. There are good and bad varieties. The appeal of these vinegars to our modern palates is their sweetness, created by sugar, caramel and sweet grape must.

Very cheap mass-produced balsamic vinegars can be highly acidic and unappealing. The traditional balsamic producers have created a range of middle-priced products. These are made with Trebbiano grapes but using faster, more economical methods of ageing, and then blended with white wine vinegar. The best ones are sweet, low in acid and with a fresh clean taste. I use them in salads and for deglazing fats from a roasting pan.

BREAD

THE WORD 'COMPANIONSHIP' IS DERIVED from the Latin 'con pane', meaning 'with bread'. To break bread together and eat with companions or family, gives fundamental nourishment to body and soul.

Our table is always set with freshly baked, crusty, chewy bread. The bread is torn and eaten as it is, without butter or oil. It is used to soak up the oils and juices on the plate, very like naan bread in Indian cooking. Italian plates are always wiped clean with bread. A great compliment to the cook!

For my grandparents, bread made with wheat was a luxury.

Their bread would most likely have been made with a mixture of unrefined grains – ground corn, barley, rye and wheat. This 'pane nero', or black bread, was sturdy and heavy and kept well for a week. It had no salt, because salt was an expensive luxury, not one that could be wasted in bread. It was most likely baked in a communal oven that was lit only once a week, all the women taking it in turn to fire their bread. They made large loaves, 2–3 kg each. To slice it they unceremoniously tucked the loaf under one arm and sliced across with a sawing action towards themselves, pressing the bread against their chest. Any leftover pieces were kept and served in soup or toasted by the fire. Dry bread was grated for use in stuffing vegetables, particularly peperoni and zucchini. It was also used to coat thin slices of meat before frying.

On the last day before the next baking day, the bread would be brick hard. It was splashed with cold water and allowed to soak for a while until it softened. It was then dressed with a little chopped garlic and doused with some green olive oil. Some slices of ripe, fragrant tomatoes and a sprinkling of dried oregano would add some extra flavour, transforming a hardship into a treat.

In most European countries, towns and villages all have their own bakers who make bread by traditional methods every night. However cleverly supermarkets manufacture 'freshly baked' bread, it is never as satisfying as naturally risen hand-baked bread. If there is a baker near you, make sure you support him.

Italian Country White Bread
PANE CAMPAGNA D'ALBERTO

Other than finding a good baker, you may want to try baking bread at home. Choose organic strong white bread flour; it makes all the difference to the flavour and chew factor of the bread.

Alberto, the best baker I know, taught me how to bake this bread. If you want to make it at home you need a warm atmosphere and a bit of patience. There are five steps. The bread is started 3 hours before it's mixed with a starter dough, a 'biga'. It has a slow proving over another couple of hours, so prepare to be in and out of the kitchen. Having said that, the actual work involved is minimal and the result is worth waiting for. Weigh the ingredients and water accurately. The malt syrup is easily available in supermarkets. (I remember getting a spoonful of 'Virol' when I was young. I'm sure this is the same thing.) This recipe makes two loaves.

1 kg organic strong white bread flour
575 ml hand-hot water
30 g fresh yeast
25 g fine sea salt, or Maldon sea salt, crushed
25 ml malt syrup

Step 1: Make the biga
Firstly make the starter dough, the 'biga'. Put 100 g of the flour into a bowl. Add 100 ml of the hand-hot water and sprinkle in 10 g of the fresh yeast. Mix everything together with a spoon until the mixture looks like a thin batter. Cover it with clingfilm and leave it for 3 hours in a warm room. The biga will get bubbly and double in size.

Step 2: Make up the dough

Warm the rest of the flour, 900 g, in a low oven (160°C/325°F/Gas 2) for 10 minutes or so, just to take the chill off it. Add the sea salt, crumble in the rest of the yeast and add the malt syrup. Tip in the risen biga. Add the rest of the hand-hot water, 475 ml.

Use the dough hook on the mixer and mix the dough, first for 4 minutes on low speed, to mix everything together, then a further 8 minutes on a higher speed. The dough should be elastic but firm, easy to work with. Of course, you can knead it by hand, much more satisfying and smug!

Mould the dough into a round ball and put it into the bowl. Cover it well with clingfilm and cover that with a damp tea-towel. Leave it to rest for 30–40 minutes. Alberto told me that it's best to put it in a cupboard, a warm one if possible. Bread hates draughts more than cold. An airing cupboard or hot water cupboard is ideal.

Step 3: Shape the dough

Remove the dough from the bowl and, on a clean floured work surface, knock the air out it. Divide the dough evenly into two 800 g pieces and shape them into round balls. Place them on a tray, cover them again with a damp cloth and leave them in your snug cupboard for a further 25 minutes.

Step 4: Shaping the loaves

Shape both balls of dough into loaf shapes. (Don't knock the air out of them again.) Grease a baking tray and put them on. Sprinkle them with a little flour and prove them in a cosy, draught-free place for 40–60 minutes.

Step 5: Baking the bread

Preheat the oven to medium (180°C/350°F/Gas 4).

Make three cuts with a sharp knife on each loaf. Put a baking dish in the bottom of the oven with a good handful of ice cubes. This will make steam, simulating a commercial steam oven. Bake the loaves on the middle shelf for 40–50 minutes. The loaves are baked when they are golden to dark brown and you can tap them on the bottom to get a hollow thud.

Leave them to cool on a wire rack for at least 2 hours. These loaves will last at least two days. The bread toasts beautifully.

It is a bit daunting baking bread, but, once you've got the hang of it, it's like riding a bike. It's well worth the bother. To inspire you to try, close your eyes and think of the smell of home-baked bread warm from the oven and biting into a slice slathered with lots of fresh butter and home-made strawberry jam!

SEASONS AND ORGANICS

As a cook who shops regularly for fresh food, I tend to look out for produce that is local and seasonal. If I have the choice I prefer to choose organic vegetables, especially if I intend to serve them raw. It reassures me that they are guaranteed not to have a residue of preservatives in them that may be harmful. In my style of cooking I do use a high proportion of fruit and vegetables and I am aware that the benefit of this in health terms may be negated by inadvertently consuming a higher quantity of residue chemicals. Because organic vegetables are not artificially spurred on with chemicals to make them grow faster, their tissues are formed more slowly. This means they have a slower uptake of water resulting in more concentrated natural sugars.

As long as the produce is fresh, this can result in crisper and better flavoured food.

I always make sure I wash any fruit and vegetables really well. I pay particular attention to perishables like salads and herbs that are more likely to have preservative chemicals sprayed on them. Soak them in a couple of changes of chilled water to dilute and wash away any unwanted ingredients. By the way, Francesca, organic produce is more likely to have livestock nestling inside – greenfly or caterpillars and the like! I remember my mum always added some salt to the soaking water of salads. This helps clean out any such visitors.

I often serve fresh berries to children. They love them and as they are packed with healthy vitamin C, they are very good for them. Or should be! I have become suspicious of the length of time some berries last in the fridge and question what is sprayed on them to stop them spoiling. As we tend not to wash berries very well as they taste better if they aren't waterlogged, I have started choosing only organic berries. It is a real pity, because they are much more expensive. Do we have the right to know what harmful residue may be lurking on our food?

The organic movement is raising awareness in the food world about the quality of our food and the husbandry of our animals. We should support it as much as possible, though it is in danger of being hi-jacked by the marketing people of big companies to promote products that are not necessarily beneficial in other ways.

TASTE

Francesca, when it comes down to it, your own sense of taste is the most valuable tool when cooking. An experienced cook will pay close attention to the flavour of the food as it is cooking.

Taste. Taste. Taste. It is a great pleasure to sip the food as it's cooking and adjust the amount of the ingredients you add as you go along. 'Adjust seasoning' is the key to every recipe. Your taste is your best guide.

Although these recipes are written out with quantities, I never learned them like this. I learned to cook by helping in the kitchen and by always eating good and varied food. My taste memory bank has been well stimulated from an early age. Letting children help in the kitchen as soon as possible is the easiest way to get them to eat well.

Francesca, use all your senses while cooking: sight, smell, hearing and taste. Pay attention to what is happening and adjust as you go along. The quantities written out are only as a guide. All raw ingredients are different and no matter how many times you make a dish, it will taste different each time. I hope the ideas in this book will free you to cook without recipes. It is designed to teach the skills and an understanding of the principles of the way I cook, then, I leave the rest to your own imagination and skills.

Most important, have fun! 'Buon appetito.'

NOTE

The recipes all feed four unless stated otherwise. The pasta recipes feed four as a starter, three as a main course. Having said that, I've noticed that we always eat whatever quantity I make, there are seldom leftovers. The recipes are also very simple. Depending on your appetite, you should be able to adjust the quantities easily as you become familiar with my style of cooking.

WEDDING LIST

Francesca, it's really not worth buying lots of different gadgets to cook with. They clutter up the kitchen and end up with pieces missing or broken. Here's a list of the equipment I can't live without. No, you can't take any of them to your new flat. Add them to your wish list!

Good stainless-steel pots of different sizes. A couple of small pots, 1 litre capacity, a couple of 3 litre pots and at least one large 4 litre pot for boiling pasta. My biggest pot holds 8 litres, for boiling pasta on Christmas Day!

More often than not, I have to cook something quickly for one person.

A few *stainless-steel shallow saucepans* are really handy. I have two-handled 20 cm ovenproof pans that I use constantly. Cast-iron gratin dishes are also useful.

A *stainless-steel butter melter* is handy for all sorts of things.

A *large colander* to drain pasta. A couple of sieves. A stainless-steel tea strainer is useful for skimming broth. (My plastic one melted!)

A *large heavy-bottomed enamelled cast-iron saucepan* for slow-cooking stews and sugo. I like to have 2 or 3 and 4 litre ones. These pots can be used on the cooker and in the oven. They last a lifetime. Don't forget that the handles and lids get hot!

You really need a couple of *heavy frying pans.* I like a small 18 cm non-stick one for frittata and a large, deeper cast-iron one for most other jobs.

A *cast-iron griddle* is a great tool to use to cook food quickly, healthily and with maximum flavour. They can generate a lot of

Marietta and Cesidio's wedding in Picinisco, c.1916

smoke. *Don't buy one if you don't have good ventilation in your kitchen or a strong extractor fan.*

Knives *are very personal items. Choose knives that are comfortable in your hands. You need a heavy large knife, and a few small sharp ones for general chopping. When I'm on holiday in Italy I always buy a pack of plastic serrated steak knives at the local markets. They're really cheap but I use them for all sorts of jobs. (I use a mezzaluna, a two-handled, half-moon blade for chopping herbs and onions really finely, but you could live without one.)*

A sharpening steel *is almost as essential as the knives. (Ask a butcher to show you how to use it.)*

An old-fashioned heat diffuser *is very handy when cooking sugo or soffritto slowly. Tucking it under the pot prevents the contents burning.*

I have an ancient **Kenwood mixer** *for cake-making and bread-making. It has a liquidiser attachment, which is very useful.*

Francesca, I'll get you a **hand-held electric whisk**. *It's just as good.*

I use a **hand-held electric blende**r *to whizz and liquidise soups and tinned tomatoes. Very useful.*

I use an old-fashioned **porcelain pestle and mortar** *to make pesto. It needs to be at least size 3, 450 ml, otherwise there's no room to work.*

I've got a **small pestle and mortar** *to grind spices only, size 00, 110 g. Apart from anything, it looks pretty.*

I don't own a food processor or a microwave. After a lifetime of cooking I've never missed either.

If you want to make home-made pasta, you'll need an **Imperia pasta machine.**

If you want to make ice-cream, you'll get better results if you use a machine. I prefer the type that has a container that is kept in the freezer for 24 hours, then the ice-cream is churned outside the freezer in 20 minutes or so. The downside is that they only make about a litre at a time, not much good in my house. I prefer to make semi-freddo and sorbet, as they don't need to be churned. Don't invest in an ice-cream machine if you aren't going to use it often. (Come and live near Luca's ice-cream shop in Musselburgh instead.)

I would like a **double boiler** for melting chocolate and making custards. I use a bowl balanced in a pot of boiling water.

I use a simple **conical grater** for grating Parmigiano and vegetables. Choose one with a good selection of large and small serrations. Elbow grease is the best tool and if the Parmigiano is in good condition and moist it will grate with little effort.

A good solid, **wooden chopping board** is my preference. I keep a separate wooden board for bread, one that looks nice on the table.

A serrated bread knife.

If you want to deep-fry you need a **chip pan and chip basket.** You can buy great electric fryers that absorb the smell of fat, but they don't hold very much oil at one time. I love 'fritto' but hate the smell of frying in the house.

*When you choose **baking trays, oven trays and baking tins**, buy the best quality you can afford. They'll last much longer and will conduct the heat better. Don't get bogged down with lots of different sizes. I've tried to use as few sizes as possible.*

*Oh yes, you'll need a **stainless-steel ladle, spoon, slotted spoon and potato masher.***

*Stocking fillers: **pastry cutter for ravioli, pastry brush, swivel potato peeler, a wooden rolling pin, a good pepper mill and a dish for Maldon sea salt. A good solid tin-opener for tomatoes, some wooden spoons and pasta tongs.***

*It's worth investing in **good scales** for baking recipes. Work in metric. We're in the twenty-first century! I prefer electronic scales.*

*Good coffee at home is a must. Only two recommendations, the sublime to the ridiculous: an old-fashioned Moka espresso machine or a full-blown, bank-breaking **Baby Gaggia.** Put it on your wedding list. You may have a generous auntie.*

***Crystal glasses**, don't put them on your list. Francesca, when your dad and I got married, Edinburgh crystal glasses were the 'in thing' to give (probably bulk-bought at Jenners' sale). We still have lots of unopened boxes and — until they come back into fashion — you can help yourself.*

ANTIPASTI

'Mangiando, mangiando, viene l'appetito.'
'Eat, eat, and your appetite will come.'

Annunziata, second from left, front row, and Luigi, far right, with their family

'NGOPPA 'A TERRA, POZZUOLI, ITALY 1934

The area of Pozzuoli, north of Naples and Vesuvius, has a dramatic history. It is steeped in fumaroles and hot springs, and is a centre of seismic activity. 'Ngoppa 'a terra' is Pozzuoli dialect meaning 'Rione Terra', the 'earth district', on which the ancient town of Pozzuoli was founded. Around the seventh century BC the Greek colony of Dicearchia was founded on this site, overlooking the port. By 194 BC it had become a flourishing trade centre and an important Roman stronghold.

Around ten centuries later the Rione Terra quarter, 'ngoppa 'a terra, was built on a crop of land that juts out into the sea, high ancient walls protecting a medieval village inside. A single bridge and door was the only entrance. By the beginning of the twentieth century, the Rione Terra was inhabited by the poor of Pozzuoli, crammed into crumbling houses and rooms piled high on top of each other, clinging to the side of the hill, and reached only by hundreds of steps, winding high between the houses.

In a flat high in 'ngoppa 'a terra, overlooking Ischia and Capri, Luigi Silni always sat at the head of the table. Carlo, his first son, sat on his left, the rest of his eight children gathered round. His was an open house. His mother, father and any or all of his brothers and sisters, their wives and husbands, nieces, nephews, boyfriends and girlfriends were always welcome. Priests, doctors or passing policemen were given pride of place.

Annunziata, Luigi's wife, cooked what she could afford. Those who came ate a share of what had been prepared. Like the loaves and the fishes, there was always more than enough. Anyone who protested, out of politeness, that they weren't hungry, would be encouraged to eat even more enthusiastically. Luigi would begin a comical ritual. He had an instinctive understanding of human nature. To him, it was obvious that every man, woman and child was hungry twice a day. And, it went without saying that everyone had an equal right to eat.

'Mangiando, mangiando, viene l'appetito!' Luigi would gesticulate, as if the protestor was mad. It was a waste of energy to resist good food and deny hunger. 'Eat, eat and your appetite will come.'

Sure as fate, once Luigi had tempted them with a little slice of prosciutto cut slightly thick from the ham, the objector was made to feel comfortable. Once Luigi teased with a few spicy, pickled courgettes, salty and sharp but with a decidedly hot kick of chilli to shock the taste-buds, they conceded a little hunger. By the time Luigi offered a spoonful of roasted peperoni, dripping with caper-laden olive oil, the reluctant diner had changed sides and was eating ravenously and with gusto.

The others round the table, who until now had been offered nothing, were starving and agitated. They had watched this ritual temptation and had, by sheer self-control, avoided shouting to the objector to 'Mangia, e stai zitto!' 'Eat up and shut up!'

After what seemed like an interminable wait, Luigi made the sign of the cross and said Grace Before Meals, the signal for all to eat.

He sliced some mozzarella, sprinkled a little salt on it and offered it around. Then, without further discussion, more small plates of food were passed, each person taking a little, judging how much was needed to share among them all. Artichoke hearts; slivers of fresh pecorino; creamy, sweet buffalo milk ricotta; silvery anchovies marinated in olive oil; flakes of baccalà, salted cod pungently prepared with garlic, chilli and olive oil; thick, bulbous tentacles of octopus and calamari or squid.

We seldom prepare antipasti like this at home, except for high days and holidays when lots of different treats are laid on the table. More often one type of antipasti is prepared and eaten as a simple starter before the pasta is served. A few bits and pieces on the table as you sit down with plenty of good bread is a civilised way to relax and settle to enjoy your meal.

I remember, Francesca, that as a child you enjoyed these foods. The children at Luigi's table, and there were always many, quickly learned that it is worth tasting things that look unfamiliar or unusual. More often than not they are delicious and even if you don't like them, you become part of the adult ritual. It takes the pressure off children if they can take little tastes of food to try, helping themselves to those they like, and leaving the rest. Each time they get more adventurous, always tempted to try something new. If you watch their behaviour, an interesting pattern develops. Their memories are selective. As long as the food they tried produced no ill-effects the next time it comes along, it's no longer regarded as unfamiliar. Within a few days or weeks, without realising it, the new food is their favourite!

The most worrying element of relying entirely on ready-prepared food for children is that it stops this process of experimentation. Processed food is by definition always exactly the same. A child will have very limited experience of different flavours and will come to expect food to always taste the same. This will stunt their palate and inevitably make them less likely to try new foods. This also applies to breast-feeding. Depending on what she eats, a mother's milk tastes slightly different every day. Formula milk tastes exactly the same every feed, and may be one of the reasons our children are reluctant to try new flavours. The more varied the tastes a baby experiences between the ages of four and nine months, the more adventurous its taste-buds will be.

Invite and encourage children at a young age to eat a varied diet, and their appetite will come. 'Mangiando. Viene l'appetito!'

Celery Sticks and Extra Virgin Olive Oil
SEDANO E OLIO EXTRA VERGINE

My mum often put a long glass of celery sticks on the table when we were kids. This was accompanied by a small bowl of tasty extra virgin olive oil, and a dish each of sea salt and crushed black pepper. We had great fun dipping the celery into the oil and salt – pepper if we were brave – and crunching it noisily as we waited to be fed.

Choose organic celery if you can find it, but definitely some that is very fresh and crisp. Snap the celery off at the base and wash each stick well in cold water. Trim off the ends. If it is stringy, use a potato peeler to whip off the outside of the ridged edge. Really fresh celery usually isn't stringy. Leave any leaves attached.

To eat, simply dip the celery sticks into the salt, pepper and extra virgin olive oil. Kids love the fun of this; it's a good after-school snack. Do the same thing with carrots, chicory, fennel or even artichokes if they are very fresh and young, chewing the pale fleshy part at the base of each leaf.

Artichokes
CARCIOFI

Artichokes are seductive and alluring but they're part of the thistle family and can be a bit nippy! They do grow easily in Britain, but you are most likely to find Italian or French arti-chokes on sale – if you find them at all. Look for them in specialist fruit shops and farmers' markets. Early spring Roman artichokes are exceptional and easy to prepare. As the season progresses the artichokes get bigger and meatier. In the autumn you may find the beautiful French artichokes. Only buy them if the stalk is firm and the head tightly closed. They need a bit of time to prepare but, like anything that takes a bit of effort, the end result is worth it.

Work at the sink, with the cold water running, rinsing the artichoke all the time. Have a bowl of cold water ready with a couple of lemon halves floating in it. The acidity of the lemon stops the prepared artichokes from discolouring.

Cut off all but 4 cm of the stalk. Use a small sharp knife to trim a little of the outside of the stalk, paring away some of the outer fibres. Rub any cut surfaces with a piece of lemon. Now tackle the head. Work round the artichoke, snapping off each of the outer leaves just as they naturally break, usually about two-thirds down the leaf. Keep working, snapping away, until all the dark green leaves have gone and the lighter yellow, inner ones are showing through. Lay the artichoke down on a chopping board and trim off the spiky leaves that are still sticking out the top. You will now have a pretty devastating pile of discarded leaves, none of which is edible. Don't be afraid that you will throw away too much. Once you cook the artichokes you will soon realise that any dark green parts remaining are inedible and you'll wish you had cut them away.

The only remaining problem is the spiky, fibrous choke that nestles in the centre of the artichoke. The easiest way to get it out is to cut the artichoke head lengthwise in half, then into quarters. Rub the cut halves with the lemon half as the cut sides discolour very quickly. Looking at the middle of the artichoke you will see the sharp, hairy spikes, the choke. With a sharp knife, cut them away, leaving the white solid base clean. Alternatively, if you prefer to keep the artichoke head whole, bash the head down on a chopping board and prize the leaves apart. The choke can then be scraped out with the end of a sturdy teaspoon. Frankly, I find this more work and usually avoid it. Rinse the artichoke as you work, rub with lemon again and pop it into the cold-water bowl.

It really is a learning curve. It's a hassle the first couple of times, but once you work out which bits eat well once cooked, the whole process becomes easy. Beware that if you set out to prepare a lot of artichokes your fingers and nails will get pretty stained. Now to cook them.

4 large or 6 small artichokes,
prepared as above, either left whole or cut, as you prefer
1 clove garlic, peeled and finely chopped
a handful of flat-leaf parsley, washed and finely chopped
about 1 teaspoon Maldon sea salt
about 4–5 tablespoons extra virgin olive oil

about the same amount of cold water
6–8 fresh mint leaves

Mix the chopped garlic, parsley and salt together to make a rough paste. Rub the mixture into the base and between the leaves of the prepared artichokes and pop them into a saucepan large enough to hold them. Add the extra virgin olive oil and cold water. Bring the liquid to a slow simmer, cover the saucepan with a lid and steam gently over a low heat for about 15–20 minutes. Add the mint leaves towards the end.

Push a sharp knife into the thickest part to check that the artichokes are cooked.

Serve them warm with the juices from the saucepan. (Don't refrigerate them.) We usually eat them with our fingers, scraping the best of the juicy flesh from each leaf and using plenty of crusty bread to soak up the juices.

Fresh Anchovies Marinated in Olive Oil
ACCIUGHE MARINATE

This recipe is only worth attempting if you find really fresh anchovies. The fishmonger may have them in spring, but you may have to order them.

500 g very fresh anchovies or small sardines
Maldon sea salt
some peperoncino (dried chilli) to taste, crushed
juice of 2 lemons
extra virgin olive oil, a light-flavoured one if possible
a handful of flat-leaf parsley, very finely chopped

Ask the fishmonger to scale and gut the anchovies for you. I would really flirt badly with the fishmonger to get him to fillet and butterfly them for me as well, but you can do that at home.

If you have to clean them at home you need a small, very sharp knife. Working with plenty of cold running water scrape off the scales with the knife. Hold the body of the fish firmly in your left hand and pull the head and spine away from the fish in one. Cut away the tail and fins. The flesh is soft so the bones and head pull away easily. You will be left with a flat, butterflied fillet. Lay it flat down on a chopping board and check with your fingers that there are no bones or spikes left. Wash each one again in cold water, dry on kitchen paper.

Lay the fillets, skin side down, on a plate in a single layer. Sprinkle with the sea salt and crushed peperoncino, pour the lemon juice all over them and then give a good drizzle of the extra virgin olive oil. The lemon acts to cook them. Leave them covered in the fridge until the next day so that the flavours develop together.

Before serving them sprinkle with chopped parsley. Serve them with wedges of lemons and plenty of crusty bread.

Another way we prepare anchovies is 'all'Ischitana' where the filleted anchovies are sprinkled with extra virgin olive oil, a few breadcrumbs, some lemon juice and wild marjoram (here, you may have to use freshly dried oregano). These are baked in a fairly hot oven (200°C/400°F/Gas 6) for 10–15 minutes until cooked.

Salad to Your Good Health
INSALATA BUONA SALUTE

The Spanish produce fabulous marinated anchovies which are every bit as good as those you could make at home. These 'boquerones' are marinated in olive oil and vinegar and are really succulent, sweet and tasty. They are very useful to serve as antipasto, just on their own with plenty of crusty bread. Alternatively you can prepare them as a salad. The quantities here are per person.

2–3 slices smoked pancetta or bacon
a narrow baguette or 'sfilatini', sliced diagonally into crostini
some Cos lettuce leaves and some Belgian endive, enough to make a
big salad for one
Maldon sea salt and black pepper
extra virgin olive oil
red wine vinegar or lemon juice
6 boquerones (anchovies preserved in oil)
shavings of Parmigiano Reggiano

Lightly fry the pancetta and leave it to cool slightly. Use the flavoured juices that have seeped from the pancetta to oil the bread, and grill these to make some warm crostini.

Wash and dry the salad leaves. Salt them sparingly: the pancetta and anchovies are both fairly salty. Toss the leaves with 2–3 tablespoons extra virgin olive oil. Sprinkle on a little red wine vinegar or some lemon juice.

Choose a deep plate, and place the crostini on the bottom. Pile on the dressed leaves and drape the pancetta and anchovies on top. Finally add the shavings of Parmigiano, adding a last-minute splash of extra virgin olive oil. I like to add a good fresh grinding of pepper. Eat while the crostini and pancetta are still warm.

Puntarelle with Roman Anchovy Sauce
PUNTARELLE CON SALSA DI ACCIUGHE

We enjoy eating in Rome best of all. The dishes are unchanged over centuries and have flavours we are very familiar with. In the 'osterie' and 'trattorie' away from the tourist trail, we eat well. It is the same food our great-great-grandmothers cooked. The sugo tastes like Maria used to make. The salad has carrots and celery chopped through it, just like my Nonna Marietta served it.

Francesca, you and Olivia always eat really well when we visit. You feel at home!

I first tasted this dish in Testaccio, the Jewish ghetto of Rome, on the west bank of the Tiber. The recipes used here have remained unchanged since Ancient Roman times. The curled, crisp, slightly bitter salad was served with an evocative dressing which was creamy, light and delicious. Although it had anchovy and garlic in it, it was neither fishy nor overpowering.

Puntarelle is an ancient type of chicory particular to Rome. It is a magnificent plant with long spiky green leaves and a thick bulbous centre. As always, nothing is wasted. The outer dark green leaves are often blanched and sautéed in oil and garlic and eaten as a vegetable. The white stems and centre have to be painstakingly cut lengthwise, trimmed, sliced and curled. No matter how I tried I couldn't work out how they made the puntarelle curl.

After four years, on another visit to Rome, I worked it out. In the Piazza dei Fiori, an old nonna was sitting with the puntarelle cut into long strips. She had a large tub of iced water at her side. She also had a little square wooden implement on her lap, threaded with guitar wires in a criss-cross, like a fine mesh. As she slowly pulled every strip through the wire mesh, it curled perfectly, just as it had been served in the salad.

Ever curious about the mundane, I asked her what the implement was called and where I could find one to take home. She answered with a knowing look, 'E una macchina per le puntarelle.' 'It's a puntarelle machine!' She shrugged with a wry smile. Was I stupid! It had always been curled like this.

I asked her if I could buy it from her but she declined. I hovered around watching her work, fascinated. Her husband joined in the conversation and ran off to get me one of the tools. I was flattered. What a kind gift. He charged me the modest price of 60,000 lire, nearly £20. A favour, cheap at half the price!

It's highly unlikely you will find puntarelle in Britain and I doubt if you'll find the tool to twirl it with. Mine is not for sale! Don't worry. Make the dressing and serve it with Belgian endive, chicory, celery or even fennel. It really is good!

2 cloves fresh garlic (or less if the garlic is very pungent), peeled
3–4 anchovies preserved in oil, or 2 salted anchovies, de-boned and
rinsed
Maldon sea salt
4–5 tablespoons extra virgin olive oil
1 tablespoon red wine vinegar

Pound the garlic and anchovies together in a pestle and mortar to make a smooth paste. Make a good job of this so that the garlic is smooth and creamy. Add a few grains of salt to give a bit of friction in the pestle. Gradually add enough extra virgin olive oil to make a sauce the consistency of runny honey. Add a couple of splashes of red wine vinegar, just enough to sharpen the flavour of the oil. Taste and adjust the flavour, adding a little more sea salt if required.

It is a perfect accompaniment to any bitter salad leaves or as a dip for raw vegetables.

WILD SMOKED SCOTTISH SALMON

FRANCESCA, I REMEMBER WELL THE TREAT on Hogmanay when we had a midnight feast after the bells at twelve o'clock. Instead of being packed off to bed, three or four in each room, my father pragmatically let us stay up late. We were all bathed, scrubbed and wrapped up in pyjamas, slippers and dressing gowns. Hair had been washed and – yes – the girls usually had rags in to encourage a bit of curl into our straight black hair. We waited excitedly, desperately trying not to squabble and be sent to bed before the fun.

On the stroke of the first bell of midnight – the Presbyterian church next door providing live acoustics – we all had to kneel down and with reverence say a decade of the rosary to ask God to bless the year ahead.

There were never less than twenty of us in the front room: a set of parents, my mum and dad, eight children, Uncle Alex, Aunty Betty, Marietta, Laura, Nonna Café, a dog, a priest, the

Fish sale at Port Seton, with Marietta in white apron, lower right, 1924

73

doctor and a passing policeman or two. The fare was standard every year – a strange mixture of Scottish and Italian traditional festive foods. We children were always as high as kites and tipsy on stolen gulps of champagne, spumante and lemonade. We had Nonna's pizza, 'ham and egg pie', prawn cocktail – made with fresh langoustine, a gift from the local fishermen – black bun and shortbread! There were bowls of olives and 'giardiniera' (pickled vegetables) and prosciutto and melon laid out on scattered small tables and on top of the telly.

Best of all, and a real treat, there was a whole side of Scottish wild salmon smoked by James Dickson, the local fishmonger. He always brought the salmon on the morning of Hogmanay, a gift for my father for all the business he had given the fishmonger all year.

We were allowed to stay up for the party as long as we hid under the table and didn't breathe a word when the doorbell rang. My father knew that if any 'first footers' came in with their bottle of whisky and lump of coal for luck, they would never leave till the wee small hours. So every ten minutes or so we giggled and sniggered in fits of hilarity, hiding with the dog, Aunty Betty, Uncle Alex, Nonna Café, Marietta, Laura, the priest, the doctor and the policeman, all behind the couch or under the table until the unwelcome would-be visitor gave up ringing the bell and moved on. Any squeal, squeak or smart crack was given a sharp threat that any more noise and we would all be sent to bed!

If any first footer persisted and managed to gain entry, they had to join the game and hide with us the next time the doorbell rang!

Wild smoked salmon is far more distinctive and satisfying than farmed, with firm flesh and a rich flavour. Then it was a treat to have salmon at all. Farmed salmon is so common now, that it's still a treat to have wild salmon. Pay the price for wild salmon and buy it for a special occasion. If wild stocks don't improve, it may be that in the future we'll no longer have the choice.

Marinated Wild Salmon
CARPACCIO DI SALMONE

The principle at use here is very similar to the marinated anchovies on page 68. The acidity of the lemon juice 'cooks' the fish and changes its flesh to a pinky, whitish colour.

8–10 slices wild Scottish salmon
3–4 tablespoons lemon juice
3–4 tablespoons light extra virgin olive oil
1 tablespoon small salted capers, soaked for half an hour and rinsed
2–3 tablespoons very finely chopped dill
Maldon sea salt

Use raw salmon or sea trout, not smoked fish. Ask the fishmonger (flirt again!) to cut slices from a wild salmon fillet, no more than 1 cm thick, just as if he was giving you thin slices of smoked salmon. His very sharp knife can do this a lot easier than you would manage at home.

Lay the slices on a chopping board and check with your fingers that there are no bones lurking in the flesh. (Use sterilised tweezers to yank them out if there are any.) Rinse the fish in cold water and dry with kitchen paper. Lay the salmon slices on a flat plate, not overlapping, and dress with plenty of lemon juice. Drizzle on the extra virgin olive oil and sprinkle the capers and most of the dill across the surface. Cover with clingfilm and leave to marinate in the fridge for 1–2 hours.

Taste the salmon and adjust the seasoning depending on how salty the capers are. You may need to add some salt. Sprinkle on some fresh chopped dill.

Carpaccio di salmone is best eaten with thin, lightly buttered slices of fresh rye or sourdough bread.

Squid Salad
INSALATA DI CALAMARI

This is so easy to make. If you're frightened of preparing the squid, ask the fishmonger to do it for you (see page 303). Make him guarantee they are fresh! Always wash the squid before you cook it to get rid of any residual smelly water.

500 g fresh squid, cut into 1 cm thick rings, washed
1 litre water
lemon juice
2 lemons, quartered
DRESSING
2–3 tablespoons extra virgin olive oil
1 clove garlic, peeled and chopped
Maldon sea salt
1 tablespoon black olives, stoned
2 tablespoons finely chopped flat-leaf parsley
1 raw carrot, peeled and thinly sliced
½ red pepper, skinned and thinly sliced

Put the water into a large saucepan and add a good squeeze of lemon juice. Add the washed squid rings and bring the water to the boil. As soon as it's boiling turn off the heat. The squid rings will be cooked. Check by cutting a piece of squid to see if it is tender. Drain the squid and refresh by running cold water over it. Drain again and leave to cool.

Once the squid is cool, mix the dressing ingredients together and drizzle all over the squid. Mix well and check the seasoning, adjusting to taste.

I like to serve this with plenty of lemon quarters to squeeze more juice on just before eating. (It's probably best to eat this the day you prepare it. The garlic will become more pungent the next day.)

MOZZARELLA DI BUFALA

THERE ARE BUFFALO IN THE SOUTH OF ITALY. When I first visited I was amazed to see them grazing on the muddy fields at the side of the road from Rome to Naples, the ancient Roman Appian Way. These days they have been moved inland away from the coast, but are still farmed and produce vast quantities of milk. Fresh mozzarella 'di bufala' is soft and creamy and produces a voluptuous, seductive sensation in the mouth. It is sweet, slightly acidic and vaguely salty.

Maybe it was because her grand-father taught her to love mozzarella so much when she sat at the table with him, but Luigi's granddaughter, Nunzia, became a chemist. She and her husband have the enviable job of testing the buffalo milk every day for the many mozzarella creameries in the region. Luigi used to buy mozzarella from the farm every single day. He knew all the producers by name and

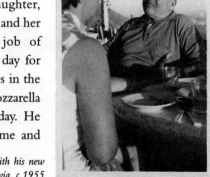

Luigi Silni with his new daughter-in-law Olivia, c.1955

visited so frequently they would direct him to the best day's production, even if it were to a rival's door.

He lifted it from its briny, milky water bath and cut it in slices, drizzled it with extra virgin olive oil and sprinkled it with salt. Nothing else. Every day. Even when Luigi eventually bought a refrigerator, he never chilled the mozzarella. It should be eaten at room temperature.

We are really lucky. We can buy really good buffalo mozzarella these days. Check the label. The fresher it is the better it tastes. Only buy it suspended in its own milky whey. This preserves it naturally and keeps it from forming a skin.

'Bocconcini' are small cherry-tomato-sized mozzarella cheeses, which are especially good to eat with tomatoes or in a mixed salad. There is also a similar style of cheese made from 100 per cent cows' milk, 'fior di latte'. It is in fact better to cook with as it goes stringy rather than rubbery when heated.

PROSCIUTTO CRUDO

'PROSCIUTTO CRUDO', OR RAW HAM, is the cured hind leg of a pig, cleaned, shaped and salted for up to eighteen months to produce a characteristic, sweet, moist cured product. The prosciutto we are most familiar with is that made in Parma where the pigs are fed the whey left over from the Parmigiano Reggiano production. The ham is chilled, cleaned and moulded into the characteristic shape before being salted and aged. This process is carried out all over Italy, each region's ham having subtle differences in flavour.

Probably the most frequently ordered antipasto in Italy and in Italian restaurants the world over is 'prosciutto e melone', Parma ham and melon. When it is at its best it's probably the finest flavour combination on earth. San Daniele prosciutto and deep orange-fleshed Charentais melons are my favourite. Serve it with a fresh grating of black pepper.

At its best, the sweet, juicy prosciutto should be sliced freshly by hand from a ham still on the bone, balanced perfectly on a specially designed stand. The rapier-sharp knife slides smoothly across the surface of the ham, producing a perfectly cut slice, not too thin, and with the creamy, silky band of white fat draped at the edge. The ham should be at room temperature. Otherwise buy prosciutto freshly sliced and use it the same day. Vacuum-packed, ready-sliced prosciutto pales beside the fresh product.

Even better, in the summer, I love to partner the prosciutto with green figs. If only you could taste a ripe warm fig, picked in the morning straight from the tree. A mouthful of intense perfumed sweetness, soft, moist and seductive. Sadly, such ripe figs don't travel well. The purple perfect figs often on offer here may disappoint. Try sweet mango as an alternative.

Air-dried Beef, Wild Rocket and Parmesan
BRESAOLA, RUCOLA E PARMIGIANO

Bresaola is air-dried beef from Valtellina, north-east Italy. It is lean and pink in the middle and should be sliced transparently thin. As with all cured meats it is at its best freshly sliced. The packaged ready-sliced meats have extra preservatives added to stop them discolouring. This inevitably changes their flavour for the worse.

wild rocket leaves
Maldon sea salt and black pepper
extra virgin olive oil
very thin slices of bresaola, freshly sliced, about 8 per person
some Parmigiano Reggiano, shaved from a block
lemon juice

Rinse the rocket and break off any long stalks. Shake it dry. Dress the leaves with a good sprinkling of Maldon sea salt and some extra virgin olive oil. Toss it well, so that the rocket is well flavoured. Taste to check.

For each person arrange seven or eight slices of bresaola on a plate and pile some dressed rocket on top. Shave on some Parmigiano Reggiano and add a drizzle of extra virgin olive oil and a good grinding of black pepper. Just before serving, add a good squeeze of lemon juice, which just lifts the flavour perfectly. (Don't be tempted to add the lemon juice too early. The bresaola goes white and discoloured.)

SALSICCIA, SALAME, COPPA, LARDO

THE BEST ANTIPASTO, AND THE ONE WE PREFERRED as children, is when slices of salame and prosciutto are cut by hand at the table and offered around. Freshly cut, the salame is slightly thicker than usual and is moist, sweet and juicy. Just be aware that the outside skin of the salame is treated to keep out bacteria and can smell suspiciously sour. We always use a sharp knife to peel away the skin of the salame, then a clean knife to cut the slices. This way there is no contamination of flavour or bacteria from the skin into the salame. It's worth noting that pre-sliced salami in vacuum packs have usually been treated with extra preservatives to stop them discolouring. Unfortunately this affects the taste and can be slightly overpowering. When the salame is cut so perfectly thin in these packs, you also miss out on the most satisfying part of salame eating – chewing!

The curing of pork is an ancient tradition in Italy, so the types and style of salami and salsiccie is vast. Salame is eaten raw, and although sometimes used in cooking, I don't. Sausage

is either cured or fresh. Cured sausage or 'salsiccia' can be
eaten raw or used in cooking. Fresh Italian pork sausage must
always be cooked and is perfect for making tomato sugo or
for grilling. (Unfortunately you can't substitute British sausage
in Italian recipes.)

There are many types of salame and cured sausage from
Italy; use as many or as few as you like. These are just a few
of our favourites.

Fonteluna Sausage: *a 100 per cent pork sausage cured with
spices to the Crolla family's original recipe. It is hot and spicy, can be
eaten raw, in thin slices, or used in cooking.*

*Salame di Napoli: a 100 per cent pork salame. This is roughly
textured and is seasoned with whole and crushed black peppercorns.
The spicy kick of the pepper complements the fat in the salame
perfectly. Salame is best served lightly chilled: not too cold, but just
firm enough to slice.*

*Salame Finocchina: if you can find it, try this wonderful pork
salame. It is a 12–15 cm round salame, moist and sweet with a
wonderful fennel-aniseed flavour.*

*Mortadella: a very finely minced pork sausage from Bologna,
this is especially good when sliced paper-thin. As well as antipasto, it
makes the best panini on earth. (During the Second World War
mortadella became associated with donkey meat . . . which, of course,
was only a rumour!)*

*Coppa or, better still, **Culatello di Zibello**: cuts of boned
shoulder of the pig, which are cured in saltpetre, salt, pepper and
nutmeg. It is especially good when flavoured with juniper berries. It is
cured for a minimum of three months and has a sweet, clean pork
flavour, not unlike prosciutto. It is made of equal parts of lean pork
to fat and is best eaten sliced thinly.*

*Knuckle of prosciutto: ask at your local delicatessen for the
knuckle of the Parma ham. This narrow ankle of the ham tastes just*

the same as the rest of the prosciutto but as it doesn't slice into the long traditional slices it is more often than not sold off cheap – or at least it should be! Use the skin to flavour soup or minestrone and cut the prosciutto into chewy slices . . . the best! (I rarely use prosciutto for cooking except for saltimbocca. I think it loses its delicate flavour. If you do want to cook it, use the knuckle for flavour and value.)

Lardo: *in the old days lardo was a valuable source of cooking fat and calories. The fat is taken from the pig and cured in salt for a few months to preserve it. It is usually bashed and tenderised with flavourings of garlic, parsley and black pepper and melted into soups and sugo to give creamy substantial flavour called a 'battuto' (see page 108). It is also eaten raw, sliced very thinly with a sharp knife. Lardo d'Arnad is famous, made in the Val d'Aosta in northern Italy. They leave a little of the flesh of the pork marbled through it and flavour it with rosemary and black pepper. Sliced very thinly it is especially good in a mixed antipasto or as a pizza topping with wild rocket. I had stopped using lardo in my cooking trying to cut down on fat. Having just read that it has fewer calories than olive oil or butter, I'm going to reconsider!*

Guanciale: *the cured jowl of a pig. It is similar to pancetta, but with more fat, like lardo. It is often seasoned with black pepper on its surface.*

WILD CHICORY, BITTER GREENS

WE HAVE INHERITED THE ROMAN PRACTICE of serving a plate of bitter greens as an antipasto. The Romans are mad about their greens, eating them with every meal. They grow a great variety of different types throughout the year: cicoria, cime di rapa, spinach, Swiss chard and escarole. Most are bitter and ferrous, obviously good for you. Blanched and then simply sautéed with olive oil and lemon or flavoured with garlic and chilli they are amazingly tasty, leaving a strong sense of well-being when consumed. Not unlike a workout at the gym!

If you can find Roman cicoria, simply wash it well, trimming away any coarse stalks and discarding any dull leaves. Boil in boiling salted water for 5–8 minutes and drain it well.

If it is very young and tender all you need to do is dress it with a good-flavoured extra virgin olive oil and a generous splash of lemon juice.

If it is a bit older, warm some oil in a large frying pan and add a flavouring of garlic and peperoncino. Toss the cicoria in it. Again simply flavour it with lemon juice. Bitter greens are an acquired taste, but are addictive once your body subconsciously realises the benefits of eating them.

SOUP

'Si non può magnà carne, accuntienté a ò broro.'
'If you can't eat meat, be content with soup.'

Marietta and Cesidio and their children outside the Cockenzie Café, East Lothian,
c.1930

COCKENZIE, EAST LOTHIAN, SCOTLAND
1930–1960

Over time, Marietta had four children. She was a simple cook,
preparing fresh satisfying food every day. She was also an astute
businesswoman, eventually running three cafés and a catering
business. As a child, I spent a lot of time in her kitchen. I loved
being with her and thought of her as a source of good food
and 'half-crowns'.

She was strong and honest, with a tendency to scheme.
Cesidio had gradually bought the shop in Cockenzie, then the

flats above it and then the flats above them. She knocked every-thing together and what had been home to ten or twelve fami-lies became her family home. It was higgledy-piggledy with odd-shaped rooms and long corridors, but for the first time in her life she had an inside toilet, a gas stove and electricity. She had a sink in her kitchen with running water. Hot and cold! There was no luxury like central heating, however. The main living room was heated with a single coal fire: coal delivered on Mondays on the horse and cart from the local mine. The rest of the rooms were stuffy in the summer, freezing in the winter.

She went back to Italy every second or third summer, taking money and clothes, chocolate and tea to her sisters and their families who had remained there. They were still living in the poverty she had left behind.

Francesca, Nonno Cesidio died while quite young, and Marietta always mourned. From then on she always wore black, and still dressed modestly in long skirts with shirt collars buttoned at the throat. She always had a spotlessly clean white apron on, reaching down over the whole of her skirt. She wore neat, polished black lacing shoes, with a thick chunky heel. (Rumour has it that during the war she had the heels hollowed out and used the space to hide money.) For a woman so tall, five foot six, it made her look statuesque and powerful.

Gradually she bought more and more properties in Cockenzie and neighbouring Port Seton, and opened a very busy second café. Though we always ate Italian food at home, she learned how to make Scottish dishes and provided food for the hordes of holidaymakers who visited the coast east of Edinburgh for their summer holidays.

There was no market for pizza and pasta, but there was for ice-cream, fish and chips, steak pie and Scotch barley broth. I remember her carrying huge 40 litre pots on her head, balanced on a round tea-towel. She walked, as she would have in Italy up the mountain, with one hand on her hip, supporting her back, the other stretched high, balancing the side of the pot on her head.

As a child, it was always a great treat to visit her in the café and help her: chopping vegetables, peeling potatoes, mixing ice-cream. She had a great sense of fun but was strict and very hard-working. We called her 'Nonna Café'.

Having been brought up without running water she had a great passion for the liquid silver coming out of a tap. When she got up in the morning she turned on the cold tap and left it running the whole time she was in the kitchen, which was the best part of the day. She had a natural instinct for hygiene. All food was kept spotlessly clean. All food was washed endlessly under the running water. Everything was covered or kept in separate dishes in the refrigerator. Hands were washed, washed and washed again. Pots were scrubbed clean, not a speck of fat or grease allowed to stay on the base. She always encouraged us to help in the kitchen and to taste everything. The only down-side was she made us help with the washing-up which had to be done to perfection.

Nonna Café made 'pastina in brodo' every week. It's a lovely light soup, easily digestible and a favourite with all children. She served it with freshly grated pecorino which melts and goes a little stringy in the soup . . . we loved it.

But the soup that made her fortune and helped pay for her string of properties was Scotch barley broth, which she made by the gallons for her customers.

Scotch Barley Broth

1 tablespoon split peas, soaked overnight
2 carrots
2 onions

2 leeks
1 small white turnip, about 150 g
1 or 2 lamb shanks
1.5–2 litres cold water
2 tablespoons pearl barley
Maldon sea salt and white pepper
finely chopped flat-leaf parsley

Remember to soak the peas in cold water overnight.

Wash, peel and trim the vegetables as appropriate, cutting them into small pieces, all roughly the same size. Discard the coarsest parts of the dark green leaves of the leeks.

Trim the lamb shanks of any fat and give them a rinse. Put them into a large saucepan and cover with the cold water. Bring to the boil and turn the heat to low. As the water simmers gently use a tea strainer to skim off any scum that rises to the surface. This takes about 20 minutes: just keep skimming now and then, using a piece of wet kitchen paper to wipe the inside of the pot.

Rinse the barley and the pre-soaked peas, and add them with a teaspoon of Maldon salt. Simmer gently for about an hour.

Add the fresh vegetables and leave the soup simmering for another half-hour or so, adding more water if necessary. Check the seasoning.

Remove the lamb shanks and cut the tender juicy meat into bite-sized pieces. Add them to the soup. Add a grinding of white pepper.

This lovely filling soup somehow tastes even better the next day. Serve it with plenty of finely chopped parsley.

Small Pasta in Broth
PASTINA IN BRODO

Francesca, please make this soup. It's a great standby and really easy to prepare. Apart from anything you love it, so that gives it pride of place in my book! Look for a piece of beef that is well hung, with a thin slice of fat. The beef should be dark purple-red, and look appetisingly tender.

1 x 500 g piece boiling beef, with the bone in
2–2.5 litres cold water
1 small onion
2–3 sticks celery
2 carrots
1 small leek
3–4 fresh tomatoes or ½ x 400 g tin Italian plum tomatoes
a bunch of flat-leaf parsley (I remember Nonna Café added a clove of garlic and a teaspoon of tomato purée but these have fallen by the wayside in my kitchen)
Maldon sea salt
3–4 handfuls pastina (120–150 g)

Wash the beef, trimming away any excess fat. Put it into a medium-sized pot and cover with cold water. Bring the water to the boil and as it simmers gently, use a small tea strainer to skim off any scum that rises to the surface. (Now, don't tell me this is too much bother. I did it when I was eight!) Once the water looks clear, just take a wet piece of kitchen paper and clean round the inside of the pot. That's the limit to the hard work here.

Wash and peel all the vegetables, but there's no need to chop them. Just cut them so they'll fit in to the pot. Now, simply, add them to the pot with the tomatoes, parsley and a teaspoon of Maldon salt. Cover the pot and leave the soup to simmer slowly for 1½ hours or so. Leave the lid slightly off-centre, the broth should reduce by about a quarter at the most. Taste the broth. Isn't it lovely? Check the seasoning. If you prefer to get rid of any fat, you can strain the broth and leave it to cool. Any fat will solidify on the top and can be lifted off. I usually just lift any excess fat off with a ladle and discard it.

When you're ready to eat, cook the pastina in a separate pot of boiling salted water for 8–10 minutes until it is al dente, and strain it. Put it back into its pot and strain the cooked broth on to it. Aim to have about half pastina to liquid broth. Bring the soup back to the boil and add a little finely chopped parsley. We always eat this with freshly grated pecorino or Parmigiano.

The broth will keep in the fridge for two to three days, or it freezes very well.

I buy a chunk of boiling beef or a lamb shank when I'm in the butcher's and make this soup while I'm cooking other things. It looks after itself and the next day's supper can be ready in minutes.

This broth is also a good stock to use for risotto, in which case dilute it with half its volume of cold water. It is perfect for risotto Milanese flavoured with saffron.

Boiled Beef and Carrots

The beef boiled in the broth becomes deliciously tender and juicy. We used to eat it with the carrots and celery from the soup and soft, fluffy mashed potatoes. Sometimes I just cut it up and put a little tender piece into each bowl of soup.

Alternatively, you can jazz it up with a pungent salsa verde, made with herbs and capers (see page 226).

Chicken Broth
BRODO DI POLLO

So many great cuisines have chicken broth as a central ingredient. It's the 'penicillin' of Jewish cooking, the base for so many
exotic, aromatic broths in Chinese and Thai cooking, and the
substance for Scottish cock-a-leekie. It is also the basis for the
best, creamy risotto. It's the broth offered during illness to tempt
a patient back to health. (What do ill people get to tempt them
back to health in households that just eat ready-made foods?)
It's the broth offered to me by my mother-in-law when I
returned home from hospital with her first grandchild. (We hadn't
organised a carry-cot for you, Francesca, so you spent the lunch
in an orange, plastic laundry basin, the one I still use to wash
your sweaters in!)

The modern, fast alternative in all these instances is the ubiquitous chicken stock cube. But believe me, it's no bother at all to
make at home. The best chicken broth or stock is made with a
boiling fowl. This is traditionally any old chicken that has spent
its life rummaging and pecking around the farmyard but is now
over the hill! When it's boiled gently in water it provides a good-
flavoured stock that will set like jelly when cool. Its flesh is juicy
and tasty and good eating itself. Modern, battery hens will just
not do the job. There is no substance in their bones!

It's almost impossible to buy boiling fowl these days, except
in a Chinese supermarket. (These come with head and feet
attached, a bit off-putting to a city girl!) Frozen chicken wings
from the Chinese supermarket are good, but I tend to use free-
range chicken legs or thighs, which work just as well. Alternatively,
if I buy a free-range chicken I cut off the breasts and legs to
roast separately, and use the carcass for soup. (This isn't as difficult as it sounds. Just use a sharp knife to cut away each breast
and then cut each leg away from the side of the carcass. Trim off

any excess fat, give the bones a good wash in cold water and you have the basis for a good chicken stock.) Some butchers will sell you chicken carcasses. Make sure they're from free-range birds.

Is it worth the bother? Undoubtedly, yes. Once you get into the swing, it isn't even a bother at all.

> *4 free-range chicken legs or a 500 g pack chicken wings,*
> *or a carcass as described above*
> *2–3 sticks celery with leaves*
> *a large bunch of flat-leaf parsley, with stalks*
> *Maldon sea salt*

Wash the chicken pieces and trim off any excess fat. Put them into a medium-sized saucepan and cover them with cold water, about 1.5–2 litres. Don't be tempted to add too much water. Just cover the chicken by a couple of centimetres. You will get a full-flavoured broth that you can dilute later. Bring the water slowly to the boil. You may see some alarming scum rise to the surface. Lower the heat to a very slow simmer and use a tea strainer to skim the scum away. Keep skimming intermittently for 10–15 minutes until the surface of the broth looks clear. Use a damp piece of kitchen paper to clean the inside of the pot. This is really worth the effort if you want a clear stock that's not greasy.

Add the celery, the parsley and some salt, and simmer very gently for about 1½-2 hours with the lid half on, half off. Taste and add more salt if you think the broth needs it.

Let the broth cool. Strain it and keep aside any bits of chicken that look tasty. The broth can be stored in the fridge for two to three days. Any fat will solidify on the top and can be removed. Frozen, the stock keeps for three to four months.

Use the broth for risotto or for any of the following soups.

Chicken Broth with Pastina
BRODO DI POLLO CON PASTINA

I make this at least once a week. It's quick when you're hungry, light when you just need a snack and has never been refused by old or young. If you use fine egg vermicelli you're making the original pot noodle!

3–4 handfuls, 125 g, pastina or egg vermicelli
Maldon sea salt
1 litre (or so) chicken broth (see page 90)
a small handful of flat-leaf parsley, very finely chopped
freshly grated Pecorino or Parmigiano Reggiano

Cook the pastina or vermicelli in boiling salted water. (The pastina takes about 8 minutes, the egg vermicelli no more than 4.) In a separate saucepan, warm the chicken broth, checking its seasoning.

Drain the pastina and add it to the hot chicken broth. Add the parsley and sprinkle with some grated Parmigiano cheese.

I often add the cooked chicken pieces to this to add substance. As a child I really loved sucking the juicy chicken wings, which are meltingly tasty and good.

Broth with Egg
STRACCIATELLA

Stracciatella is a delicious egg mixture lightly whisked through broth to add substance and flavour. Maria thickened her mixture with a little flour, Marietta made a more cheesy version using grated Parmigiano Reggiano. Both are delicious.

1 litre chicken broth (see page 90)
2 free-range eggs
2 teaspoons plain flour, or 2 tablespoons freshly grated Parmigiano
Reggiano
1 teaspoon lemon juice
1 tablespoon very, very finely chopped flat-leaf parsley

Bring the broth to a fast boil. Taste it to check its seasoning. Whisk the eggs and mix in all the remaining ingredients.

Stir the egg mixture into the boiling broth, pouring it over a fork and stirring as if drawing a figure of eight. The idea is to cook the egg very quickly in the hot broth and to make it form long, light ribbons. This makes a very elegant light soup.

You can add pastina as well for a more substantial dish.

THINGS TO PUT IN SOUP

KIDS LOVE ADDING BITS AND BOBS TO SOUP. They love the sense of independence it gives them. It's also one of the best ways to develop their palates using their natural sense of curiosity and adventure to try anything that looks or smells nice.

Freshly grated Parmigiano Reggiano is the most popular. Who can resist? I love fresh, young pecorino grated as well. It goes stretchy and stringy in hot broth.

We used to be able to buy little, light round soup balls from Italy, not unlike modern-day corn pops without the sugar. They floated on the soup and slowly absorbed the hot liquid. When you ate them they oozed delicious flavour into your mouth. Sadly, I don't think they're made any more. Alternatively, little squares of bread, lightly fried in olive oil or doused in oil and toasted in the oven, are lovely floating on soup.

One step ahead of this is the fashion for floating crostini in soup: squares of crispy, thin bread, toasted and soaked in good-flavoured olive oil. Add a topping related to the ingredients in the soup, or a little cheese like Gorgonzola or Stilton. Keep it simple.

Cesidio's children, Anna, Carmela and Johnny, with Alex in front, c.1927

You can cook a piece of the washed skin of the Parmigiano in the soup. It imparts a lovely flavour and is deliciously chewy and stringy to eat.

Cream or soured cream can be added to thick soups that are based on milk like Cullen skink or potato and porcini soup.

Fresh herbs sprinkled in at the end freshen and lift the flavour. Young kids enjoy making patterns and stirring everything in. This way, they build up their familiarity with different flavours, get more nutrients and vitamins, and gain confidence in tasting and assessing flavour . . . without an inkling of what's going on! It's just fun at teatime.

I often poach an egg in soup, especially in broths. It makes the soup into a complete meal as the soft yolk oozes out into the broth giving a creamy delicious flavour.

Cream of Chicken Soup

Marietta's café become a flourishing catering business that my parents took over as she got older.

Francesca, my mother and father did the catering for my wedding, all 350 guests. The second course was cream of chicken soup. We were amazed at how delicious the soup was. It was full flavoured and creamy. Daddy was thrilled to serve it. He had been very worried about delegating the serving of the food to hired chefs. Delighted, he left the top table, and went into the kitchen to thank them. It wasn't until the dessert that we all realised why the chicken soup had tasted so good. They had poured all the cream set aside for the Scotch trifle into it. No wonder it was good!

My father never got over the shock. From then on, every time he met my mother-in-law he asked her if she had forgiven him for serving the trifle with no cream on top . . .

Make this soup only if you have good, intensely flavoured, home-made chicken broth.

500 ml full-fat milk
1 bay leaf
1 small shallot
30 g butter
3 tablespoons plain flour
Maldon sea salt and white pepper
450 ml hot, good-flavoured chicken broth
(see page 90)
2 tablespoons of the chicken pieces reserved from the stock
some very finely chopped flat-leaf parsley,
or a few chopped fennel fronds
2 tablespoons double cream

The base of the soup is a classic white sauce or béchamel (see page 223). (I remember when Mummy went through her 'French phase'. After a holiday in Paris she had her seventh child - John Mark! She also took to making vol-au-vents, very posh pastry cases filled with a white sauce flavoured with concentrated chicken stock and little cubes of chicken. Ooh là là!)

Firstly pour the milk into a saucepan, add the shallot and the bay leaf, and warm it up. Take it off the heat and leave to let the flavours infuse.

Melt the butter in a saucepan, add the flour and stir to make a paste (a 'roux'). Cook it for a couple of minutes over a medium heat, taking care not to let it burn. Keep stirring and strain in half of the warm milk. Stir the sauce until the milk is absorbed and comes to the boil. It will be lumpy at first but it will become smooth as you stir. Gradually add the rest of the milk, stirring as it comes back to the boil. Let it simmer for 5 minutes or so to cook the flour. Don't let it singe or boil over. Season the sauce with salt and pepper. Taste it.

Now incorporate the hot chicken broth. Add it gradually, stirring as it blends together. You can use a blender, but a wooden spoon does the job just as quickly. Keep stirring to get a smooth soup. Taste the soup and check the final seasoning.

Add the chicken pieces and the herbs, and serve with a swirl of cream.

If you cool the soup, it will solidify somewhat and form a skin. Don't worry, this will stir in and disappear as you heat the soup again.

You can add a little more milk if the soup is too thick.

Cock-a-leekie

Marietta, my Nonna Café, learned how to cook Scottish recipes from the friends she made in Cockenzie. She went down to the harbour every day to buy fish from the boats. No doubt she chatted and talked about food, listening and learning.

Gertrude. Johnny and Marietta at one of the Caterings, c.1960

Prunes are traditionally served with cock-a-leekie, but surprisingly, I don't remember her adding them.

2 large leeks
1 medium onion
50 g unsalted butter
1 large potato
1.5–2 litres hot chicken broth (see page 90)
pieces of chicken from the broth

white pepper
2 tablespoons finely chopped flat-leaf parsley or chives
8–10 semi-dried prunes
2 tablespoons double cream

Wash the leeks, removing the very course outer green leaves. Loosen the leaves of the leek to make sure you wash out any grit. Peel the onion. Chop the leeks and onion fairly small.

Melt the butter in a medium-sized saucepan. Add the chopped leek and onion, stir and cook slowly with the lid on until they are soft and translucent. (The lid allows the vegetables to steam in the butter and concentrate their flavour.)

Peel and chop the potato into cubes, and add them with the hot broth. Simmer for 30 minutes or so until the vegetables are nice and soft.

Add the chicken pieces, and check the seasoning, adding a good grinding of white pepper. Make sure the cock-a-leekie is nice and hot, and stir in the chopped parsley or chives and a couple of soft prunes. Serve with a swirl of cream.

If you prefer a smooth soup, whizz everything in a blender before you add the chicken pieces, prunes, herbs and cream.

Chinese Noodle Soup

Francesca, look how easy it is to make Chinese broth. Use Chinese rice noodles. Simply soak them in boiling water for a few minutes before adding them to the hot broth.

1 litre hot chicken broth (see page 90)
2 nests soaked rice noodles
a 4 cm piece of fresh root ginger, peeled and cut into matchsticks
2 tablespoons chopped fresh coriander

1 fresh green chilli, de-seeded and chopped
some frozen won-ton from the Chinese supermarket, defrosted (optional)

Heat the chicken broth. Add all the ingredients, heat through, and check the seasoning. Serve in bowls with chopsticks for fun. Home-made pot noodles!

Pasta and Potato Soup
PASTA E PATATE

At home, this soup was made religiously (!) every Friday. We strictly kept the Catholic tradition of not eating meat on Fridays. This was no great hardship as 'pasta e patate' is one of the most satisfying, comforting soups on the face of the earth. No matter what the priest says, no Italian mother would willingly deprive her family. In practice, the rule was obeyed in spirit only.

2 tablespoons extra virgin olive oil
1 clove garlic, peeled
1 small piece peperoncino (dried chilli)
1 onion, peeled and very finely chopped
1 x 400 g tin Italian plum tomatoes
1.75 litres hot water
2 floury potatoes, peeled and diced
Maldon sea salt
a handful of ditali rigate pasta (or small chunky pasta)
freshly grated Parmigiano Reggiano

Warm the oil in a saucepan and add the garlic and chilli. Add the chopped onion, stir and coat with the oil. Put the lid on and cook the onion slowly until it is soft and translucent. Don't let it burn.

Whizz the tomatoes in a liquidiser and, if you can be bothered, strain out the seeds by pressing the purée through a sieve. (You can use a packet of tomato passata instead.) Add the sieved tomatoes and 1 litre of the water. Add the potatoes and a teaspoon of Maldon salt. Cover and cook for 30 minutes or so until the potatoes have softened. Remove the garlic.

Add the remaining water and the pasta. Stir and simmer for 10 minutes until the pasta is al dente. Check the seasoning, and serve in big warm bowls with plenty of freshly grated Parmigiano Reggiano.

I often poach a couple of eggs in this soup. When the pasta has started to cook, break one or two eggs on to the surface and let them poach gently as the pasta finishes cooking.

Nonna Café's Tomato Soup

Marietta made tomato soup with a ham stock. It is most likely that she had learned to make it originally with smoked pancetta, Italian bacon, which had been cured from the farm's pig when it was slaughtered.

I remember when I was very young, spending half an hour or so passing this soup through a sieve for Nonna. I hated the job. She insisted on squeezing every scrap of flavour out of the tomatoes, which, for my small hands, meant heavy work. She rewarded me with morsels of pecorino, cut regularly from the whole cheese. Fair exchange!

To make the stock, soak a ham-end in cold water overnight to get rid of the excess salt. Rinse it and put it into a saucepan covered with 3 litres fresh water. Bring it to the boil and skim off any scum that rises to the surface. Let it simmer gently for a couple of hours until the ham is tender and cooked. (Any extra stock can be frozen.)

Alternatively, use a 4 cm slice of smoked pancetta or bacon and cook it slowly with the butter, shallots and carrots. In this case, add hot water instead of stock.

For a vegetarian variation leave out the ham or pancetta, make the soup with water and just add a little more salt.

3 shallots
3 carrots
2 large potatoes
75 g unsalted butter
1 kg sweet ripe tomatoes, washed, or 2 x 400 g tins Italian plum
tomatoes
1.5 litres hot ham stock
Maldon salt and black pepper
double cream
fresh basil

Clean and peel the shallots, carrots and potatoes, and shred them coarsely.

Melt the butter in a small saucepan. Add the shredded shallots and cook them very slowly until they are translucent. Don't let them burn. Add the carrot and potato. Let this mixture cook slowly in the butter for half an hour or so.

Transfer this soffritto to a larger saucepan and add the tomatoes, stems, skins and all. Stir everything round, cover with the lid, and cook the soup for a further 20 minutes or so until the tomatoes soften down.

Push the soup through a sieve or a mouli if you have one. Bring the soup to the boil. Add the hot ham stock. Taste and season and finish the soup with a swirl of cream and a good handful of fresh basil to lift the flavour.

Serve the boiled ham with some mashed potatoes as a main course.

Porcini and Potato Soup
ZUPPA DI PORCINI E PATATE

Fresh porcini mushrooms are packed with flavour. It is an acquired taste, but one which seduces. I used to be put off using fresh porcini because they do have a tendency to house maggots. Not appealing at all. My cousin Renzo, a ranger in the Abruzzo National Park, pops the porcini into a clear plastic bag for 10 minutes or so. Any 'visitors' crawl out and stick to the sides of the bag. The porcini can then be carefully extracted from the bag, clean. (Francesca, this reads like one of those Chinese game shows where the contestants have to perform spine-curdling feats! Don't worry. It's not that bad.)

If you do have some fresh porcini, do try this soup. If not, use cultivated chestnut or Paris brown mushrooms instead. It's still very good.

2 shallots, peeled and finely chopped
2 sticks celery, very finely chopped
125 g unsalted butter
2 medium-sized potatoes (Maris Piper or other floury potatoes),
peeled and grated
1.5 litres hot water
300–400 g fresh porcini (or chestnut mushrooms), wiped clean and
sliced
Maldon salt and black pepper
250 ml single cream
fennel fronds taken from the stem, or finely chopped flat-leaf parsley

Soften the shallot and celery in the butter until they are soft and translucent. Add the potato and the hot water and cook for 10 minutes.

Now add the sliced porcini or cultivated mushrooms and simmer the soup for another 20 minutes or so. Taste and season then blend the soup until it is smooth. Porcini have a lovely velvety smooth consistency. The soup will probably be very thick. Adjust the consistency with the single cream and a little more hot water if you prefer it thinner. Add the fresh herbs and serve it piping hot.

Dried porcini or ceps are another alternative you can use if you don't have fresh porcini. Use cultivated mushrooms and about 10–15 g dried mushrooms. Soak the dried mushrooms in a cup of warm water for about 15 minutes. Drain them through a sieve lined with kitchen paper, collecting the soaking water to add to the soup. Give the reconstituted mushrooms an added wash. They can be gritty and there is nothing more off-putting than grit in a smooth soup. Chop them, add to the soup and blend.

Green Soup
MINESTRONE VERDE

Tell kids they're having 'spring vegetable soup with pesto genovese' for tea and they'll throw a wobbly. Offer them 'green soup with shells' and they'll be impressed. Funny creatures, kids! They can eat something week in week out for months and then, out of the blue, push it away and refuse to admit they've ever eaten it in their lives before.

Francesca, in my experience, husbands are much the same.

It's a bore, but it makes all the difference if you chop all the vegetables neatly and approximately the same size, into 2–3 cm cubes. This lets them cook evenly. Always add hot liquid, water or stock, when making soup. Maintaining the heat keeps the vegetables simmering instead of stewing, keeping them bright and flavoursome.

1 onion, peeled
3–4 sticks celery
300 g greens, cime di rapa, Swiss chard or spring cabbage
2–3 courgettes
a good handful of freshly podded peas
(don't use frozen or tinned, they're too soggy here)
2 tablespoons extra virgin olive oil
1.5 litres boiling water
Maldon sea salt and black pepper
a handful of gnocchetti sardi or conchigliette (small shell-shaped pasta)
2–3 tablespoons fresh pesto (see overleaf)
freshly grated pecorino or Parmigiano Reggiano

Get the vegetables all washed and chopped fairly equally in size. Soften the onion and celery in the oil until they are translucent.

Always add the vegetables you are using in order that they need to cook. Basically the harder ones take longer. So, add the chard and chopped greens, pour over the boiling water and cook for 20 minutes or so until the vegetables are tender.

Add the courgettes, then finally the fresh peas. (Use your discretion. If some of the greens are very young they can be separated from the tougher stalks and added later on in the cooking. This will keep them brighter and preserve some of the vitamins in them.) Season the soup well.

At this stage, I usually use a hand blender to whizz half of the soup. This leaves some of the vegetables chunky in a thick broth. Stir in the pasta and a little more hot water if the soup is too thick, and simmer for the last 10 minutes. Once the pasta is cooked, adjust the consistency and check the seasoning again. Stir the pesto into the soup with a good grating of pecorino or Parmigiano Reggiano just to finish it off.

Wonderful!

In a pestle and mortar make a very quick pesto by grinding the leaves from a good handful of fresh basil, a ½ clove of garlic and a sprinkling of Maldon sea salt. Grind it together, adding enough extra virgin olive oil to make a rough paste. Check the flavour.

Adjust the basic recipe depending on what vegetables you can find. I like to add a few spears of asparagus. For a more substantial soup, add a peeled and cubed potato at the beginning.

Ring the changes, using a handful of arborio rice instead of the pasta. The rice will take about 20 minutes to cook and will probably absorb more water, so adjust accordingly.

You can let kids add their own pesto and cheese to make a pattern on the soup. Just make sure they eat it all up!

'Celtic' (Cream of Spinach) Soup

Francesca, I used to give you this green spinach soup with white cream drizzled across the surface in stripes. The Glasgow Celtic Football Club's strip is green with white stripes. They called themselves 'The Hoops'. Grandpa Hugh Hilley, who played for Celtic in the 1920s, scored an own goal in the Cup Final against Rangers! This is your Celtic soup.

The 'ready-to-use' young spinach that you can buy is great. It saves all the work of washing the spinach in several changes of water to get rid of all the grit.

Hugh Hilley, top left, and the Glasgow Celtic Football Club, 1922–1923

50 g unsalted butter
2–3 shallots, peeled and finely sliced
4 sticks celery, washed, peeled and chopped
2 potatoes, peeled and finely sliced
1 small white turnip, washed and peeled (about 50 g)
1 x 250 g bag fresh washed young spinach
a good handful of very finely chopped flat-leaf parsley
Maldon sea salt and black pepper
lemon juice
freshly grated nutmeg
double cream or crème fraîche to serve

Warm the butter and add the shallot and celery. Coat them in
the butter and cook very gently until they are soft and
translucent. Add the potatoes, the small turnip in one piece
and 1 litre boiling water. (The turnip just adds some extra
flavour; leave it out if you don't have one.) Simmer the soup
gently until the potatoes have softened. Remove the turnip
and discard.

Add the spinach, pressing it down into the water. Add the chopped parsley and cook for a further 10 minutes or so. Use a hand blender or liquidiser to blend the soup and if you want it to be really smooth pass it through a sieve. Bring back to the boil. Now, firstly check the consistency, adding more water if necessary. Season the soup well with salt, pepper, lemon juice and nutmeg.

Serve the soup with a good blob of softly whipped cream or crème fraîche, or make the white stripes of the Celtic strip!

Sausage and Cabbage Soup from the Fontitune
ZUPPA DI FONTITUNE

I love this soup. It's thick and substantial and very welcome on a cold winter's evening. With the sausage, rice and cabbage it's a meal in itself. I use Fonteluna, an Italian pork sausage that is made the same way my great grandparents made it when they slaughtered the pigs in the autumn. Use a cured, spicy, 100 per cent pork sausage. Alternatively, use 200 g chopped smoked pancetta. Remember there is spicy heat in the sausage, so judge how hot you like this and adjust the amount of chilli you add. Err on the side of caution the first time!

2–3 tablespoons extra virgin olive oil
1 medium onion, peeled and finely chopped
a small piece of peperoncino (dried chilli)
about 250 g spicy Italian Fonteluna sausage made with 100 per cent pork
5 good handfuls chopped white or Savoy cabbage, kale or cavolo nero, washed and shredded
2 handfuls arborio rice

Maldon sea salt
BATTUTO
a couple of thin slices of lardo, about 50 g
2 tablespoons very finely chopped flat-leaf parsley
1 clove garlic, peeled and finely chopped

Heat the oil in a saucepan. Sauté the onion, chilli and sausage to soften the onions and infuse the flavours. Add the shredded cabbage, turn it in the oil and add enough boiling water to cover. Simmer gently for 20 minutes or so.

To make the 'battuto', put the lardo on a wooden chopping board. Bash it with the back of a rolling pin until it is smooth and creamy. As it softens, put the chopped parsley and garlic on top and bash them in.

Add the rice to the simmering soup and a little more hot water if needed. Stir it in and add the battuto on top. The flavoured lard melts down into the soup, adding a delicious, creamy texture. Check the seasoning: the sausage can be quite salty, so I usually don't add salt until the end.

Serve this soup as a one-bowl meal with plenty of crusty bread.

Pasta and Chickpea Soup
PASTA E CECI

Francesca, this is your dad's favourite soup of all time. Prepare for him a big thick plate of creamy, sweet nutty chickpeas with a hint of garlic and chilli, nestling in between some chunky pasta, and he'll give you anything!

It's easy to get good-quality dried chickpeas. As long as they're this season's dried pulses, they will swell up and cook nicely. Old, ancient dried pulses will take forever to cook, if they ever do. I confess to burning more than one pot in an effort to get old chickpeas to cook.

To prevent the liquid in the soup evaporating, I find it more successful to cook the chickpeas in the oven.

If you're in a hurry, make this soup in 15 minutes with tinned chickpeas. Just remember to rinse off the water they are canned in before use.

300 g dried chickpeas
1 teaspoon bicarbonate of soda
4 tablespoons extra virgin olive oil
2 small cloves garlic, peeled, one left whole, one finely chopped
a small piece of peperoncino (dried chilli)
a sprig of fresh rosemary
120 g ditali rigati (or any small, chunky pasta)
Maldon sea salt
a small handful of flat-leaf parsley, finely chopped

Soak the chickpeas in plenty of cold water overnight.

Drain the chickpeas and rinse them well. Put them in an ovenproof saucepan or casserole and cover them with cold water, to about 5 cm above the surface, and add the bicarbonate of soda. Boil them on a high heat for 10 minutes. Drain the chickpeas and rinse them again. This gets rid of any scum.

Now, in the saucepan, heat half the extra virgin olive oil and sauté the whole clove of garlic and the chilli just to flavour the oil. Add the drained chickpeas, the rosemary and 1.5 litres hot water. Bring to the boil and place in a low oven (150°C/300°F/Gas 2) for about an hour until the chickpeas are cooked. The timing depends very much on how old the chickpeas are. You just need to keep checking to judge when they're cooked.

When the chickpeas taste nice and soft, remove the

rosemary and the garlic clove. Add the pasta and a little more hot water if necessary. The soup should be eaten fairly thick, more like a pasta dish. You decide. Season with Maldon sea salt. If you add the salt earlier the chickpeas tend not to cook so well.

Continue simmering the soup on top of the cooker until the pasta is cooked. Just to finish it off, sauté the finely chopped garlic in the remaining oil. As it sizzles, pour it over the soup. Add the parsley.

If you are using tinned chickpeas it couldn't be easier. Drain the chickpeas and warm them through in the flavoured oil. Cook the pasta separately in boiling salted water, drain it and add it to the chickpeas. Add enough boiling water to make a thick soup and season to taste. Make up the flavoured oil with chopped garlic and pour it over the cooked chickpeas and pasta. Add the parsley and check seasoning and consistency.

Smoked Haddock Chowder (Cullen Skink)

This is a traditional east coast of Scotland's fishwife's broth. It's not surprising that we absorbed the recipe into our family's cooking repertoire. Marietta was used to cooking with salted cod, baccalà, so using cured haddock was a natural alternative for her.

The traditional finnan haddock used for the soup comes from the village of Findon in Aberdeenshire. The haddock are gutted, headed and split. The bone is left in and they are dry-salted overnight then cold-smoked over peat for 8–9 hours. Smoked, undyed filleted haddock can be used as well. They are milder in flavour.

As children, Margaret, a girl from the fishing community of

Peterhead, looked after us. She taught us how to dance Scottish country-dances to the tunes of Jimmy Shand, how to eat stovies (see page 216) and how to cook Cullen skink. I find it easiest to cook the soup in two separate pots.

1 large finnan haddock or 2 undyed smoked haddock fillets
300 ml full-fat milk
1 fresh bay leaf
100 g unsalted butter
1 large onion, peeled and finely sliced
500 g floury potatoes, peeled and finely sliced
Maldon sea salt and white pepper
2 tablespoons double cream
very finely chopped dill fronds or flat-leaf parsley

A word of caution! The haddock is salted. Don't add salt until the end.

Rinse the fish and place it in a small saucepan with the milk and the bay leaf. Bring the milk gently to the boil then switch off the heat. Leave it to cool. The fish will gently cook through and infuse the milk with all its delicious flavour.

Melt the butter in a separate saucepan. Add the sliced onion and, over a very low heat, cook until soft. Add the sliced potato and 1 litre hot water and simmer gently until the potato starts to soften. Use an electric blender to whizz the soup to smooth out the texture. (I quite like to keep some of the potatoes chunky.)

If you are using finnan haddock, take it from the milk and carefully remove the bones and skin, adding the pieces of flesh to the soup. Similarly, add flaked pieces of smoked fish to the soup. Still check for bones, there may be a few lurking. Strain in the infused milk and heat the soup through. Don't let it boil, as the milk may curdle. Adjust the consistency by adding water or milk. Check the seasoning. Finish with a swirl of cream and some fresh herbs.

'Shells'
ZUPPA DI COZZE

If you put a shelled mussel on a plate and asked a child to eat it, chances are they would think you were playing a joke on them. They'd push the plate away in disgust. Sit with a child, two to three years old, and eat a plate of 'shell soup', scooping up the mussels in the shell, slurping and dripping juice down your shirt, dunking bread in the liquid and mopping the plate clean, and I'll bet you won't be able to stop the child pulling the plate from you to work out what this exciting, delicious smelling food is.

Rope-grown mussels from the north of Scotland are some of the best in the world. Shellfish and seafood may be available all year round, but we only eat mussels in the cold months. The fishermen here say that you should only buy shellfish when there is an 'R' in the month. I think they know best.

It's always a bit tricky knowing how to buy mussels. Judge about 500 g per person though mussels were traditionally sold in pints.

The great thing about farmed, rope-grown mussels is that they are usually fairly clean and free of barnacles. This makes preparing them very easy. Run each mussel under cold water, pull off the beard, and use the blunt edge of a knife blade to crack off any barnacles. Discard any mussels that are wide open, that float to the surface of the water, or that won't close when tapped with the knife.

I usually prepare the mussels as soon as I get them home to get rid of any stale water hanging around them, and then store them in a large bowl of cold water in the fridge until I'm ready. Always use mussels the same day you buy them.

The recipe is simplicity itself.

2–2.5 kg mussels, cleaned
3 tablespoons extra virgin olive oil
2 cloves garlic, peeled and finely chopped
a piece of peperoncino (dried chilli), crushed
a good handful of flat-leaf parsley, chopped
lemons to serve

Drain the prepared mussels in a colander.

Heat the oil in a large, deep saucepan with a tight-fitting lid. Add the garlic and chilli and let the flavours infuse. Don't let the garlic burn. Add half the parsley. Turn it once in the flavoured oil and then tip in the mussels. Put the lid on, give the saucepan a good shake to make sure the mussels are well coated in the oil, and allow them to cook over a high heat until the shells have all opened. This takes as little as 2–3 minutes. Give the pot another good shake to get the mussels on top nearer to the heat so that they all cook evenly. Discard any that remain closed.

Add the rest of the chopped parsley and serve the mussels in deep soup plates, spooning the tasty juices over them. I love slices of crusty bread, drizzled with extra virgin olive oil and toasted in a warm oven to dunk in the juices. Add big wedges of lemons to squeeze on the mussels.

Remember that you don't need to add salt to the mussels. The liquid they release as they cook provides a perfectly seasoned soup to eat with them.

PASTA AND PASTA SAUCES

Luigi Silni, right, with his family around the table, c.1970

Most southern Italians eat pasta every day. The variations of pasta and sauces are endless. It is usually quick and easy to prepare, the original fast food. We eat pasta in soup, as a main dish, as a light starter or as a midnight snack.

I remember Marietta, my nonna, making pasta by hand. She formed a mound of flour on the middle of the table, made a well in the middle with her hands and broke some eggs into it. With a fork she lightly whisked the eggs, supporting the sides of the flour with her left hand. Gradually she incorporated the amount of flour the eggs needed to make a stiff dough. No weighing, no recipes, no instructions.

She kneaded the dough by hand then let it rest covered in a perfectly ironed, clean tea-towel. She rolled it out with a long broom handle she kept only for her pasta. The sheet of dough would cover the whole of the table, as long as her arms could stretch. It would then be folded over and over and niftily cut with a knife, unceremoniously making perfect, light, flavoursome tagliatelle. She then balanced the broom handle between the backs of two chairs and hung the pasta over it to dry.

Dry, durum wheat pasta was first manufactured in Naples in the late nineteenth century. Marietta and Maria couldn't afford the luxury of buying pasta. When they did get it, it was a real treat for them, they wouldn't have to work so hard. Gradually, as they became better off, and the pasta became more widely available, dried pasta became the norm. Innumerable pasta shapes were produced, to mimic all the different shapes that had been made by hand over the centuries.

Francesca, when your Nonna Olivia visited Annunziata on her honeymoon in 1952, she wanted to show her new mother-in-law that she was a good cook and would look after Carlo well. She offered to make home-made pasta. Annunziata was shocked. 'We don't make pasta at home any more. Our neighbours will think we are poor and can't afford to buy it.'

These days, dry durum wheat pasta is still the norm in Italy and among Italians in this country. We never buy ready-made manufactured fresh egg pasta. It's rubbery and slimy and doesn't resemble home-made pasta at all. On the other hand, dried 'hand-made egg pasta', made in Italy by 'artigiani' firms, especially in Campofilone, is exceptionally good and the best alternative to making egg pasta at home.

In our house, home-made egg pasta is made on high days and holidays and is regarded as a special treat. We make the pasta very fine with a good bite. I confess we bicker and fight over our home-made pasta and compete to make the longest, thinnest, and finest ever. Francesca, Uncle Cesidio's are the best!

Egg pasta made by hand at home is referred to as pasta 'all'uovo fatta in casa'. 'Home-mades' to you and me. The recipe on page 118 is the way all our mothers, grandmothers and great-grandmothers before them have made it for hundreds of years, although the ingredients have become considerably more refined. Where we use '00' durum wheat flour, our grandmothers would probably have used a mixture of unrefined polenta and whole-wheat flour.

Be prepared to spend some time getting the knack of making pasta by hand. It is an acquired skill. If you want to stay sane, don't try to make home-made pasta for guests the same day they're coming. Make it the day before and let it dry as explained. It doesn't affect the flavour. If anything it tastes better if it is allowed to dry a little.

Only use Italian double zero, '00', durum wheat flour. This has an especially high gluten content and is finely milled. When it is kneaded the gluten joins to make long, strong bonds, producing very good textured dough with good workability.

Use organic eggs. They have a good flavour and rich yellow yolks.

We don't use any salt in the dough, as it tends to make the pasta go black as it dries. Salt is added to the water as the pasta cooks where it absorbs just the right amount to flavour it.

Neither do we add any oil to the dough. It makes the pasta slightly slimy and sticky. We don't actually use anything else, just hard work. The more the dough is kneaded, the better the bite. You'll find the basic recipe on page 118.

Never buy ready-made pasta sauces. There is nothing easier or tastier than a home-made sugo, and most can be put together in the time it takes to boil some pasta. The right shape of pasta with the right sugo is a learned instinct that comes with eating pasta every day. A general guideline is that most olive oil based sauces go well with thin, long pasta: spaghetti, spaghettini and linguine. A light tomato sugo tastes good with thin pasta, but a slow-cooked, winter-warming tomato sugo invariably matches chunky stubby pasta like penne or rigatoni. Creamy sauces like any shaped pasta – but your hips don't like creamy sauces!

Most of the sauces I cook are based on one of the following ingredients: extra virgin olive oil, dairy products or tomatoes. They're based on simple principles, which once learned, can be adapted to produce an infinite number of variations. The measurements are given as a guideline. Please enjoy ignoring them!

The only thing that is written in stone is that pasta must be drained, dressed and eaten immediately. The bite of perfectly cooked pasta al dente is achieved 2–3 minutes or so before the pasta is cooked through. Add the pasta to a large pot of boiling, well-salted water. Move it around with a fork to separate the strands and keep the pasta on a rolling boil. Don't put a lid on the pot.

As the pasta cooks it starts to become pliable and will become slightly paler in colour. I really enjoy continually pulling a strand out of the pot and offering it to a waiting, hungry family to test. The advantage of this ritual is that everyone gradually congregates in the kitchen, their appetites are heightened and willing hands will help with the final jobs to prepare the table.

We eat at the table, but with very little fuss. The cutlery is simple: spoon, fork and knife, laid together on a side plate with a serviette. Two glasses are placed at each setting, one for wine, one for water. Bread and salad will be laid out, but no butter or olive oil.

I usually put one or two vegetables in the middle of the table. I prefer them warm rather than hot, most likely with an olive oil and lemon dressing. I always delegate the job of grating the Parmigiano. I did it too often when I was young. A black pepper mill is placed on the table for those who want it, but no salt. A good cook, that's you, will taste the food as it's cooking and season it perfectly before serving it, so extra salt shouldn't be needed. The water and wine will be poured, the pasta checked again, and everyone will gradually sit down to eat.

Drain the pasta at the sink into a big colander. Give it a couple of good shakes to get rid of excess water, and tip it back into the pot, with a little cooking water still clinging to it. Add the sugo, enough to coat it well, but not drown it, and mix it through. Serve it right away.

Grace before meals is – or should be – said, and everyone eats.

'Home-mades'
PASTA ALL'UOVO FATTA IN CASA

300 g '00' Italian durum wheat flour
2 large organic free-range eggs
3 large organic free-range egg yolks

You'll need a pasta-cutting machine: we use the Imperia brand.

1. Traditionally the flour is piled in a mound on a clean work surface, a well is made in the middle, and the eggs and yolks are placed in this. I find it less messy in our modern kitchens to put the flour in a large, wide bowl. Make a well and put the eggs and yolks in the middle.

2. Use a fork to whisk the eggs, flicking the flour so that it gradually gets incorporated into the eggs. The light mixture will naturally become denser and eventually form into a ball. Don't be too enthusiastic. Work in the middle of the egg mixture all the time. If you start to stir everything together you may end up with too dry and crumbly a mixture that won't form into dough.

3. Use your hands to press the dough together, tossing it in any flour that is still not incorporated, trying to let the dough take as much flour as is comfortable to handle. The dough should be quite stiff, but pliable and not sticky. (You'll be glad to hear, this stage can be reached using a food processor with the dough attachment. Add more flour if the dough is sticky.)

4. Remove the dough to a clean, floured work surface and begin to knead it with the palm of your hands. Push the dough away from you, constantly folding it over, rotating it 90 degrees, and kneading it again. Keep working the dough until it becomes smooth and elastic, dusting it with a little flour if it's sticky. The more you knead the dough and the more flour you can incorporate, the better bite the pasta will have and the lighter it will be.

5. When you can ease the dough apart between your hands to show a smooth silky surface with no cracks, it's ready.

6. Cover it with clingfilm and let it, and you, rest for half an hour.

7. Divide the dough into six pieces. Take one and keep the others covered with the clingfilm. Make sure the pasta machine is attached to a table that is at a comfortable height for you to work. I usually put greaseproof paper on the floor to catch all those bits of pasta that fall down while I'm working.

Now, pass the dough through the widest setting of the pasta machine. Fold it equally into three by folding the narrowest side a third of the way across the length of the dough, and then fold it over again. The idea is to keep the edges tidy so that it is easy to work with it. Pass the even folded edge through the rollers again. Continue to roll and fold at the widest setting about eight times. This works the dough and helps the bite of the finished pasta.

We always look for the 'bubble-gum pop' when we're making pasta. At some point when the dough has been worked enough, an air pocket will form in the dough as it passes through the rollers. This gives a noise like bubble-gum popping and is the best way to judge that the dough is ready. (Don't worry if you don't hear it. It's not the end of the world!)

8. At this stage you can start to thin out the dough. Reduce the width of the setting between the rollers, passing the dough through so that it becomes thinner and longer. It shouldn't be sticky, but if it is, add a sprinkling of flour. Don't fold the dough any more, just pass it once through each reduced setting. I usually take the dough down to the second thinnest setting, but it depends on each machine. It needs to be fine, but is it is too fine it will be difficult to handle. Experiment and make it the way you like it.

9. When the dough is in a strip, let it dry for a few minutes before cutting it. The easiest thing is to do what Marietta did, hang it over a broomstick balanced between two chairs. Put greaseproof paper over the stick and on the floor to collect any pieces that drop down.

Prepare the rest of the dough in the same way. This is going to take the best part of an hour the first time you make pasta, but as you practise it can be a lot quicker.

10. Once all the dough is in sheets you can use it for lasagne (see page 172) or to make ravioli (see page 125). Alternatively you can use the cutters on the machine to make tagliatelle or tagliarini.

We usually use the narrower of the two cutters that are on

the standard machine. There is a knack to turning the handle while you feed the long delicate strip of dough through the machine and catch the tagliatelle at the other end. Get a little help at this stage if you don't have three hands! The cut pasta can then be hung again to dry a little over the broom handle. If you want to keep the pasta for the next day lay it on a tray between sheets of greaseproof paper once it has dried completely. It will keep like this for up to four to five days.

Practice makes perfect. I have to say that I have taught pasta-making to Primary One children with great success, so it is not impossible by any means. It just takes a bit of getting used to and, if you find it difficult the first time, the second time will be much easier.

We don't bother making flavoured or coloured pasta. Carefully made 'home-mades' are the best, pure and simple.

Home-made pasta needs a very large pot of boiling, well-salted water. There is no salt in the dough so the pasta will absorb the salt it needs from the water. You can add a splash of olive oil to the water, but it's really not necessary. The pasta will sink to the bottom. Don't put the lid on the pot, and keep the heat up high. Use a long-handled fork to stir it around and as the water comes back up to the boil the pasta will start to float. Lower the heat. Test it at this stage. It should only take 2–3 minutes at the most to cook, nearer 3–4 if it has been dried overnight. Drain the pasta well: it tends to stay wetter than dry pasta so pour it all into a big colander in the sink and give it a good shake.

Home-made egg pasta needs twice as much sugo as dried pasta. We traditionally use a meat sugo (see page 164) with it. We prefer our traditional treats to be familiar and nostalgic, just like we remember as kids when Nonna cooked for us.

Judge an egg per person when making pasta for a big crowd (a yolk and 3 whole eggs makes pasta for six to eight). I nearly always make the pasta and the sugo the day before, so that the worry is taken out of the whole thing. At Christmas we serve the pasta on a large ashet. It's carried to the table held aloft and is always greeted with a loud cheer for the cook. Well deserved, I say!

Just a note about your pasta machine. Read the instructions and note that it should never be wet or washed. The stainless-steel rollers will rust and the machine will be ruined. When I've finished using mine, I wipe it with a dry cloth and use a dry pastry brush to whisk away any flour or dough. I then wrap the whole machine in a clean tea-towel and the attachments, handles and clamp in another towel. Everything is stored in the original box until the next time. When you bring it out to use it take a little bit of dough and run it through the machine to get rid of any dust. Discard this dough.

A new machine sometimes marks the edge of the pasta with a black oil mark. If this happens just trim the marks of oil away before you put the pasta through the machine again. As you use the machine this will stop happening.

HOME-MADE RICOTTA

FOR CENTURIES, SHEPHERDS HAVE MOVED THEIR FLOCKS according to the season in search of pasture. There were no good pastures high in the mountains so the 'pecorari' from the Fontitune came down to the coast in the spring to lowland pastures. They went every spring to the same area, very near Mondragone, a village twenty miles north of Naples that Annunziata and Luigi eventually moved to after the Second World War. The marshlands near the coast were covered with spring vegetation, particularly wild thyme and oregano. It was also naturally salty from the winds blowing in from the sea.

The sheeps' milk was very rich and creamy and made

exceptionally good cheese. The shepherds collected the juices from the lining of the stomach of a slaughtered sheep for the rennet to make their cheeses. The whey, a watery, liquid by-product of the pecorino cheese-making, was heated to boiling point and cooled back down to blood heat. It was then mixed with the sheep's rennet and was allowed to separate. 'Ricotto' means 're-cooked'. Cheese has been made like this since Roman times. The women took the cheeses and ricotta into the towns and sold them to the locals who looked forward to their visitors every year.

You can buy ricotta easily these days. Tubs of pasteurised ricotta are available, but can be a bit dull and heavy. Freshly made ricotta or farmhouse ricotta has a soft, smooth light texture with a creamy sweet flavour. Sometimes you may find buffalo milk ricotta from the mozzarella producers in Naples. It is exceptionally good, perfect eaten with fresh fruit or raw 'fave' or broad beans.

All my nonne and bis-nonne made ricotta frequently at home, with far better results than any that can be bought. You can most likely buy rennet from a chemist or health-food store (or you may find it in a passing sheep's stomach!). Vegetarian rennet is available. Ricotta is obviously made traditionally from the whey of the milk, but at home with bottled rennet, you need to use full-fat milk.

However, it is telling that some full-fat milk on sale has so little protein and fat left in it, that you can't make ricotta with it. I tried many times to make ricotta with no success. Then, by coincidence, I used a different milk. The ricotta was beautiful and ready in an instant. It amazed me that even a standard ingredient like milk could be so different. Obviously some milk, even full-fat milk, has most of its goodness removed when the top cream is taken away. Use full-fat milk, Ayrshire, Jersey or Gold Top, or three-quarters milk and a quarter of double cream.

As with all cooking, personal experience and patience is the most valuable ingredient. If you're in the mood, experiment!

1 litre good-quality full-fat, organic milk, Ayrshire or Jersey
2 scant teaspoons rennet

Put the milk into a wide saucepan and gently bring it slowly to blood heat, 37.5°C/98.6°F. Take it off the heat and stir in the rennet. Leave it to stand in a warm place until the milk separates into solid curds and liquid whey. If the milk is rich it will take only a few minutes.

Put the pot back on to the heat and slowly bring it back up to blood heat. Tip the pot to one side and use a slotted spoon to gently lift off the curds.

Strain the curds into a plastic strainer lined with a double layer of muslin or cheesecloth, and balance over a bowl. Or tie the muslin and suspend it on a wooden spoon over a bowl for a couple of hours, so that the curds can drain and solidify. You should be able to make about 180–200 g of ricotta from a litre of full-fat milk.

Traditionally the ricotta was drained in small rush baskets made just for that purpose, creating the characteristic ridges along the sides. Interestingly I couldn't find any baskets in the south of Italy recently. Apparently they don't make ricotta in their homes any more. One old street vendor in Naples told me he remembered long conical baskets, just like my nonna told me. These were strapped to the sides of a donkey and the ricotta would drip and set as the shepherds made their way home.

Home-made ricotta is very light. Eat it with crusty bread and a salad of wild rocket dressed with olive oil. Use it for stuffing home-made ravioli or pancakes, 'crespelle', or in pasta sauces. Try adding chopped rocket to the milk before you add the rennet. It's also very good drizzled with honey and eaten as a dessert, or sweetened with sugar, flavoured with orange-flower water and chopped peel, and used as a stuffing for cakes or in ice-cream.

Ricotta Ravioli
RAVIOLI DI RICOTTA

Francesca, you have a sweet temperament just like your bis-nonno Cesidio had. Since you were eleven or twelve you have, on occasion, made lovely home-made pasta and, when you give me a real treat, make the best ravioli I've ever tasted.

250 g fresh ricotta, bought or home-made
2–3 tablespoons freshly grated Parmigiano Reggiano
1 egg yolk, beaten
1 scant teaspoon caster sugar
1 tablespoon finely chopped herbs (flat-leaf parsley, mint or rocket),
or 2–3 tablespoons finely chopped cooked spinach, squeezed dry
a grating of nutmeg
Maldon sea salt and black pepper
a squeeze of lemon juice

You will need home-made pasta dough (see page 118), but made with about 200 g flour, 2 egg yolks and 1 whole egg. Cut it into sheets on the finest setting on the pasta machine.

Make the filling for the ravioli very simply by blending together the ingredients above. Add a grating of nutmeg, some salt, freshly ground pepper and lemon juice, and taste it to check the flavour.

Lay out one sheet of the pasta on a floured work surface and put teaspoonfuls of the filling along the middle, spaced about 4 cm apart. Use the egg white left over to brush along the edges of the pasta and between the mounds of filling. Now, simply fold the sheet of dough over so that both edges meet each other, just like folding a letter in half. Use your fingers to press along the edges to stick the dough together and to press out any pockets of air. Press between the filling to stick the pasta dough together around each mound.

Use a pastry wheel to easily cut out the squares of ravioli, cutting along three sides only, the fold forming the first edge. As it cuts, the cutter seals the dough. Lift each one up, pressing the edges together with your fingers to check that the dough has sealed well. The knack here is to have the dough thin enough so that the ravioli aren't stodgy, but not too thin that the filling will burst through. Test one in a small pot of boiling salted water to see how it cooks, and adjust accordingly.

If you are cooking the ravioli right away, add them in batches to boiling salted water. They take about 4–5 minutes, as the filling has to cook as well.

Normally we prepare these to cook later on or even the next day. Beware. If the filling is wet at all, it can ooze through the pasta and spoil. To prevent this, it does no harm to pop the ravioli into the freezer, laid out on trays. They can then be cooked straight from frozen, taking about 6–7 minutes. (They'll keep frozen for three to four weeks easily.)

You may have some pasta dough left over. Cut it roughly by hand and cook it in clear broth or serve it with some Parmigiano and butter.

Ravioli need a simple sugo. Any of the creamy ones are lovely but I prefer butter and fresh sage (see page 148).

You can experiment with the filling. I don't really like meat fillings for ravioli but roasted pumpkin mashed with some ricotta and sage is wonderful. Season to taste.

*Try lightly cooked, finely chopped smoked pancetta, grated
pecorino and a grating of nutmeg blended into the ricotta.*

ANNUNZIATA AND LUIGI, POZZUOLI, ITALY
1915–1940

She was very pretty and delicately boned, with jet-black hair
tied austerely back from her face. She was very elegant. She
walked like a ballerina, proud and straight. When she laughed
her world lit up. Her eyes flirted, her chin lifted and her smile
broke to display her sparkling white teeth. She was admired for
her charm and compassion, combined with a strength of spirit
that made her everyone's favourite. She fell in love. She was only
thirteen. 'Sono innamorata. Innamorata per sempre.'

He wasn't handsome. He was short and coarsely featured. He
had a bit of a reputation for being 'nu' scugnizzo' – a charmer,
a flirt and a ladies' man. He was a true Neapolitan: 'furbo', fly
and cunning. He had learned that in life, you had to use all your
wits to survive. You had to be admired by your pals, so you
needed to be popular with the girls. You had to make the most
of every situation. He quickly worked out that if you didn't have
the looks to draw the ladies, then charm and flattery were
successful substitutes. He was only fourteen.

Her father was furious! 'Who? Luigi Silni. Quello? Him? Per
mia figlia? Mai! Never!'

Her mother agreed. 'No. You're too young. It's too soon. He's
a fast one!'

Annunziata was adamant. She wanted Luigi. The more her
parents objected the more she pushed up her pretty little chin
in defiance.

Luigi hung about on the street. He made friends with
Annunziata's brothers. He became indispensable to her mother.
He was always at hand to carry her shopping, sweep the yard

or pay her a compliment. The poor lad was losing weight with all that extra work. What a nice boy!

Her father was furious. That 'scugnizzo' was always hanging around. He was always 'just passing'. 'He's getting on my nerves!'

Her father was a skilled and respected carpenter. Exasperated, he took an important job in another town and went away to work for two weeks to get some peace. Luigi still hung around.

Mamma was tired of the commotion the lovesick daughter was causing in the house, and of quarrelling with her husband. What was wrong with the boy? She was irritated with her husband. What a fuss he made. Deep down, she knew the truth. Annunziata and Luigi were in love, and it was a good match. She decided to take the law into her own hands.

She started to invite Luigi to eat with them at lunchtime. He was in the street anyway. What harm would it do? She invited him for dinner. Well, he was here most of the time anyway. She invited him to stay!

When his work was finished, Papa came home. The break had done him good. He was calm and peaceful and hoped Annunziata had forgotten that layabout who was always hanging about. He approached the house. The good-for-nothing wasn't there. Thank God!

He whistled to announce his arrival. His daughter, Annunziata, ran out to meet him. She looked so beautiful and happy. She looked different. He immediately suspected something was wrong.

The boy was in his house! He was furious. 'Why are you here? What do you want, you layabout?'

'Papà, I was just passing.'

'Papà?' And like the volcano in whose shadow he lived, Annunziata's father blew his top. He'd been tricked! 'You're not just passing. You've been staying here. Ho annusato il tuo odore! I smell a rat! Va via! Get lost!'

He shouted and yelled, bellowed and screamed, stamped his foot and laid down the law. Then, having shown all of Pozzuoli who was boss, he took them to be married. His wife and daughter had outsmarted him. With a shrug of his shoulders he admitted defeat.

'Questa è la vita!' 'That's life!'

Things quickly settled down to a peaceful existence. Luigi worked with his father-in-law as a carpenter and proved to be as skilled and as talented a 'falegname' as he was a flirt.

This all happened in Pozzuoli, an ancient fishing village just north of Naples, where seismic tremors, uncertainty, laughter and optimism were part of everyday life. It happened in 1916, when sanitation was rank, electricity a rumour and superstition rife. Where people genuinely believed that men could change into werewolves on a full moon and you had to lock your door at night to protect against evil. Where the anticipation of new life brought hope and reassurance. Where everyone rejoiced when Annunziata became pregnant.

Her first son was born. They called him Vincenzo, in honour of her father. He had beautiful dark hair, deep blue eyes, ten fingers and ten toes. He was perfect. 'Che bella vita.' 'What joy and celebration.' What a feast they had!

But, without warning, things started to go wrong. Vincenzo became ill. Someone had cast the 'malocchio', the evil eye. He didn't breathe well. His skin paled and his eyes grew dull. Everyone started to pray. The doctor was called. There would be an understanding about payment. 'Do anything you need to do to make the baby well.'

Within days Vincenzo was dead.

Annunziata was distraught. She cried and cried. Nothing terrible had ever happened to her. She had always been blessed. She was shocked.

Her mother reassured her. 'These things happen. You're young. It will be fine.'

Before long, she was pregnant again.

Ernesto was born, named after Luigi's father. They fussed him and spoiled him, thrilled with the new arrival. They were ready to put their sadness behind them. What a feast they had!

Annunziata was worried. Her mother said it was natural to worry. Annunziata was afraid. 'Calm down!' Annunziata panicked. Ernesto wasn't breathing well. He looked pale. He seemed hot. Annunziata was right. Something was wrong. Four days later he was dead.

Antonio was born within the year. He was such a scrawny, ragged little fellow, but Mamma said he was a fighter; he would be strong. Annunziata was so relieved. At last they could stop worrying, it was going to be all right. Life was hard in this rough, inhospitable environment but, as Luigi always said, you had to keep your wits about you to survive. Things settled down to a peaceful existence.

Antonio died before he was a year old. The next two children, Marianna and Antonietta, both only survived a few months.

'Povera ragazza!' Poor Annunziata. She was inconsolable. Devastated at the loss of her babies, she became ill. She wouldn't eat and wept all day and night.

Luigi was terrified. He was petrified at what was happening to them. He felt so helpless. He had to think. He had to find a way to change things. When he had married Annunziata he had promised her father he would look after her. He had to do something.

'L'ospedale!' The foundling hospital in Naples . . . . There were plenty of babies to choose from. He would bring a baby home for Annunziata, and make her better. With his mother and mother-in-law, he went to choose a child.

Wandering amongst the cots, they saw a beautiful little girl with jet-black hair, smiling and gurgling. Next to her a little blond boy, sleeping peacefully, looked settled and contented. In another cot there was a round-faced, sturdy-looking baby wrapped in a cotton shawl. How could they choose?

Then Luigi noticed a cot pushed against the wall. Inside was a very thin, neglected-looking child, pale faced and whimpering. He looked so lost. Luigi felt a pang of recognition, this one was different. This one was just like him. The card above the cot read 'Carlo Contini'.

Annunziata fell in love with baby Carlo. Luigi fell in love with Carlo. Everyone fell in love with Carlo. They welcomed a stranger's baby into their lives, a good omen to ward off the 'malocchio' that had haunted them.

Italian law dictated that an adopted child keep the surname of the natural father. In order that Carlo would not be ostracised and would be protected within their community, Annunziata and Luigi changed their surname from Silni to Contini. They moved to a room and kitchen, 178 steps up into the ancient heart of Pozzuoli, 'ngoppa 'a terra. There, high up, overlooking the glistening blue sea, with the islands of Ischia and Procida in the distance, they started a new life with their son. He grew strong and healthy and was adored and indulged by them both.

Carlo, the Prince of Pozzuoli, c.1952

Annunziata had another twelve pregnancies. Only seven of her children survived. To console herself, and always willing to help others, she acted as wet-nurse for other mothers, loving many babies in her own grief.

Her natural children were all small, like her and Luigi. Carlo, on the other hand, grew to be well over six feet tall. He had distinctive aquiline features, was extremely handsome and incredibly charming. Annunziata adored and spoiled him. She called him 'the Prince of Pozzuoli'. He fitted into the role instinctively. He sometimes wondered why his brothers were short, his sisters petite, and why he towered over his parents. He wondered why he felt different; but then, he was different, he was 'the Prince of Pozzuoli'!

He wanted to make the most of every situation. He wanted to escape the poverty and hardship of Pozzuoli. At twenty-one, he left home and joined the police force. Annunziata and Luigi were devastated. No-one in the family had ever left to work elsewhere. There had always been work. They were carpenters. Carlo should be a carpenter like his father and his grandfather before him.

But Carlo was different. He was frustrated living in poverty. He had to escape. He was so handsome. In uniform, mounted on his horse, he looked like a movie star, like royalty. He travelled all over Italy and when he was offered the opportunity to visit Britain to learn English, he couldn't refuse.

Carlo was posted to Edinburgh. A charmer and a social being, he was welcomed into the immigrant Italian community. It should be noted that he was very popular with the girls. They argued over him, flirted with him and set their caps at him. This was nothing new to Carlo. He was used to being regarded as a 'scugnizzo', a charmer and a ladies' man, just like his father. He took it as his right. He enjoyed the attention. He was 'Prince of Pozzuoli' after all!

One girl was not quite so interested. Independent and single-minded, Olivia Crolla was also extremely beautiful. She was nursing in the local hospital, unusual for an immigrant Italian girl to work outside the family.

Her indifference attracted Carlo. Her spirit impressed him.

But what really caught his eye were 'the seams of her stockings. You see, they were always perfectly straight.' He was smitten. He fell madly in love, head over heels, and, against all the odds, decided to marry and set up home in Edinburgh.

He wrote to tell his parents about Olivia. In the letter that came back, Luigi and Annunziata poured out their love for their son and revealed the painful truth to him for the first time. They were not his natural parents. They had never told him that he was a

Olivia Crolla, c.1950

foundling who had been given up for adoption. He was stunned. He couldn't believe it, but it all fell into place. It made sense. He'd felt different all along. He loved Annunziata and Luigi all the more when he understood all the sacrifices they had made for him.

He married Olivia and took up his new position in life, 'King of Elm Row'!

Annunziata's 'Stones'
GNOCCHI DI PATATE

Francesca, when your dad was very young, he spent many long summer holidays with his grandparents, Annunziata and Luigi. He learned to speak Neapolitan, to understand the Italian mentality and to enjoy the best Italian food. Annunziata loved him with a passion and cooked for him all the best she could afford. She was an instinctive cook. She never read, never owned a cookery book, but had learned from her mother and mother-in-law how to feed her family.

Like us all, she did have one or two blind spots. She knew that her grandson loved gnocchi. She always made them for him the very day he arrived. He enjoyed the ritual of pleasing her by eating two or three platefuls. Her gnocchi were quite heavy and, as she got older, they got heavier. By the time she was eighty-five, they were referred to as 'pietre di piombo', 'lead stones' – though never in her presence!

On honeymoon, when we visited, she insisted on showing me how to cook her gnocchi for my new husband. It was now my duty, after all to provide him with all his needs. Gnocchi included! To prove to her how he loved her, and I suspect to let me know who was going to be boss, your dad ate not one, not two, but three huge plates of 'stones'.

Let me just say that it took him three days to recover, and he didn't quite keep up his air of authority at all times.

These are my mummy's gnocchi. Many Italian women add some baking powder to prevent them being heavy. Mummy uses a little self-raising flour to the same effect. You need to choose floury potatoes to make gnocchi. Waxy or new potatoes don't work.

450 g floury potatoes such as Maris Piper, King Edward or Desirée,
peeled weight
1 organic egg yolk, beaten
200 g plain flour
25 g self-raising flour
Maldon sea salt

Cut the potatoes into quarters, and boil until cooked in unsalted water. Drain them and put them back on the cooker, letting them dry off on a very low heat for a few minutes to get rid of any excess water. Mash them really well or preferably pass them through a mouli or potato ricer. Leave them to cool a little.

Mix the egg yolk into the potatoes to lighten them a little, then sift in the flour. Blend everything together with clean, floured hands. Lightly knead the mixture a little to make sure it is mixed well. You need a soft, light mixture that is not too sticky but isn't dry.

It's a good idea to test the dough before cutting out the gnocchi. In a small pot of boiling salted water cook a small piece of dough for a minute or two, until it floats to the top. Taste it and test its consistency. It should be light, but firm. If it's too soft, add a little more flour. If it's too dry, add a little more egg yolk.

Once you are happy with the dough, pat the mixture into a flat, round shape, 2–3 cm thick. Cut off six to eight strips of dough and lightly roll them into cigar shapes. Cut each of these into 2–3 cm bite-sized pieces.

Use a fork with slim prongs to indent each one. The purpose of the exercise is to make a dent and a few ridges in each 'gnoccho' to let it cook evenly in the middle and to let the sugo nestle nicely in the ridges. With the inside curve of the fork facing up, press it lightly into the middle of each one. With a single action, flick the dough over the prongs, making fork marks and a dent on half of it. Have a light touch; you'll soon get the hang of it. If the dough gets sticky as you work, dust your hands, and it, with a little flour.

Lay the gnocchi on to trays or baking sheets covered with clingfilm. It's best to cook these as soon as you've made them. You can make the dough earlier in the day but don't cut out the gnocchi until you need them. Don't refrigerate them. They'll turn black.

Prepare a large pot of boiling water. Add enough salt so that it tastes nicely salted. There's no salt in the gnocchi, but they will absorb salt from the water. Use the clingfilm to slide layers of gnocchi into the boiling water. The clingfilm magically shrivels up into nothing, letting the gnocchi slip into the water in one go. Don't over-crowd the water. I usually cook these in three batches.

The gnocchi sink to the bottom of the pot. They look a bit uninspiring, but don't panic. Within a couple of minutes they float to the top and are cooked. Use a slotted spoon or sieve to lift them out of the water. Drain them well and lay them on a warmed dish with a few spoonfuls of sugo. Keep them in a warm place until the rest are cooked. Whichever sugo you use, remember to have it ready so that you can dress the gnocchi as you cook them. Add a good sprinkling of freshly grated Parmigiano between each layer.

I love gnocchi best with the butter tomato sugo. You can use melted Gorgonzola sugo or simply butter and fresh sage with pecorino (see pages 149 and 148).

Try adding some slices of bocconcini mozzarella, 'fior di latte', to the dressed gnocchi and melting it under the grill. Delicious! (Remember, the mozzarella made with cows' milk melts better.)

Traditionally, gnocchi were made by eye. The women never weighed the potatoes and the flour. They just judged when they had added enough. Use the recipe as a guide and make them how you like them.

Francesca, don't let Nonna Annunziata know that your dad likes my gnocchi better than hers!

EXTRA VIRGIN OLIVE OIL BASED SUGO

Olive oil based sauces usually originate from the south of Italy. They are never served with grated Parmigiano but usually with a generous fresh grinding of black pepper.

The basic method is always the same, but can be used to give an infinite number of variations.

Spaghettini with Garlic, Oil and Chilli
SPAGHETTINI AGLIO, OLIO E PEPERONCINO

360 g spaghettini
Maldon sea salt
5–6 tablespoons extra virgin olive oil
2 cloves garlic, peeled and finely chopped
a piece of peperoncino (dried chilli), crushed
1 tablespoon very finely chopped flat-leaf parsley

Put the pasta on to boil in salted water. Spaghettini takes about 8–10 minutes to cook, depending on the brand. Meanwhile, warm the extra virgin olive oil in a small saucepan. Add the garlic and chilli and let them cook very slowly. Just flavour the oil gently. Be careful not to brown or burn the garlic.

Keep testing the pasta. Pull a strand out with a fork and check it. Before the middle of the pasta changes from yellowy to white and it is still very firm when you bite it, it's ready. Take the pot to the sink. Drain the pasta into a colander, give it a good shake and return it to the pot.

Add the chopped parsley to the oil and pour the hot oil over the pasta. Use two forks to toss everything together, and serve immediately. This smells so appetising, it is a relief to be able to eat it so quickly!

Add about 10–15 bite-sized broccoli florets to the pasta as it cooks. This has the advantage of flavouring the pasta a little while it's cooking. When the oil is added to the drained pasta and broccoli, the flavour of them both together is exquisite. Increase the oil to 8–9 tablespoons to coat the broccoli well.

Add some cauliflower florets to the pasta water and cook in the same way.

In the south of Italy it is common to add more chilli and a couple of preserved anchovies to the oil mixture. Press them down with the back of a spoon to melt them into the oil. The flavour changes subtly, but don't worry, it's not fishy at all. If the anchovies are salted, remember to rinse and de-bone them before adding them. You can also add the anchovy with the broccoli or cauliflower combination.

This is my favourite of all. I add a couple of good handfuls of fresh spinach to the oil mixture. In this case I use a little more oil and warm it in a larger frying pan with the oil and chilli. Then I add the spinach and cook it down in its own steam by covering the frying pan with a lid. When the pasta is ready, drain it and toss it in the frying pan with the spinach and oil, on a medium heat to keep everything piping hot.

My mother used to add the garlic in whole cloves and cook it until it browned, then discard it. This is the way that the Romans eat their 'aglio e olio'. When I got married, Philip didn't like his pasta like this. He was used to the Neapolitan way. Heavens!

Spaghettini with Scottish Chanterelles
SPAGHETTINI CON GALLETTI

This, for me, is the ultimate Scottish-Italian recipe: the marriage of wonderful Scottish wild chanterelle mushrooms and the garlic and olive oil combination of 'aglio e olio'.

Chanterelles are prolific in Scotland from late summer until the first frosts of autumn. Apricot coloured and aromatic with a firm texture, their delicate flavour is perfect with pasta. It goes without saying that, even although chanterelles are distinctive and easy to identify, don't collect mushrooms from the wild unless you have been trained to identify them by a mycologist. Wild mushrooms can be bought in specialist shops, though I wouldn't buy them in a plastic tub from a supermarket.

200 g chanterelle mushrooms
5–6 tablespoons extra virgin olive oil
1 clove garlic, peeled and finely chopped
1 smallish piece peperoncino (dried chilli), crushed
Maldon sea salt
2 tablespoons finely chopped flat-leaf parsley
360 g spaghettini

Pick over the chanterelles carefully, trimming off the base of the stem and using a damp paper towel to wipe off any soil or moss that may cling to them. Unlike porcini (ceps), they are usually free of maggots. As long as they have been picked in good condition and aren't waterlogged, they are really easy to handle. Don't be tempted to wash them; they soak up water at an alarming rate. Cut any large chanterelles into pieces, but they do shrivel down a lot as they cook, so I prefer to leave them whole where possible.

Warm the olive oil in a large frying pan. Add the chopped garlic and chilli, and cook them gently to flavour the oil. I like this to have quite a kick so I use a generous amount of chilli. Raise the heat a little and add the chanterelles. They do release quite a lot of moisture as they cook, but don't worry, this reduces to make a lovely natural sauce for the pasta. Cook the mushrooms over a brisk heat to evaporate some of the moisture, tossing the mushrooms in the flavoured oil.

Don't overcook the chanterelles. They can become rubbery. Season with Maldon sea salt and add the chopped parsley.

Cook the pasta in boiling salted water until al dente, drain it well and toss it in the frying pan with the chanterelles, coating it well. Serve it piping hot in hot pasta bowls.

Spaghettini with Mussels
SPAGHETTINI CON COZZE

This is what I love about the way we cook. One technique evolves into a myriad of different dishes, adapted to what ingredients are available and what time of year it is. It is so simple and logical that I hope you are very quickly empowered to cook without a recipe, guided by your own palate and mood.

Prepare the mussels simply as described in the recipe on page 112, but don't add the parsley at the end.

500 g mussels, cooked (see page 113)
1 clove garlic, peeled
1 piece peperoncino (dried chilli), crushed
2–3 tablespoons extra virgin olive oil
2–3 tablespoons finely chopped flat-leaf parsley
5–6 ripe cherry tomatoes or a couple of tinned plum tomatoes
and a tablespoon of their juice
360 g spaghettini

In a wide frying pan sauté the garlic and chilli in the extra virgin olive oil. Add the chopped parsley and stir it around, adding the tomatoes as well. I usually squash the cherry tomatoes with my hands, watching not to blind myself as the juice squirts everywhere. Cook this for 5–10 minutes. Adding the parsley at this stage subtly changes the garlic's flavour.

Add the cooked mussels and a tablespoon or so of the liquor they cooked in. (You can take most of the mussels out of most of their shells, but leave some in; it looks nice.) Check the flavour.

Boil the pasta until al dente. Drain it well and toss it in the frying pan with the mussels, mixing all the flavours together and heating everything through.
Simple!

If you can get a hold of very small flat carpet clams, 'vongole veraci', cook them in exactly the same way. They are really delicious. Clams can be gritty. I find the best way to deal with this is to rinse them well in a few changes of cold water and cook them as the mussels on page 113, but for the briefest of time. They are so small they open in seconds. Then, use a slotted spoon to lift the clams out. Use a ladle to spoon off any remaining liquor and strain it through a sieve lined with kitchen paper. With a bit of luck, any sand will be at the bottom of the pot or in the sieve. I find the bigger clams available here can be too gritty. They annoy me so much I rarely cook them.

Spaghettini with Courgettes
SPAGHETTINI CON ZUCCHINE

I love courgettes but frustratingly I'm the only one in the house who does, so I cook this when I'm alone. Choose small organic courgettes. They are usually crisper and firmer and have less water in them.

4–5 courgettes
4–5 tablespoons extra virgin olive oil
2 cloves garlic, peeled and finely chopped
2 sprigs fresh rosemary

360 g spaghettini or any pasta
Maldon salt and black pepper

Wash the courgettes in cold water and trim off the top and tail. Grate them on the coarsest side of a conical grater.

Warm the oil in a large frying pan. Add the chopped garlic and cook it gently to flavour the oil. Add the courgettes and cook them in the oil, keeping the heat high enough to let them brown a little at the edges. Season the courgettes with some Maldon sea salt. Add the sprigs of fresh rosemary. (Adding it here, at the very end of cooking and simply warming it through, gives a fresh, light rosemary flavour, perfectly delicate with the courgettes.)

Cook the pasta in boiling salted water until al dente. Drain the pasta and add it to the frying pan. Toss everything together and serve it with plenty of black pepper.

Orecchiette with Artichokes
ORECCHIETTE CON CARCIOFI

We tasted this pasta in Puglia, the area far down the east coast of Italy towards the heel. It's one of the most unspoiled and fascinating parts of Italy, well worth a visit, though go in spring or late summer to avoid the intense heat.

I love the extra virgin olive oil from Puglia. The land is covered with olive groves. Everywhere you look there are olive trees. The best oil comes from the ancient gnarled trees that look as if they're about to give up! These have in fact been pruned more extensively, and yield a lower crop of olives that are better quality and give sweeter flavoured oil.

Orecchiette, 'little ears', are local hand-made pasta rounds made from a simple flour and water dough. They're pressed with

the thumb to look like a little ear. The sauce sits nicely in the
scoop of the pasta, perfect for a rich sugo. In Puglia the garlic
is often left whole and allowed to brown, giving a subtler,
aromatic flavour.

hearts of 2 medium or small artichokes, cleaned and thinly sliced
(see page 66)
4–5 tablespoons extra virgin olive oil
2 cloves garlic, peeled but kept whole
1 piece peperoncino (dried chilli), crumbled
2–3 fresh bay leaves
Maldon sea salt
360 g orecchiette pasta

The most time-consuming part of this dish is preparing the
artichokes. If you can't find fresh artichokes substitute 'carciofi
sott'olio', artichokes preserved in olive oil. If you're using fresh
artichokes, pare them down, cut them in half and after
removing the choke, cut the white central heart into fine thin
slices. Keep them in a bowl of water with a couple of lemon
quarters to stop them discolouring.

Warm the extra virgin olive oil in a wide frying pan. Add
the garlic and cook it slowly, allowing it to brown. The
flavour changes very noticeably. Add the chilli, the bay leaves
and the sliced artichokes, and season the artichokes with some
sea salt. Turn them in the flavoured oil for a few minutes. Add
2–3 tablespoons water, covering the frying pan with a lid so
that the artichokes soften and cook in their own steam
without frying. Taste the sauce to check the seasoning. The
flavour is distinctive.

Cook the orecchiette in plenty of boiling salted water
until al dente. They usually take about 12 minutes. Drain
them and toss them into the artichoke sugo, reserving a few

tablespoons of the cooking water to add more moisture if necessary.

The pasta is usually served with a bay leaf and whole garlic clove on the plate, but neither is eaten.

Aromatic Spaghettini
SPAGHETTINI AROMATICI

1 tablespoon salted capers
2–3 salted anchovy fillets
360 g spaghettini
Maldon sea salt
3–4 tablespoons extra virgin olive oil
1 clove garlic, peeled and roughly chopped
a piece of peperoncino (dried chilli)
1 tablespoon black olives, Taggiasche if possible, stoned and chopped
4 fresh mint leaves, finely chopped
2 tablespoons very finely chopped flat-leaf parsley

Soak the capers in cold water for 20 minutes or so to get rid of any excess salt, then drain and chop them. Wash the salted anchovies under lots of cold running water. Pull the fillet from the bone, pat dry and chop roughly.

Start to cook the spaghettini in plenty of boiling salted water.

Warm the extra virgin olive oil in a frying pan. Add the garlic and a good pinch of chilli, and cook gently to flavour the oil. Remove both before they start to brown. Add the chopped anchovy and fry gently until it starts to dissolve, mashing it down into the oil with a wooden spoon.

Drain the pasta while it is still a bit undercooked, saving a cup of the cooking water. Toss the pasta into the oil in the frying pan. Add the olives, capers and fresh herbs and cook everything together, adding a little of the pasta cooking water if necessary.

Genoese Pesto
PESTO ALLA GENOVESE

If you see large bunches of fresh basil or you grow it in abundance on your windowsill, make some fresh Genoese pesto. It is a real treat. It freezes well, so it's worth making more and keeping some for later, cooler months.

3–4 large handfuls fresh basil (at least 100 g)
1 clove fresh garlic, peeled and chopped
Maldon sea salt, about ½ teaspoon to start
1 tablespoon pine nuts
2 tablespoons freshly grated Parmigiano Reggiano
3 tablespoons freshly grated pecorino romano
(slightly salty, hard pecorino)
6 tablespoons fruity extra virgin olive oil, Ligurian if at all possible

Pesto really tastes best when it's made in a pestle and mortar. There is a knack to using one and it does take a bit more elbow grease, but the result is worth the effort. 'Pesto' means to crush or pound, just what you need to do.

Pick the basil leaves from the stalks, discarding any that are bruised or damaged. Don't wash them.

Put the chopped garlic, a pinch of Maldon sea salt and some of the basil leaves, torn up, into the mortar. The rough salt provides some friction needed to grind the basil leaves. It also helps to preserve their vibrant, bright green colour. Gradually add more and more leaves to the mortar until it is all ground down.

Now add the pine nuts and the two cheeses. (Or use the combined quantity of one cheese.) The pesto is more appetising if it is rough and textured. I like to see some of the pine nuts just crushed and no more. Lastly blend in the oil, enough to make a nice, thick consistency. Check the flavour and adjust as necessary. I don't like it too garlicky.

Spoon this on to drained, piping hot pasta, and toss it well with a fork and spoon. A spoonful in soup or spring vegetable risotto lifts their flavour from good to sublime.

If you store the pesto in a sterilised jar with a lid it will keep a few days in the fridge. I usually cover the surface with a little olive oil to stop it oxidising and going brown. Don't be tempted to store it for too long, as the garlic may become too overpowering. I prefer to make a little as I need it and freeze any excess in ice-cube trays, tipping it out into soups or pasta as I want.

Just a word on commercial ready-made pesto. Some of them have nuts other than pine nuts in them. Walnuts and even peanuts can be used. They may be made with a blend of different oils, not just olive oil. Be careful if anyone has a nut allergy.

DAIRY SUGO

THE GREAT ADVANTAGE OF THESE PASTA SAUCES is that they're also incredibly quick and easy to make. Based on cheese, butter or cream, they can be made in the time it takes to boil the pasta. They're practical for any working person who needs to prepare something to eat very quickly. I usually serve these as emergency food, when I'm starving, exhausted and need some real spoiling.

Pasta with Parmesan and Butter
SPAGHETTINI CON PARMIGIANO E BURRO

Parmigiano Reggiano really must be freshly grated to release its distinctive moist, creamy flavour. Ready grated or old, stale Parmigiano from the bottom of the fridge won't give the complete sensation of unadulterated luxury that this pasta should have.

These quantities serve one portion; I usually make it for Philip.

Philip aged three, eating his pasta

85–100 g spaghetti
Maldon sea salt and black pepper
a good blob of unsalted butter
3–4 tablespoons freshly grated
Parmigiano Reggiano

Cook the spaghetti in well salted boiling water. As soon as it is al dente, drain it, keeping a little of the cooking water.

Put the butter into the saucepan, add the drained pasta and quickly heat the two together over a high heat, turning the pasta with a fork so that it gets well coated. Add a splash of the cooking liquid to add moisture. Take the saucepan off the heat and toss in the grated Parmigiano. Grind plenty of black pepper on to the pasta and eat it, preferably in front of the telly. Enjoy!

You can use freshly grated pecorino instead. The pecorino is often slightly sharper than the Parmigiano, so add more black pepper to complement this with a kick.

147

Pasta with Butter and Sage
PASTA CON BURRO E SALVIA

It seems too obvious to write down, but a classic dressing for pasta is simply unsalted butter flavoured with a couple of fresh sage leaves. This is particularly good with home-made stuffed pasta like ravioli (see page 125) or is fabulously brilliant with home-made gnocchi (see page 133).

Melt 100 g of unsalted butter in a frying pan. Add 3–4 fresh sage leaves. The sage flavours the butter and gives a wonderful, aromatic smell. As soon as the sage just starts to change colour the flavoured butter is ready. Toss it over cooked pasta or ravioli. Add plenty of freshly grated Parmigiano Reggiano or pecorino and freshly ground black pepper.

Pasta with Ricotta and Lemon
PASTA CON RICOTTA E LIMONE

360 g spaghettini
Maldon sea salt and black pepper
4 tablespoons fresh ricotta, bought or home-made (see page 122)
a good blob of unsalted butter
2 tablespoons finely chopped flat-leaf parsley
1 unwaxed lemon
freshly grated nutmeg or some basil leaves, torn

Cook the pasta in well-salted boiling water until al dente. The water should be a bit saltier than usual because there is no salt in the ricotta. Drain it, keeping some of the cooking water aside.

Tip the pasta back into the saucepan or into a wide frying pan. Add about 80 ml of so of the cooking water and the ricotta and butter. Heat everything through, breaking up the ricotta with a fork.

Add a generous squeeze of lemon juice and a few fine gratings of the washed rind. Grind on plenty of black pepper to lift the flavour. Check the seasoning and adjust to taste. Finish with a scraping of nutmeg or some torn fresh basil leaves.

Tagliarini with Gorgonzola
TAGLIARINI CON GORGONZOLA CREMIFICATO

I use dried egg tagliarini for this pasta so that the creamy sauce just slides and coats the pasta. Buy a really runny, ripe Gorgonzola 'dolce'. This is the creamy, sweet version of the traditional mountain Gorgonzola, which is firmer and sharper. Or, even creamier, a Gorgonzola cremificato.

Melt about 200 g Gorgonzola cremificato into a saucepan with a couple of tablespoons each of milk and double cream. Gently use a fork or a wooden spoon to break down any of the green strands, melting the cheese into a sauce. If the strands don't melt down and the sauce tastes gritty, strain it through a sieve.

Cook about 360 g tagliarini until al dente. Egg pasta takes only 4–5 minutes. Check the packet. Drain the cooked pasta, saving some of the cooking water. Toss the pasta in the Gorgonzola sauce, adding a couple of tablespoons of the water if needed. Finally, season with plenty of freshly grated black pepper.

Fettuccine with Cream and Butter
FETTUCCINE CON PANNA E BURRO

I was a mini-skirted twelve-year-old when I first visited Italy. Anita, my sister, was thirteen, slightly taller, slightly thinner and slightly – ever so slightly – prettier! We spent three weeks in Picinisco, thrilled to be in Italy and excited by all things Italian. Nonna Marietta took us to Rome to visit the Vatican, the Sistine Chapel and for lunch at the famous Ristorante Alfredo. Everyone

Gertrude and Johnny at Ristorante Alfredo, Rome, 1952

visited Ristorante Alfredo when they were in Rome. My mum and dad had visited while on honeymoon and told us all about it. We were very excited about the visit. This would be cool!

Alfredo made his name not only because his fettuccine were wonderfully light and coated with a perfect combination of cream, butter and Parmigiano Reggiano, but also because he had a very good marketing gimmick. As his fettuccine were the best in Rome and merited the best presentation, they were ceremoniously tossed in front of the customer with a solid gold spoon and fork. It also did wonders for the ego of the lady who was being served, who was the most beautiful signorina in Rome (and for the size of the gratuity left at the end of the meal).

Naturally, Nonna Marietta ordered fettuccine for us. The waiters fussed over us both, our first encounter with Italian males was very exciting. We were impressed! This was fun. But the anticipated ritual of the gold fork and spoon was a dreadful disappointment. The waiter walked past me and prepared my teenage sister's pasta with the gold spoon and fork. I was dismissed, just a young child, with stainless-steel cutlery. I couldn't swallow my pasta for jealousy and hurt pride. What a come-down.

Francesca, I've never forgotten my embarrassment. My only consolation is that your auntie reached forty before me and will always be ever so slightly older than me!

Use good dried egg pasta for this dish. Home-made pasta is also fabulous served like this. Dried egg pasta cooks within 4 or 5 minutes, faster than you would expect. Use less egg pasta, as it is very filling.

225 ml double cream (a small carton)
80 g unsalted butter
2 tablespoons freshly grated Parmigiano Reggiano
Maldon sea salt and black pepper
320 g dried egg fettuccine or linguine

Start to heat the cream and the butter in a wide, deep frying pan or saucepan big enough to hold the drained pasta. Warm it through, but don't let it thicken too much. Add the Parmigiano Reggiano, stir it through, and season it a little with some Maldon salt, tasting to check the flavour.

Cook the pasta until al dente. Drain it, keeping some of the cooking water. Tip the pasta into the frying pan and coat it in the cream, tossing it with a fork and spoon. Keep the heat on very low. Add a few tablespoons of the cooking water if the pasta looks dry. Finally serve with a generous grinding of black pepper.

This is a very easy recipe to adapt. Just remember to keep it simple. Use one or two other ingredients only.

I like to add some strips of smoked salmon and a good tablespoon of finely chopped fresh dill to the cream as it heats. (Omit the Parmigiano.)

Or you can add strips of ham and some mushrooms, cooked first in a little butter.

Try a finely chopped shallot or onion softened in a little butter. Add some chopped smoked bacon or pancetta and cook it slowly. Add some double cream, grated Parmigiano and ground black pepper for an instant delicious supper.

Penne with Courgettes and Cream
PENNE CON ZUCCHINE E PANNA

Try to use organic courgettes here. They are sweeter and cook crisper as well. You can use egg tagliarini as an alternative.

3 courgettes (about 200 g)
a good blob of butter
Maldon salt and black pepper
360 g penne rigate
1 x 125 ml carton double cream, at least
2–3 tablespoons freshly grated Parmigiano Reggiano

Wash and dry the courgettes and grate them into strips on the coarsest side of a grater.

Put the butter into a wide, deep frying pan and cook the grated courgettes slowly, slowly, until they soften down and brown a little at the edges. Season them fairly well with Maldon salt.

Get the pasta on to boil in salted water.

Add enough double cream to the courgettes to make a rich sauce. Warm it through and check the taste. (No, don't taste it again, you know it's good!)

Drain the pasta and toss it into the cream and courgette sauce, adding freshly grated Parmigiano to taste and a good grinding of black pepper. Just let the pasta warm through in the sauce, then eat.

Pasta Wheels with Artichokes, Peas and Cream
RUOTE ALLA NONNA

Nonna Annunziata in Naples taught me how to make this pasta.

She liked pasta wheels because they were nice and soft. When I knew her, she was over seventy-five-years old and had two teeth left, one at the top of her gum, one on the bottom.

Francesca, it was she who taught me to

Annunziata and four-year-old Francesca

enjoy brandy! When I was pregnant with you I felt very sick all the time. I couldn't eat and was losing weight. I was carrying her favourite son's son's child. Boy, was I important! So important, seventy-eight-year-old Annunziata made the journey from Naples all on her own to check me out.

When she saw I wasn't eating she took me in hand. Twice a day, before lunch and supper, she took me aside and, reaching into the pocket of the short, floral apron she always wore, she pulled out a small hip flask of cognac. She would ceremoniously pour two thimble-sized glasses, one for me and one for her. Against all medical advice, we got through the pregnancy a treat, all three of us, Nonna Annunziata, me and you!

1 x 400 g tin artichoke hearts preserved in brine
a blob of unsalted butter
1 x 125 ml carton double cream
2 tablespoons frozen petits pois
Maldon sea salt
360 g ruote (wheel-shaped pasta), or any chunky pasta
2–3 tablespoons freshly grated Parmigiano Reggiano

Firstly you need to rinse the tinned artichokes. They are usually preserved in brine and the taste can be a bit over-powering in the sauce. The easiest way to do this is to rinse them under cold water and squeeze them a little to get rid of any moisture. Cut them into quarters.

Melt the butter in a saucepan and coat the artichokes. Add the cream and petits pois and warm the sauce through. Season the sauce well with Maldon sea salt.

Boil the pasta in plenty of boiling salted water until al dente. Drain it well in a colander, giving it an extra shake to get rid of the water that gets stuck in the holes in the pasta. Mix the pasta into the warm sauce and serve with the grated Parmigiano.

This is always a real favourite with children; they love to look for the peas in the wheels!

In Naples, Nonna Annunziata would almost certainly have made this with fresh artichokes and peas. In Scotland in 1980, neither was easily available. This is exactly how recipes from Europe lost some of their authenticity when ingredients were substituted. Today I make this with fresh peas and artichokes in spring and early summer.

Prepare fresh artichokes, taking away all the outside coarse leaves and the choke (see page 66). Cut them into fine slices and boil them in salted water until they are tender. Boil the peas for a few minutes as well, just to take away any hardness. Add them to the recipe above.

Marietta's Pastina Carbonara

Marietta whipped up this instant carbonara with pastina when any of her sons had been working late at night or had come home from courting a new lady friend. It instantly fills the stomach and slipped down so easily the exhausted boy didn't even have to chew!

I love making it. It's so easy, tasty and filling. The egg is cooked only in the heat of the pasta, so make sure you use a fresh organic egg. This amount feeds one hungry lad.

150 g pastina
Maldon sea salt and black pepper
a big blob of butter, softened
1 organic egg
3 tablespoons roughly grated pecorino (or Parmigiano Reggiano)

Cook the pastina in plenty of salted boiling water until al dente.

In a warm bowl whisk the butter, egg and Parmigiano together, adding a good grinding of black pepper. Drain the pastina and tip it into the mixture, whisking everything together, cooking the egg in the heat.

Let him eat it in front of the telly with a soupspoon straight from the bowl.

TOMATO AND MEAT SUGO

SURELY TOMATO SUGO IS THE WORLD'S MOST POPULAR sauce for pasta. Ask any child what their favourite food is and they are most likely to say 'pasta'. They really mean pasta with tomato sugo.

Olivia, Francesca's sister, enjoying pasta, aged six

Fresh tomatoes for sugo have to be sweet and juicy. In practice, this means that in Britain you'll only use fresh tomatoes in the summer.

The best cooking tomatoes come from Naples. This is a fact of life! Very, soft ripe San Marzano plum tomatoes cook down in no time producing a full-flavoured, juicy, wonderful sugo. Very ripe, stem tomatoes that have good flavour are also very successful.

When they're ripe, tomatoes skin very easily. Slash the side with a very sharp knife and cover them with boiling water for a couple of minutes. Drain them and, as soon as you can handle them, peel off the skin.

Sicilian Pachino tomatoes and some of the new varieties of cherry tomatoes on the stem are very sweet and make lovely sugo. Cut them in half and roughly de-seed them before using. They seem to be packed with seeds that can become very bitter when cooked.

More often than not, if I can't find the right fresh tomatoes, I use tinned San Marzano plum tomatoes. These are juicy and plump and have a good tomato juice around them, perfect for sugo.

I tend not to use passata, ready pulped or chopped tomatoes. I find their flavour too concentrated. All my grandmothers used to add some tomato purée to their sugo. I don't. I think these days we prefer our flavours lighter and even simpler.

Fresh Tomato Sugo
SUGO DI POMODORO FRESCHI

This sugo, served with spaghettini, encapsulates all I love about tomatoes, sweet, perfumed and delicate.

750 g ripe sweet tomatoes, preferably plum, skinned
3–4 tablespoons extra virgin olive oil
2 cloves garlic, peeled
Maldon sea salt
a handful of fresh basil, leaves torn
360 g spaghettini

Cut the tomatoes into even-sized pieces. If you are lucky enough to find ripe, sweet San Marzano plum tomatoes, then simply skin them and cut them into quarters lengthways.

Put the tomatoes into a large flat frying pan. Pour over the extra virgin olive oil. Slice the garlic thinly on to the tomatoes. (This way the garlic cooks very gently and imparts a more delicate flavour than if cooked in oil first. The slivers are easily left on the plate when eating.) Cook the tomatoes over a low heat until they soften and collapse. Move them around from time to time; they'll take about 15 minutes.

Add Maldon salt to bring out all the sweetness and flavour of the tomatoes. Check the seasoning. Stir the basil into the tomatoes.

Cook the pasta in boiling salted water, and drain as soon as it is al dente. Give it a quick shake in the colander before tipping it into the tomato sugo. It will have a little of the cooking water clinging to it which will just moisten the tomatoes enough. Warm it through and serve.

In the winter I make this sugo with a tin of plum tomatoes, chopped roughly, and cooked with oil and garlic and some imported fresh basil. You can make a quick sugo for the price of a tin of tomatoes and a little olive oil. No need for expensive ready-made sauces.

Annunziata used to make a sugo with peperoni in exactly the same way (see page 212). You need really good red and yellow peppers. The knobbly odd-shaped Italian ones are the best, but use organic home-grown ones if you can find them.

Penne with Tomato and Butter Sugo
PENNE CON SUGO DI POMODORO E BURRO

Francesca, I don't care what you say. This is the most indulgent sugo on earth and especially because it's so simple to prepare. It's perfect for home-made gnocchi, or serve it simply with penne rigate. And by the way, the butter quantity is not a misprint! I'm sure my Nonna Marietta used more.

2 x 400 g tins Italian plum tomatoes
1 small shallot, peeled but not chopped
300–400 g unsalted butter, preferably Italian
1 teaspoon caster sugar
a sprig of fresh rosemary

Maldon sea salt
360 g penne rigate
freshly grated pecorino or Parmigiano Reggiano

You need to get rid of the seeds in the tomatoes to do this sugo justice. Pass the tomatoes through a sieve or mouli. I used to do this for Nonna Marietta as a child, stirring and pressing the tomatoes through the sieve with a wooden spoon. I hated that job . . . and still do. I cheat and whizz them briefly through a liquidiser and then through a sieve. A bit easier! After that it's plain sailing.

Put the tomato, shallot, butter and sugar into a small saucepan over a low heat and cook very, very gently for half an hour, with the lid balanced on a wooden spoon, half on, half off the saucepan. The sugo will reduce by about a third. Stir it from time to time to stop the butter separating. Remove the shallot, and add the rosemary. Heat it through, then season with Maldon salt. You may have to add more salt than you expect. It acts to sweeten the tomatoes.

Boil the penne in salted water until al dente. Drain and put back into the saucepan. Spoon over enough tomato sugo and serve with plenty of grated pecorino or Parmigiano Reggiano. Any extra sugo will last two to three days in the fridge.

You can make this with fresh basil instead of the rosemary, adding it at the last minute, to maintain its fresh flavour.

Fresh Tomato Sugo with Ricotta and Pecorino
SUGO ALLA CIOCIARA

Francesca, 'le ciocie' are the traditional leather-strapped sandals that our ancestors wore. 'Ciociaria' is the geographical name for the area relating to the Province of Frosinone and some parts of Isernia and Caserta, south of Rome. The whole area, down to the coast, is famous for its wonderful fresh produce, its pecorino cheese, ruby-red, fruity Montepulciano wine and, according to legend, its beautiful women!

'I ciociari' is the name of the people who come from this area. Remember Nonna Marietta's young brother who was so happy to get his first pair of 'ciocie'?

To capture the exquisiteness of the flavours of this southern dish you need really sweet cherry tomatoes, fresh basil and soft, creamy fresh ricotta, all easily found in the summer at least. These ingredients serve two.

2–3 tablespoons extra virgin olive oil
a couple of handfuls of sweet cherry tomatoes
1 clove fresh garlic, peeled and sliced into 4
180 g spaghettini
Maldon sea salt and black pepper
2 tablespoons fresh ricotta, bought or home-made (see page 122)
freshly dried oregano or fresh basil
freshly grated pecorino

Warm the oil in a wide frying pan. Wash the tomatoes and squeeze them through your hands into the oil, just letting their juices mix with the oil. They splash and squirt out, so be careful. You can chop them into quarters if you prefer. Add the garlic and let the tomatoes cook for 10 minutes or so, just to soften the skins.

Boil the spaghettini in salted water while they're cooking.

Crumble the ricotta with a fork. Sprinkle it on to the tomatoes and add a couple of generous pinches of freshly dried oregano. Alternatively tear on some fresh basil. Let the ricotta warm through. Taste the sugo and adjust the flavour with some sea salt. The tomatoes should be sweet enough to allow the salt just to lift their flavour.

Drain the pasta well and toss it in the sugo. Add a good grating of black pepper and some grated pecorino. The whole dish is beautiful in its simplicity and fresh flavour.

BRUNTON PLACE, EDINBURGH, SCOTLAND
1930–1940

Alfonso Crolla was charismatic. He had a natural affinity for people and was a great socialiser. He became an important leader in the immigrant Italian community. He organised passage for cousins and their wives to emigrate from Italy. He helped Cesidio when he came over. He lent money to those arriving with

Alfonso, Maria and Domenico, centre, with visiting friends and family, c.1917

nothing, helping them find work and start businesses. He supported community clubs and helped the young Italians settle in their new country. He acted as the link between the old and the new, forging friends and contacts in the local Scottish community as well. Alfonso enjoyed every minute of his new role. He travelled around Scotland keeping in touch with his compatriots and selling them provisions. His house was always full of business acquaintances, friends, family and priests.

Maria had a hard life. By now she had six children to bring up. They lived in a top flat in Brunton Place, close to their ice-cream business in Easter Road. Like all women in those days, she had to wash all the clothes by hand, bent over the bath, scrubbing with carbolic soap. She had no drying area so had to wring the clothes out as best she could and hang them, dripping, from the pulley in the kitchen.

She worked in the shop, and kept control of things while Alfonso was away on business. She spoke little or no English, so relied on her young children to help her communicate with her customers. She often despaired at the difficulties of her new life, blaming her husband. 'Why have you brought us here? Why have we left our beautiful country? How will we manage with all the work we have to do?'

Her great pleasure was feeding her family. She was a skilled, natural cook. Like all Italian mothers, she was prone to spoiling her sons Domenico and Vittorio, while her daughters Margherita, Olivia and Filomena were pulled into the kitchen to help. Gloria, her favourite, was a bit spoiled too.

Sunday was the most important day. A big pot of sugo was prepared in the morning, simmering away gently while the family all trooped out to Mass. Maria would add pork or beef to the sugo with some spicy Fonteluna sausage to give a rich, sweet flavour, exactly as her mother had shown her. In Rome, they say 'follow a priest at lunch time and you will eat well'. In

Edinburgh, you just needed to follow them from St Mary's Cathedral at the top of Leith Walk, along London Road to Brunton Place. You would have been welcomed at Maria's table, and would have eaten extremely well!

Alfonso usually arrived late. Without warning he invited friends, relatives or strangers he'd just met, for lunch. Maria quickly set more places and prepared more food. He sat at the head of the table, handsome and proud of his family and his wife. Like all Italian fathers he had a duty to keep up appearances as the head of the household. To this end, he constantly tormented Maria about her cooking. No matter how good it was and how carefully she had cooked for them all, he always tasted his food, looked up, paused for a moment and said, with a thoughtful nod to the left: 'Cara, è buono, ma . . . ci manca qualcosa . . . ' 'Darling, it's good, but . . . there's something missing . . . '

The sugo was wonderful, tasty and nourishing, made with wisdom and love. He really enjoyed it, and was happy to see his family eating well around his table. But somehow he couldn't let Maria know. He needed to show a little restraint and keep the upper hand. Everyone round the table needed to know who was boss.

The girls would be cross with him for tormenting their mother, but she never said a word. She just nodded her head and gave him a look, that look that passes between husband and wife when they really understand each other. She loved him, he knew that, and they both knew who really was boss.

Tragically, he died during the Second World War.

She mourned him all her life. She stayed in Edinburgh and kept working hard, looking after her family and cooking wonderful meals for them, but from then on, Francesca, 'ci manca qualcosa', there was always something missing.

Slowly Cooked Sugo
'CI MANCA QUALCOSA'

Francesca, I learned to make this traditional, slowly cooked sugo by watching my Nonna Marietta and my mummy and, once I got married, by listening to my mother-in-law, Olivia.

Learn how I make it with spalebone and then you can adjust the recipe to make countless variations. Always use a good, heavy-bottomed saucepan for cooking sugo slowly. Use a heat diffuser if you have one.

The skill is to take time over the slow cooking of the onions so that they form a sweet natural body for the sugo. The meat or sausage that is cooked in the sugo becomes tender and flavoursome, and is eaten either with the pasta or is placed on the table to be eaten as the main course. Either way it is perfect!

This sugo is really versatile. Serve it with chunky pasta like rigatoni or penne, but also with spaghetti or bucatini. There is enough sugo for up to 1 kg of pasta, which would serve eight to ten people. Use what you need and keep the rest in the fridge. It will last easily three to four days, or freeze it for up to three months.

The same technique is also used to make ragù for lasagne.

Francesca, come over here, I'll show you how.

300 g spalebone beef or blade steak, in one piece
1 clove garlic, peeled and thinly sliced
1 tablespoon finely chopped flat-leaf parsley
3–4 tablespoons extra virgin olive oil
1 onion, peeled and very, very finely chopped
1 piece peperoncino (dried chilli)
3 or 4 x 450 g tins Italian plum tomatoes, sieved or liquidised
and de-seeded
½ Fonteluna sausage or salsiccia napoli (150 g)
Maldon sea salt and black pepper

First, prepare the spalebone or blade steak. This cut of meat has a fine glutinous vein in the middle. It's an inexpensive cut because it needs very slow cooking. Having said that, it becomes exceedingly tender and sweet, the vein melting into the sugo, making it especially good. Use a sharp knife to make three or four slits in the meat. Push a sliver of garlic and some chopped parsley into each slit.

Warm the extra virgin olive oil in a wide, heavy saucepan. Add the meat and brown it well all over. This will take 10 minutes or so. Remove the meat from the flavoured oil and add the chopped onion and the chilli. Stir around in the oil and cook the mixture very, very slowly until the onion is transparent and soft. This is the key to a good sugo. There shouldn't be any hint of onion at the end so, the softer this soffritto is, the better the sugo. Add the sieved tomatoes and return the meat to the saucepan. Take the outer fine skin from the Fonteluna sausage, and add the sausage to the sugo. (If the sausage is dry it is easiest to run it under warm water: score the side with a sharp knife and the skin will peel off easily.)

Bring the sugo to a slow simmer. This sugo takes 2–2½ hours to cook on a very low heat. Put a wooden spoon over the pot and balance the lid on top. This way the sugo can reduce slowly, but most of the water that evaporates will drip back into the pot. Use a heat diffuser under the pot if you have one to prevent the sugo burning. If you don't have one, pull the pot to the side of the heat.

(Right, get out to Mass! Francesca?)

After a couple of hours, the sugo will have reduced by about a third. Taste it and season it with Maldon sea salt. The seasoning in the beef and from the sausage will have already added some flavour. If it still tastes a little sharp, a little more salt does the trick.

This sugo is best with chunky pasta like rigatoni rigate or

penne, and is the one we always prepare for home-made pasta at Christmas. It freezes well and keeps in the fridge for four to five days.

The delicious tender meat and sausage are usually placed in the middle of the table and shared with everyone.

'SOCKS'

'Socks' Cesidio during the First World War, far right, with three comrades

RIGATONI ARE TUBULAR CHUNKY PASTA WITH RIDGES, 'righe', along their edges. In our house we always called them 'socks'. I never knew why till my Nonna Marietta died.

Just after they were married, her beloved Cesidio was called up to fight in the First World War. A pacific and gentle man, he hated being away from his family. He desperately wanted to go home. In the freezing cold of the trenches, he took his socks off and pushed his already frozen feet deep into the snow. Many soldiers did this to deliberately get frostbite so that they could be sent home. Unfortunately, he never got frostbite and had to stay his term.

When he wrote to tell her jokingly of his antics, she was distraught. She was afraid he would be ill. He'd catch pneumonia. She spent the rest of the war agitatedly knitting socks for him, her fingers working ten to the dozen. She became obsessive, sending him parcels of socks at every opportunity.

Years later, after he died, she knitted socks for her two sons and then for her grandsons. As she got older and her fingers became less nimble, she could only manage to knit the leg. She had to have help to 'turn the heel'. Because of that she always had a backlog of long woollen knitted tubes, ridged up the sides, waiting to be finished. . . . 'Socks'!

Francesca, while I'm thinking, I remember she used to use a 'battuto' at the beginning of her sugo. She bashed a slice of lardo with some parsley and garlic and melted it down with the soffritto. It gave a creamy, rich sweetness to her sugo. Maybe that's what was missing in Brunton Place!

Mince Balls
POLPETTE

The method of making a slow sugo is always the same. Instead of the spalebone and the Fonteluna sausage, a soffritto of onions in olive oil is flavoured with beef 'polpette', meat balls, pork, oxtail or rabbit, and then slow-cooked with the tomatoes.

These polpette are favourites. I usually add them directly into the tomatoes but you can brown them in a separate frying pan before adding them. Make the soffritto simply with chopped onions and peperoncino. I don't add garlic to the sugo when I make polpette. The polpette have plenty of flavourings in them.

I never buy ready-minced mince. Always ask the butcher to mince a piece of lean stewing or rump steak for you. Nonna

Marietta used to send me to the butcher with the express instructions for him to mince fillet steak for her.

To make the breadcrumbs just whizz old dry bread and crusts
in a liquidiser or food processor. They will last in a sealed jar
for a few weeks.

250 g fresh minced beef (or 125 g minced pork and 125 g minced beef)
3 tablespoons dry breadcrumbs
1 tablespoon freshly grated Parmigiano Reggiano
1 tablespoon finely chopped flat-leaf parsley
½ onion, peeled and finely grated
1 tablespoon raisins (Marietta did, Maria didn't!)
1 large egg yolk, beaten
Maldon sea salt and black pepper

Mix the first six ingredients together in a large bowl. Add the
egg yolk and mix it in with a fork or clean hands, along with
plenty of salt and pepper. The seasoning will seep out of the
polpette as they cook, flavouring the tomatoes, so make sure
you season them well to start with (I usually just taste a little
to check). With clean hands, mould the mixture into six to
eight small balls.

Start to make the sugo as in the slowly cooked sugo
above, but without the spalebone and sausage. Soften the
finely chopped onion in extra virgin olive oil and flavour it
with a little peperoncino. Add a whole clove of garlic if you
want. Add the sieved tomato, three x 400 g tins will do, and
gently lay the polpette into it. This sugo will take 1½–2 hours
to cook. Use a heat diffuser, and remember to leave the lid
balanced on the wooden spoon to let some steam evaporate.
Always taste the sugo and adjust the seasoning at the end.

You can serve this sugo with any pasta you fancy. I love
'socks', rigatoni rigate. Don't forget to sprinkle on plenty of

freshly grated Parmigiano Reggiano or pecorino to add an extra scrumptiousness to the pasta.

I usually put the polpette on a plate in the middle of the table so that everyone can help themselves. They can be eaten cold the next day with plenty of salad.

Francesca, don't get bogged down with quantities when you are cooking these recipes. Always bear in mind that although many of them are classic, some have never been written down before. In our family we have always cooked by instinct and experience. The most important ingredient is a thinking cook with a palate. Keep tasting all the ingredients as you cook and adjust the flavours as you go. A little more tomato or a little less meat won't spoil the flavour. Poor-quality raw ingredients, not enough salt or burning the onions will.

Meat Loaf
POLPETTONE

You can make one big 'polpettone' or meat loaf.

Press all the above polpette ingredients together to make one big mince ball. If I make this I usually brown it a little in some olive oil in a frying pan before I add it to the tomato. This prevents it breaking up. Cook the sugo slowly the same way and serve the polpettone sliced after the pasta. It is lovely in panini the next day.

Little Meat Rolls
BRACIOLE

Sometimes I make 'braciole', little rolls of thin steak flavoured with garlic and parsley. Just ask the butcher for thin slices of beef, veal or pork. Lay them flat and whack them with a rolling pin to tenderise them a little.

Sprinkle them with some chopped parsley and garlic. Season them well with Maldon sea salt and freshly ground black pepper and roll them up. When I was small I used to have the job of sewing them up with a needle and thread! Now I just keep them together with a toothpick threaded through.

Make a slow sugo with them in exactly the same way as in the recipe on page 164, browning them in the extra virgin olive oil at the beginning instead of the spalebone. I always add some Fonteluna pork sausage to the sugo as well.

Pork Chops

Marietta often added a pork chop to the slow sugo. I love it. It makes the sugo sweet and cooks into a sweet, juicy cut. Try it. To tell the truth, you can make your sugo with any combination you like.

Rich Pasta Sauce
RAGU

I usually only make ragù if I'm making lasagne.

2–3 tablespoons extra virgin olive oil
50 g unsalted butter

2 tablespoons each of very finely chopped shallot, celery and carrot
400 g lean beef, minced (see page 167)
Maldon sea salt and black pepper
200 ml dry white wine
100 ml milk
3 x 400 g tins Italian plum tomatoes (San Marzano if possible),
liquidised and sieved
freshly grated nutmeg

You need a heavy cast-iron saucepan. Ragù needs to cook very slowly with not much liquid, so runs the risk of burning. Use a heat diffuser if you have one.

Warm the oil in the saucepan with the butter until it melts, and sauté the shallot, celery and carrot until they are clear and soft, a good 10–15 minutes.

Turn the heat up and add the mince. It needs to be well browned so use a fork to break it up and turn it around in the heat. Season the mince well. Keep the heat up high and add the wine. Let everything bubble fiercely until the wine has been absorbed into the meat and the alcohol has evaporated. Add the milk and let things bubble away again until the milk has all been absorbed. It coats the mince and takes away the gritty feel that you can sometimes get with mince. Add the tomatoes and cook the ragù for 2 hours at least, very slowly.

This tastes and smells wonderful. I love dipping the spoon into the pot and testing to see how it's doing! Adjust the seasoning as you go, remembering that it becomes more concentrated, so don't over-salt. Add a tablespoon of water if it gets too thick. Finish it off with a generous grating of nutmeg.

This freezes very well so make a double batch and pop it into containers for fast-food emergencies.

LASAGNE AL FORNO

Lasagne is a bit time-consuming but it is very handy if we're feeding a big crowd. All the work can be done the day before, and then it just has to be reheated. I love lasagne to be moist and juicy. The very nicest lasagne is made with home-made pasta, but you really have to organise yourself to spend the morning cooking. If you start the sugo, then make the pasta and the béchamel while it's cooking, you can assemble the lasagne and have the kitchen cleaned up by lunchtime. (That's the theory!)

I tend to use dried egg lasagne sheets. Even if the packet says not to, it's worth immersing them in boiling salted water for a few minutes just to soften them a little. (My mum called it 'plotting' in boiling water.) The process ensures they cook evenly in the assembled dish.

This lasagne will probably serve four to five. Double or treble all the quantities if you need more, but go easy on the oil. Make sure you have a nice ovenproof dish to make the lasagne in. It needs to be just deep enough to hold three layers of pasta with the fillings between. I use one that is 30 x 15 and 6.5 cm deep, but use one you have at home. (It's easiest to lay the dry pasta sheets in the dish before you cook them to work out how many you'll need to cook.)

All the ingredients have to be ready and warm and should each taste good in their own right. Make sure the béchamel is not too thick. I like it to be like double cream. It tends to thicken as you work. Just stir in a little more milk if it does.

6–8 sheets dried egg lasagne pasta
1 quantity ragù (see page 170)
1 quantity béchamel sauce (see page 223)
2 cows' milk mozzarella, 'fior di latte'

plenty of freshly grated Parmigiano Reggiano
freshly grated nutmeg and black pepper

Start by 'plotting' the pasta, immersing it in boiling salted water for a few minutes, for 3–4 minutes only, until it is soft-ened slightly but not cooked. I usually add a splash of oil to the water just to stop the lasagne sheets sticking together. Stir the sheets around a little. After a few minutes put the whole pot under the cold-water tap. This lowers the temperature immediately and stops the pasta cooking any more. Use a slotted spoon to fish out the lasagne sheets and lay them on a dry clean cloth.

Spread a spoonful of béchamel, a little ragù and a sprink-ling of grated Parmigiano on to the bottom of the dish. Add a single layer of pasta, trimming it to fit the dish as needed. Now add a layer of béchamel, a few spoonfuls of ragù and a sprinkling of Parmigiano. Dot it with mozzarella and add black pepper.

Now start again and layer the next sheets of pasta on, adding the ragù and béchamel, mozzarella and Parmigiano again. Build up three or four layers, depending on what ingredients you have.

Decorate the top layer with the last of the ragù, the final scrapings of the béchamel and the last few slices of mozzarella. Don't worry if the béchamel is a bit unsightly by this stage. It all melts down in the oven and is guaranteed to look beautiful and very professional at the end! Add a final sprinkling of Parmigiano, black pepper and a nice grating of fresh nutmeg to lift the flavours.

It takes about 25 minutes or so to cook in a hot oven (220°C/425°F/Gas 7), longer if you have made a bigger lasagne. Check the lasagne to make sure it's heated right through in the middle before serving, especially if it's been refrigerated. The mozzarella will be deliciously soft and stringy, just a treat. Have some freshly grated Parmigiano ready to sprinkle on top as you serve it.

You can keep the lasagne for about two days in the fridge. Take the lasagne out of the fridge for half an hour before cooking.

If you're making lasagne for big parties just make three or four times the quantity. It always pays to make too much. It's always eaten, or at worst reheats brilliantly the next day. Remember that if you make it in one big dish it can take a good deal longer to heat through, at least an hour.

Make a lovely vegetable lasagne with a plain tomato sugo (see page 157) and use roasted vegetables such as courgettes and aubergines instead of the meat. It's especially tasty with lots of mozzarella and plenty of fresh basil. Roasting the vegetables first intensifies their flavour, and takes away some of their moisture which stops the lasagne being too wet (see page 292).

The only problem I have run into with lasagne is it being either too dry or too wet. If it's too dry, add a little milk or tomato sugo to the sides of the dish as it reheats. This is usually enough to adjust the problem. If you freeze a lasagne it can defrost with a lot of moisture coming out. If it looks far too wet just spoon some off, adding it again as it cooks if necessary. I really like it creamy and gooey and use plenty of béchamel.

Lasagne made with home-made pasta is even better, lighter and more refined. It means another job, making the pasta, but if you're in the mood give it a go. You'll need dough made with 1 egg, 2 egg yolks and about 200 g of '00' pasta flour for this amount of ragù. Reduce the pasta down to the second last setting and cut the long strips by hand to fit the dish you're using. You still need to soften the pasta in boiling salted water, but this time only for 30 seconds (see page 118).

Baked Pasta
RIGATONI AL FORNO

This is an easy way to make a pasta dish that will reheat beautifully. Prepare it in advance and it will keep nicely in the fridge
until the next day. The rigatoni are baked in the oven with a
light sugo and some mozzarella just like a lasagne.

400 g rigatoni
Maldon sea salt and black pepper
1 quantity fresh tomato sugo (see page 157) or ragù (see page 170)
1 quantity béchamel sauce (see page 223)
6 bocconcini mozzarella or 2 cows' milk mozzarella, 'fior di latte'
fresh basil
freshly grated Parmigiano Reggiano

Par-cook the rigatoni in boiling salted water for 6 minutes or
so, just to start to soften them. Run cold water in to stop the
cooking. Drain them well.

Toss the rigatoni in the tomato sugo, mixing it well.
Spread them into a baking dish and dot spoonfuls of
béchamel sauce and pieces of mozzarella all over. Add some
leaves of fresh basil, plenty of freshly grated Parmigiano
Reggiano and a good twist of black pepper.

Bake it in a hot oven (200°C/400°F/Gas 6) for 20
minutes or until piping hot.

RISOTTO

Phillip aged eight in a kilt, a Scottish Italian

Francesca, I have to say, you make lovely risotto. It's moist and creamy with just enough bite left in the rice to make the whole dish perfect.

I only like to make risotto with home-made stock, usually chicken. The stock gives a good flavour but, more importantly, combines with the starches of the rice to create that perfect, creamy consistency that is a classic risotto. I know you use a chicken stock cube very successfully, and Marigold vegetable bouillon is very good as well. If you use a stock cube, add a splash or two of cream at the end just to give the risotto a little extra creaminess.

As with all things, the better the ingredients the better the result. Look for the best-quality Italian risotto rice: vialone nano, carnaroli or arborio. All are readily available. I prefer the vialone nano, beloved of the Venetians. It has a small stubby grain and white centre which slowly absorbs the stock, keeps its shape and manages to produce an oozy, creamy sauce around the grain at the same time. Carnaroli and arborio have fatter grains.

Rice produced from small specialist farms is often better than mass-produced brands. I don't like to be precious about food, but the right ingredients actually make the job easier and the end result is so satisfyingly good that all of a sudden you're a confident cook!

A word of warning, that's what I'm here for: if you buy untreated or organic rice or grains, bear in mind that they may be contaminated with the odd moth or mite. Just be cautious. Keep each product in a sealed jar in a cool dark cupboard. Keep a note of the sell-by date. If the product has not been fumigated and laced with preservatives, naturally it won't last as long.

Basic Brilliant Risotto

Cook this risotto once or twice, learn how the principles work and then I hope you'll enjoy cooking risotto any time by instinct, without bothering about recipes and quantities. I usually judge a cup of rice, 150 g, for two people with about 500–600 ml of stock. Remember, the rice will absorb the amount of liquid it wants – not the amount you tell it to! If possible, use a wide, shallow saucepan so that the rice has plenty of room to move around in.

Once you start cooking risotto you'll quickly judge the stock you have, adding water at the end if you need more liquid. I always find we manage to eat whatever quantity I make, there are never any LOs (left-overs)! This recipe serves four.

2 shallots or 1 small onion, peeled and very finely chopped (about 2 tablespoons)
1 stick celery, peeled and very finely chopped
40 g unsalted butter, plus a nice extra blob to finish
about 1–1.25 litres home-made hot chicken broth (see page 90)
300 g vialone nano or carnaroli risotto rice
Maldon sea salt
2–3 tablespoons freshly grated Parmigiano Reggiano

Make sure the shallot and celery are very finely and evenly chopped. You could almost grate them on the course side of a conical grater. I cook the shallot and celery with the butter very slowly in a small butter-melting pot or a small saucepan. This way they are completely immersed in the butter and will not brown or burn and get the chance to soften and become translucent. This will make the soffritto, the base of the risotto. Don't add salt to the shallot. It will help it cook quicker but it also acts to flavour it and make it release water. The shallot will stew instead of sauté. The result is an onion taste in the finished risotto, not appealing.

Heat the stock in a separate pot; let it simmer slowly. It should be fairly concentrated. Transfer the softened shallot, celery and butter, the soffritto, into a warmed, wide cast-iron saucepan. Let it heat through and as it starts to sizzle, add the rice. Don't wash the rice. It is the starch on the outside that produces the creaminess of a good risotto. Turn the rice around in the soffritto for a few minutes until it is almost jumping in the heat.

Add a ladleful of the hot stock and stir it in with a wooden spoon. (If you are adding wine at this stage, add it before the stock and let it bubble to get rid of any alcohol. Don't add any stock until the wine has been absorbed.) Lower the heat to medium and continue to add the stock, a ladleful at a time, stirring as you go. This breaks down the starchy outer layer of the grain. Let all the liquid be absorbed before you add the next spoonful.

You don't need to stir every second, but it is a wonderful luxury to turn the rice in the stock, to watch it change texture and to observe how it cooks. I find risotto-making a comfort. If the stock starts to run out add some hot water and some parsley stalks, season it with a little Maldon salt and continue adding that.

The risotto takes about 20–25 minutes to cook, depending on the type of rice. After about 20 minutes start to taste it. Season it if necessary but remember that the Parmigiano and butter added at the end will give flavour.

The rice is cooked when the middle is no longer chalky but the grain still has a bite. Remember the rice still cooks and absorbs liquid as it goes to the table. Take the pot off the heat and beat in the grated Parmigiano. The cheese melts and coats the rice. Finally stir in the butter with the wooden spoon. This is called 'manticato', and is the process that adds the final creaminess to the rice.

Put the lid on and leave the rice to settle for a few minutes. When you remove the lid the rice will have settled into a creamy, soupy, perfect consistency.

This risotto is very gently flavoured. Use the technique to build in any flavours you like. I prefer to keep it simple, adding one or two extra ingredients only. The only thing to remember is to prepare anything you are adding all the same size so that it cooks evenly. Ingredients that take more than 20 minutes or so to cook need to be cooked separately, beforehand. Ingredients that cook within 20 minutes can usually be added while the rice is cooking.

Saffron risotto. Add a good pinch of saffron strands to a cup of warm water and infuse them while you cook the risotto. Strain the flavoured liquid into the risotto at the end. Alternatively, add a powdered sachet of instant saffron powder at the end. A classic Milanese risotto has beef marrow added to the soffritto, not something I use. You could make the risotto with the beef broth on page 88.

Spinach risotto, probably my favourite. Gradually stir in 200 g or so rinsed, chopped baby spinach halfway through the cooking of the risotto. The spinach takes a few minutes to melt down into the rice and its juices help to add flavour. Add a grating of nutmeg at the end and a squeeze of lemon juice as well as the butter and grated Parmigiano.

Asparagus risotto. In May we get wonderful Scottish or English asparagus. Use about 400 g to make a fabulous risotto. Break off the bottom of the stalks where they snap naturally. Trim off the top of the spears. They take less time to cook and should be added during the last 5 minutes. Rinse the asparagus, especially the heads. They can be a bit gritty if they were picked just after it has rained. Cook the stalks and the stubs in a little boiling lightly salted water until just tender. Use some of this water as well as some chicken or vegetable stock to make the risotto. Cut the stalks into bite-sized pieces and add them to the risotto halfway through cooking. Discard the stubs, these are stringy and don't eat well. Add the tips for the last 5 minutes of cooking. Lift the flavour with plenty of grated Parmigiano and a good blob of butter. The asparagus's sweetness, the salty cheese and the unctuous butter make a really beautiful risotto.

Alternatively, roast the tender asparagus heads separately with a little Maldon salt and extra virgin olive oil in a medium oven (180°C/350°F/Gas 4).

Courgette risotto. *Sauté 3–4 grated courgettes in a frying pan with a little olive oil and a few slivers of garlic. Cook them until they are just brown on the edges. Season with salt and add them to the onion soffritto at the beginning of cooking. Add a good tablespoon of finely chopped flat-leaf parsley at the end or, alternatively, a good handful of torn fresh basil leaves.*

Tomato Risotto
RISOTTO AL POMODORO

This is the only risotto my Nonna Marietta ever made for me. We were in her house in Picinisco in the dining room rather than at the kitchen table, so she must have regarded this as a special treat. She was celebrating something because after the meal she even let us have a Blue Riband biscuit. She brought these with PG Tips tea-bags by the box load from Scotland. They were so precious to her she kept them locked in her food cupboard, the key always dangling at her waist!

2 tablespoons extra virgin olive oil
75 g butter
1 shallot, peeled and very finely chopped (2 tablespoons)
200 g smoked pancetta, cut into cubes
300 g arborio risotto rice
½ x 400 g tin Italian plum tomatoes, sieved
about 1–1.25 litres hot chicken broth (see page 90) or vegetable stock
2 tablespoons freshly grated Parmigiano Reggiano
fresh basil

Warm the oil with 50 g of the butter in a saucepan. Add the shallot and sauté until it is softened and transparent. Sauté the pancetta a little, then add the rice, letting it toast a little in the soffritto. Add the sieved tomatoes and cook the mixture for a few minutes.

Now, slowly stir in the hot stock, adding it a little at a time. Stir everything and cook for about 20 minutes. When it is cooked, add the freshly grated Parmigiano, and stir it in well until it melts. Finally stir in the remaining butter and a few fresh basil leaves.

For added comfort stir in some fontina cheese and let it melt and become indulgently stringy before serving.

LIVE A LONG LIFE, EAT YOUR GREENS

'Mangia verdura ogni giorno per ottant'anni e vivrai
una lunga vita!'
'Eat green vegetables every day for eighty years and you'll live
a long life!'

Olivia, Gloria and Filomena Crolla, c.1916

Vegetables are not a punishment exercise! Vegetables have a bad
reputation in Great Britain. There's always been a limited choice
and for no apparent reason, they've often been overcooked. If
they don't taste good why should you eat them?

Please believe me, well-prepared vegetables are the most delicious part of any meal. And, no, I'm not a vegetarian, but I do eat a lot of wonderful vegetables every day. Whatever we're eating there will always be salad and vegetables in the centre of the table. The vegetables and greens are eaten warm. They are more often than not flavoured with a simple dressing of extra virgin olive oil, lemon juice or vinegar. Garlic or fresh herbs are sometimes added.

Buy salads and vegetables in season and locally where possible. Well-produced organic vegetables that are fresh will usually taste better. One thing organic production guarantees is that there is no residue of pesticides and fertilisers on the produce. But no matter whether it is organic or not, always wash and peel fruit and vegetables as a matter of course.

The rule in our house is that kids have to taste. If they don't like something they don't have to eat it, but next time, they are more likely to try it again and, before you know it, they're eating it with pleasure. There's nothing easy about feeding youngsters these days. If you make too much fuss (like me) they know they've found your weak spot, and cunningly use all the power that gives them.

If you leave the decisions completely to them, they're bombarded with so much peer group pressure they're persuaded into unhealthy habits. Don't underestimate the subtle influence of food advertising on our children. If only we had good healthy foods advertised as well as the junk food that's pushed at them now, we could turn attitudes round in a generation.

If you despair and think that it's a losing battle, look at any kids that visit a Chinese restaurant. All sorts of weird and wonderful vegetables, noodles and rice are eaten with gusto, and there are no objections to beans, greens, mushrooms or peppers. Why? Because they taste good, they're eaten at the table with adults enjoying the same food, and they can eat with chopsticks and funny plates. Simply because it's fun!

To keep them fresh, I always add green vegetables to boiling salted water. Undercooking rather than overcooking them keeps them crisp and bright. Drain them and then return them to the pot, filling it with ice-cold water. This brings their temperature down, stopping any further cooking and crisps them up. Drain them again and dress them as required. This is called 'refreshing'.

Asparagus
ASPARAGI

Of all vegetables, asparagus is the one you really should only eat in season and as fresh as possible. I have tasted asparagus that has just been cut and it is the most delicious sweet taste imaginable. The asparagus spear grows at an amazing rate, as much as 20–25 cm a day when conditions are right. The stem, when picked, is packed with the intense sweet sugars that provide the energy for this growth.

As soon as the spear is picked it stops growing and these sugars start to change to carbohydrates. The soft, sweet stems gradually become tough and stringy. This is why the best and by far the cheapest way to buy asparagus is locally or from a farm or farmers' market. Small plastic trays of asparagus from halfway round the world pale in comparison, and tinned asparagus should be banned!

Treat asparagus simply.

Snap off the base of the stem where it breaks naturally.

Wash the stems and, if it has been raining a lot, rinse the delicate fronds at the tip, which can trap grit or insects.

Steam the stems in boiling salted water for 6–8 minutes until tender. You can prop the fronds out of the water using foil if the stems are very thick so that the tips don't overcook. I usually just cut them in half, adding the thinner, top part halfway through cooking.

The nicest, easiest way is to serve with plenty of melted butter

I also like to roast asparagus in a hot oven drizzled with extra virgin olive oil and seasoned with a sprinkling of Maldon sea salt. It takes on a crispy, juicy flavour that's a little toasted around the edges. Serve this as a starter, with shavings of Parmigiano Reggiano.

Try making asparagus risotto (see page 180), one of my favourites.

Very fine young asparagus spears can be added to a mixed salad and eaten raw.

Aubergine
MELANZANE

Aubergines come in all shapes and sizes. Look out for those grown in the southern Mediterranean. Small Moroccan ones are especially tasty, as are the beautiful bulbous violet ones that come into the Italian markets and some specialist shops in the spring and summer. These are tastiest simply grilled. Slice them into rounds about 1 cm thick. Brush them on both sides with a smear of extra virgin olive oil and cook them on a preheated griddle for about 4 minutes or so on each side. Unless they're old, you shouldn't need to soak them in salt beforehand. I never do. Add salt to them after they are griddled. Dress them with a few slivers of garlic, some extra virgin olive oil, a splash of red wine vinegar and some roughly chopped flat-leaf parsley. These taste better after they have marinated in the dressing for an hour or so.

Sweet and Sour Aubergine
CAPONATA

This Sicilian way of preparing aubergines is lovely to serve with
pasta, grilled meat and especially grilled fish. The tart bite of the
aubergines and capers cuts any oiliness of the fish perfectly.

1 large violet aubergine
2 courgettes
extra virgin olive oil
10–15 sweet cherry tomatoes
1 tablespoon salted capers, soaked in a large bowl of cold water for
30 minutes, drained
fresh basil leaves

Preheat the oven to very hot (230°C/450°F/Gas 8).

Wash the vegetables thoroughly in cold water, and dry.
Chop the aubergine and courgettes into 2–3 cm chunks.
Scatter them on to a large baking tray and drizzle them with
a little extra virgin olive oil and Maldon salt. Roast them in
the preheated oven until they are cooked and the flesh is
translucent, about 10–15 minutes.

In a large frying pan, heat 2 tablespoons of the olive oil,
add the tomatoes and cook them on a brisk heat until the
skins start to soften. Add the roasted vegetables and capers.
Warm everything through and tear in a generous handful of
fresh basil leaves. Turn the leaves just to warm them through
and flavour the caponata. Adjust the seasoning. Serve this hot
or cold.

Beans, Broad
FAVE

'Fave' or broad beans are at their best when really young. They have an oddly satisfying taste, probably because they are packed with vitamins.

On holiday in Puglia, I saw a case of them being delivered at the back door of a 'trattoria'. The back door was the same as the entrance to the toilets. You had to go through the kitchen, out the back and into the owner's house next door! His four-year-old daughter showed me the way. As usual with these wonderful eating-places, there was no menu. We were simply asked by the wife, 'Che cosa vuoi mangiare?' 'What would you like to eat?'

I had seen the pile of gloriously green beans in their fleshy, woolly pods at the kitchen table. I asked for them, expecting them to be lightly boiled and drizzled with olive oil. The wife brought me a huge pile of the beans on a plate and a whole fresh pecorino cheese, a quarter invitingly cut away. A sharp knife, a side plate and a spare plate for the pods were arranged beside me and I was left to get on with it. The beans inside the pods were young and fresh. Eaten with slices of the sweet pecorino they were perfect. Try it.

To cook them, pod out the beans, and cook them in boiling salted water for 5 minutes or so until they're tender, depending on their size. Don't overcook them or they become mushy. Older beans have a very annoying outer skin on them. When cooked this becomes grey and slightly tough. You can eat it, but peel it open and two bright green tender baby beans lie inside. These are a treasure to add to light pasta dishes or soups. A few can add a subtle difference to a dish, and are well worth the bother.

Add them to a frittata with chopped chives and a little pancetta, or try the 'ruote alla nonna' recipe on page 153 with some cooked broad beans added at the end instead of peas.

Make a creamy Parmigiano risotto and add the cooked and podded beans at the end with a big blob of butter and shavings of fresh pecorino. Sublime.

Beans, Dried Cannellini
CANNELLINI SECCHI

Annunziata lived until she was over eighty-six, and never visited a dentist. When I met her, she had only four or five teeth left,

scattered randomly around her gums. She was tiny by now, shrivelled and thin with waves of wrinkles on her face. She still had an elegant straight posture, a lovely smile and a twinkle in her eye. I think she was at her most beautiful.

The side molar was giving her pain. When she chewed on a dry piece of bread she would wince. 'Oi, i mama!' She was proud of her teeth. She refused to visit a dentist though most of her contemporaries had long since given in to ill-fitting dentures. Not so Annunziata.

Annunziata asleep, aged eighty

One day, she could stand the discomfort no longer. She went out on the balcony to her rocking chair with a couple of cloves in her pocket. She chewed on the cloves, caught the sore tooth with her wrinkled, gnarled hand and, with a triumphant act of mind-over-matter, yanked the tooth out. She cleaned the tooth on her apron, popped it into her pocket and with a quiet smile settled down in the sun and rocked herself to sleep. The last time I saw her she had one proud tooth left, jutting incongruously from her lower jaw.

Dried white cannellini beans are sometimes called 'denti delle vecchie', 'old women's teeth'.

I used to hate cooking dried beans. No matter how careful I was, I always let them boil dry and have ruined many a pot. Annunziata taught me how to cook them simply in an ovenproof dish in the oven. Make sure the beans you buy are not too old. Check the sell-by date.

Cover a mug of rinsed dry cannellini beans with four mugs of cold water. Soak them overnight.

In the morning rinse them, cover them with water and bring the water to the boil. Boil fiercely for about 10 minutes. Discard the water and rinse the beans.

Cover the beans with more cold water, about 5 cm above their level in the ovenproof dish. Bring them to the boil and then simply cook them in a medium oven for anything from 30 minutes or so to a couple of hours, depending on how dry they were. You can add flavourings of extra virgin olive oil, rosemary and a clove of garlic if you like. Don't add any salt until the last 10 minutes of cooking.

These beans are delicious warm as a salad dish simply dressed with extra virgin olive oil, a little chopped chive or spring onion and some finely chopped parsley. I love them flavoured with extra virgin olive oil, which has been warmed with some garlic and peperoncino, and eaten warm with grilled meats or chicken.

If you want to use beans in soups, cook them to this stage first then add them to the cooked soup. And, if you can't be bothered cooking them, open a tin, rinse the beans in cold water and they're almost as good.

Beans, Fresh Cannellini and Borlotti
FAGIOLI FRESCHI

The most delicious beans are fresh cannellini or borlotti, which can be seen piled high in market stalls in any town or village in Italy from late spring onwards. They are sometimes found in shops or farmers' markets here. These simply need to be podded, a therapeutic job, and cooked in enough water to cover them for 15–20 minutes. They soften to a delicious creaminess and all you need to do is dress them with Maldon salt, extra virgin olive oil, freshly grated black pepper and a little chopped spring onion.

Braised Fresh Cannellini Beans
CANNELLINI AL TEGAME

500 g fresh cannellini beans, podded weight
4 tablespoons extra virgin olive oil
about 1 teaspoon Maldon sea salt
2 cloves garlic, peeled
a sprig of rosemary and a couple of fresh sage leaves
chopped flat-leaf parsley to serve

Put the cannellini into a saucepan with just enough cold water to cover them. Bring to the boil, then add the other ingredients apart from the parsley, and cook them with the lid off until they have softened and have absorbed most of the water, anything from 15–25 minutes, depending on the beans.

Take half the beans and purée them to a soft paste. Return them to the saucepan and mix the whole and puréed beans together. Take out the garlic and the herbs, check the seasoning, and sprinkle on some freshly chopped parsley.

Beans, Green
FAGIOLINI

French, runner and bobby beans are very easy to find and are simply prepared.

300 g French beans
3 tablespoons extra virgin olive oil
2 cloves garlic, peeled and halved
1 tablespoon red wine vinegar
some finely chopped flat-leaf parsley

Top and tail the beans and cook them in boiling salted water until tender, 10 minutes or so. Drain them and put them immediately into a bowl of ice-cold water. This refreshes them and keeps their colour beautiful and bright. Drain them after a few minutes.

Warm the extra virgin olive oil in the saucepan. Add the garlic and as soon as it starts to infuse the oil add the cold beans. Turn them in the oil for a minute or two just to warm them and flavour them. Add the vinegar, let it warm through then take the beans off the heat. Sprinkle with chopped flat-leaf parsley and serve warm.

French beans are very nice served as an antipasto. Simply boil them as above and drizzle them with a little extra virgin olive oil and a squeeze of lemon juice. Serve them with a bowl of home-made mayonnaise (see page 224).

Bok Choy or Pak Choi

The style, techniques and flavours of Chinese food are not dissimilar to Italian cooking: steaming, fast cooking, plenty of vegetables and simple flavours.

The best place to buy bok choy is at a Chinese supermarket. It is similar to spinach but with a sweeter flavour and bulkier, crisper stems. It is often sold as Chinese greens in a Chinese restaurant. It's very easy to prepare at home.

Prepare by breaking off the stems from the leaves, trimming them and washing them in plenty of cold water. They are usually very clean. Then, all I do is warm a tablespoon or so of sunflower oil in a large frying pan. Add a couple of cloves of peeled sliced garlic and a knob of fresh root ginger, peeled and cut into match-sticks. Add the bok choy and a good splash of oyster sauce, maybe 2 tablespoons, put a lid on and steam. The bok choy collapses in about 10 minutes. This is very nice with fish steamed with garlic and ginger, Chinese style.

Broccoli and Friends

Maybe it's because it looks like little flowers, but children are not afraid of broccoli. In fact, I've seen some actually ask to eat it!

Apart from the ubiquitous green broccoli that is available all year round, look out for purple sprouting broccoli in the spring. It is very tender and sweet and cooks very easily. You can find 'tender stem broccoli' in some supermarkets. It can be used instead of broccoli and is especially good in green vegetable soups or tossed in garlic and olive oil and used as a dressing for pasta.

Friarille is a green vegetable grown particularly in Naples. It is not dissimilar to young broccoli, with a narrow sweet stem and dark green flower head. It is distinctively bitter, but adored

by the locals. It is prepared simply, blanched in boiling water and then sautéed in olive oil pepped up with plenty of peperon- cino and garlic. They serve it as a vegetable, use it in polenta or, best of all, as a topping for

Mary and brother Cesidio on the bonnet of the car in front of the shop in Cockenzie

pizza with very hot spicy pork sausage. Fabulous greens.

Cime di rapa is an extremely tender, sweet vegetable, part of the brassica family, and is grown widely in Italy. It translates as 'turnip tops', but looks and cooks very like tender broccoli. It is a firm favourite in the south of Italy and is used in pasta and as a vegetable. It has long stalks on celery-like stems and a ragged leaf. Its flower head looks very similar to young broccoli.

Trim away any course leaves and the base of the stem. Wash it well. It cooks very easily: either lightly boiled or, if it is very young, simply sautéed and dressed lightly with extra virgin olive and lemon juice. The stems are particularly sweet.

Try it with orecchiette pasta (see page 142). Substitute tender stem broccoli, which I suspect is part of the same family.

250 g broccoli, cime di rapa or greens
Maldon sea salt and black pepper
3–4 tablespoons extra virgin olive oil
1 clove garlic, peeled and chopped

1 piece peperoncino (dried chilli)
1 anchovy preserved in oil (optional)
lemon juice

Wash the greens and trim away any yellow leaves or coarse stems. If the stems are thick, slit them into even-sized pieces, otherwise simply separate the florets or leaves. Add the stems to boiling salted water and cook until tender, 10 minutes or so. Add the florets or leaves halfway through. Drain into a colander.

In the same saucepan, warm the extra virgin olive oil. Flavour it with the garlic and dried chilli. Press the anchovy into the olive oil if you want a more intense flavour. Toss the drained greens in the oil and garlic for a few minutes, then add a squeeze of lemon juice and plenty of pepper. Serve warm.

For an interesting variation, you can change the treatment slightly by dressing the cooked broccoli Chinese style. Add a tablespoon of sunflower oil that has been flavoured with a clove of garlic cut into slivers, a 3–4 cm piece of fresh root ginger, cut into matchsticks, and a splash of light or dark soy sauce.

Alternatively, stir-fry the broccoli in the same mixture of seasoned oil. Cut the broccoli into 3–4 cm pieces and stir-fry it over a high heat.

Brussels Sprouts
CAVOLINI DI BRUXELLES

Why do Brussels sprouts get such a bad name? When they are cooked with chestnuts, olive oil, garlic and chilli they are better than chocolate.

In the autumn you can buy ready-prepared vacuum-packed

chestnuts from France. They save a lot of work and are just as good as if you have prepared them yourself. Just rinse them with a little cold water to loosen them.

500 g Brussels sprouts
Maldon sea salt
3–4 tablespoons extra virgin olive oil
2 cloves garlic, peeled
a piece of peperoncino (dried chilli)
250 g vacuum-packed chestnuts

Prepare the Brussels sprouts, peeling away any discoloured outer leaves and trimming the base. Boil them in salted water for 5 minutes until they just start to be tender. Don't over-cook them. Drain them and refresh them by pouring cold water over them to keep their colour nice and bright. Drain them again. (If you're preparing these for Christmas lunch, prepare them the day before and refrigerate them.)

When you're ready, warm the olive oil in a large wide frying pan. Add the garlic and peperoncino and gently fry them, just to start flavouring the oil. Add the sprouts and warm them through, cooking them in the oil. Add the chest-nuts and a splash of water. Put a lid on the frying pan. I like to cook these until the sprouts are a bit browned around the edges. The juices all mix together to give a lovely bitter-sweet, tart flavour.

Cabbage
CAVOLO

Oh, no! Do we have to eat cabbage?

Cabbage is good for soups but tastes at its best raw, especially when made into a crunchy mixed coleslaw.

Shred and chop the ingredients by hand, with a very sharp knife. Apart from being very therapeutic, the textures and slightly irregular shapes are more interesting than machine-shredded vegetables.

the heart of a Savoy cabbage in the winter or white heart cabbage
in the spring
2–3 carrots, peeled and sliced lengthways as thin as possible
3–4 sticks celery, peeled and sliced lengthways
1 crisp apple, cored and sliced thinly into strips
a handful each of pine nuts and juicy raisins
a large bunch of fresh coriander, roughly chopped
mayonnaise flavoured with lemon juice (see page 224)

Cut the cabbage and pull away any damaged leaves. Rinse the centre and shred it or chop it into small shreds. Mix all the fresh ingredients together, chopping and changing as you fancy. Stir in enough mayonnaise to coat the coleslaw without making it too sloppy. Serve chilled.

Remember that pine nuts – and other nuts – very easily go rancid. Buy small amounts at a time and always check the date code. I usually store them in the fridge. You can toast them in a medium oven for 5 minutes or so just to freshen up their flavour.

Use cabbage shredded in soups. Don't boil it to death. Add it towards the last 20 minutes or so. Use green cabbage, Tuscan cavolo nero or cime di rapa.

Spring cabbage and Savoy cabbage are good boiled and then dressed either with extra virgin olive oil and lemon juice or simply with lots of butter. I love to mash it very smoothly with loads and loads of butter and grated white pepper. This is especially good with steak and kidney pie (see page 259).

Cabbage also marries well with smoked bacon or smoked pancetta. Try softening some chopped smoked bacon in butter, adding some very finely shredded cabbage, a splash of water and steaming it with a lid on. Season and serve with roast meats.

Carrots
CAROTE

Francesca, you used to love raw carrots. Cut into batons and popped into your lunch box, you thought you were having a treat. I always buy organic carrots.

Annunziata's Carrots with Oregano and Vinegar

5–6 organic carrots, peeled and cut into batons
Maldon sea salt
4–5 tablespoons extra virgin olive oil
1 clove garlic, peeled
a small piece of peperoncino (dried chilli)
1 tablespoon red wine vinegar or balsamic vinegar
1 teaspoon freshly dried oregano

Cook the carrots in boiling salted water until they are just tender. Drain and refresh them in cold water to stop the cooking and keep them bright.

In a large frying pan warm the oil and flavour it with the garlic and the peperoncino. Add the cooked carrots and turn them in the oil. Warm them through for 5 minutes or so, just letting them sizzle in the heat. Add the vinegar and cook them a little longer to mellow the acidity of the vinegar. Add the oregano. Serve warm or lightly chilled.

Puréed Carrots

Dull, uninspiring boiled carrots are a no-no. However, try boiling them then puréeing them in a blender, baby-food style. Heat them through with plenty of butter and add a generous slurp of double cream. Season well with sea salt, freshly ground black pepper and a good grating of nutmeg. Cooked like this they're creamy and moist, especially good with roast turkey or chicken at Christmas.

Cauliflower
CAVOLFIORE

Francesca, I know a certain person close to us who will not eat cauliflower. He does love these cauliflower fritters, though . . .

> *1 cauliflower, washed and separated into florets*
> *Maldon sea salt and black pepper*
> *2 eggs, beaten*
> *2–3 tablespoons plain flour*
> *1 tablespoon milk*
> *1 litre sunflower or other neutral-flavoured oil for frying*

Cook the cauliflower in boiling salted water until it is just tender. Don't let it overcook, it needs to be really crisp and firm as it's going to be cooked more. Drain it and refresh it in cold water.

Mix the beaten egg and flour to make up the batter, thinning it with a little milk as necessary. It should be like thick custard. Season it well.

Warm the oil in a large frying pan. It should be at least 3–4 cm deep. Test that the oil is hot enough by dropping a teaspoon of the batter into it. When the batter starts to sizzle and move around in the oil, you can start to fry the cauliflower.

Dip each piece of cauliflower in the batter, coating it well. Use a spoon and fork to gently lower it into the hot oil. Be careful. The oil can splatter. Don't over-crowd the frying pan. It's best to cook four or five fritters at a time. As they start to brown, turn them over so that they become golden and crisp on each side. Keep the heat fairly high but don't let the oil burn. Drain the fritters on kitchen paper and keep them warm while you finish all the cauliflower.

Sprinkle with Maldon salt before serving. These are lovely all the time, hot or cold.

Cauliflower with White Sauce
CAVOLFIORE CON SALSA DI BESCIAMELLA

We often had this as kids, usually with some boiled chicken from the broth.

Break a medium-sized cauliflower into florets, discarding the centre white core. Cook them in boiling salted water until just tender. Don't let them overcook. Drain them. Run cold water over them to cool them down and stop them cooking. Put into a shallow ovenproof dish.

Make a béchamel sauce (see page 223) and pour it over the cauliflower florets. Cover the sauce with at least 5 tablespoons of grated Cheddar cheese, something good and full-flavoured like Montgomery's or Mull Cheddar. These are both white Cheddars, but use mature red Cheddar if you prefer.

Bake in a medium oven (180°C/350°F/Gas 4) for 20 minutes until the cheese is golden and melted and crispy round the edges.

Courgettes
ZUCCHINI

Francesca, it's a real pain, but zucchini are allergic to your dad and your dad is allergic to courgettes.

I absolutely adore them. I love their versatility and the way their flavour changes depending on how you cook them. Rather than use them all year round, I prefer to buy them in the spring and summer, when they are young and tender, with the flower attached if possible. Their skin can be muddy so give them a good clean in cold running water.

I never boil courgettes. They have a high water content and more water just dilutes any flavour they contain. They respond best to dry heat: grilling, griddling or roasting. Their juices become concentrated, they absorb the flavourings you add to them, and they singe well at the edges taking on a caramelised flavour that is extremely appetising. They also have an affinity to cream (see page 152) and are probably at their best deep-fried (see page 250). I particularly like to prepare them very simply.

a good blob of butter
4–5 courgettes, washed, blotted dry and sliced into discs,
cut on a slant if you like, about 1 cm thick
Maldon sea salt
lemon juice

Put the butter into a large non-stick frying pan. Add enough courgettes to form one layer. Sprinkle with salt and put the heat up to medium high. Let the courgettes cook slowly. Turn them as they brown. Nibble as you go (not fattening) and watch how the flavour changes, sweetens and browns. When they are the way you like them, remove them to a warmed dish and cook the rest the same way.

Serve them warm sprinkled with lemon juice. You could also add a splash of extra virgin olive oil and some torn basil or mint leaves as well.

If you are adding courgettes to a frittata or pizza, it's worth toasting them like this a little first. It improves the flavour no end.

Pickled Courgettes
ZUCCHINI SOTT'OLIO

The families high in the mountains had no refrigeration, local shops or delivery vans. The women inherited great preserving skills to keep the glut of produce ready for the winter. Tomatoes, vegetables and fruits were all pickled and bottled. In the late summer and early autumn fresh produce was so abundant and cheap that, unless it was preserved, it would go to waste. Take a summer stroll in the outskirts of any village or town today in the south of Italy and you will see trees and plants groaning with fruit and vegetables. Apricots, figs, peaches and nectarines will be scattered on the ground, too many to harvest. Lemons hang like giant earrings on the laden branches, low enough to stretch out and pluck.

In their remote villages, the women couldn't get their produce down the mountain in good enough condition to sell. A two-day journey on foot or with a donkey and cart in sweltering summer heat meant that their produce would start to deteriorate. Once they arrived in the Atina market they would find huge quantities of fresh produce, probably in better condition and selling for only a few lire. Their only solution was to preserve enough produce as possible, at least so that they could survive the winter. Any possible container was collected to store the preserves in, empty beer and wine bottles or any odd jars.

This is Annunziata's recipe.

5–6 large courgettes
250 ml white wine vinegar
500 ml water
Maldon sea salt
2 cloves garlic, peeled and sliced
2–3 small pieces peperoncino (dried chilli), or more if you like
these hotter
extra virgin olive oil

Wash the courgettes. Slice them lengthways, and cut them into matchstick strips, and place in a dish.

Put the white wine vinegar and the water into a saucepan. Boil rapidly to reduce it by half. Pour this over the courgettes then pack them into a sterilised jar. Add a little salt, the garlic and the chilli interspersed between the courgettes. Fill the jar with enough extra virgin olive oil to cover them.

The courgettes will absorb some of the liquid in the jar, so every few days top up the jar with more oil. The oil covering the courgettes acts to preserve them. After a couple of times the oil level will stop falling. Seal the jar with greaseproof paper and foil and leave in a cool place for three to four weeks before using them.

Apply the same method to preserve aubergines.

I must tell you that these are especially good at the beginning of a meal, just a tablespoon or so served with antipasto of cured meats are heavenly. No hardship at all.

Marietta's sisters in I Ciacca; they never left the village

Courgette Flowers
FIORI DI ZUCCHINE

The courgette plant produces two flowers. The flamboyant, large male flower produces no fruit. The discreet, smaller female flower is attached to its offspring, the courgette.

All over the Mediterranean, courgettes are sold with the female flowers attached. These are chopped and used in dishes – stirred into risotto, added to pasta or used in frittata. They add a slight sweetness as well as a beautiful bright yellow colour.

The large male flowers are prized for stuffing and deep-frying in fritters or used in soups or pizzas. They are stunning. I don't know why we never see them in shops here. You are most likely to find them at your nearest allotment (speak nicely to the gardeners) or at a farmers' market. If you do get hold of them, they are most delicious stuffed with a little anchovy and some soft, fresh mozzarella, then dipped in batter and deep-fried in light olive oil (use the batter on page 246). More simply, beautifully draped over a thin, crisp, courgette flower pizza, they become exotic.

Escarole or Bitter Curly Endive
SCAROLA

In the winter, we love to eat 'scarola'. It is a bitter curly endive, a coarser version of the summer frisée. It has fine pale yellow leaves in the middle with course curly, darker green leaves on the outside. The pale leaves are perfect for winter salad, slightly bitter and crunchy. Use them alone or mixed with other salad leaves. The coarse outer leaves can be used in broth, often added to clear chicken broth.

Marietta and Maria made a delicious dish from these coarse leaves. This shows how the most frugal ingredients can make the best food.

outer green leaves from escarole or endive, about 300 g
Maldon sea salt
3–4 tablespoons extra virgin olive oil
1 garlic clove, peeled and sliced
2–3 pieces peperoncino (dried chilli) , to taste
5–6 pieces old, crusty bread

Wash the leaves in two or three changes of water. Discard any damaged ones and trim off the coarse bases. Reserve any pale yellow leaves for salad. Blanch the green leaves in boiling salted water for 10 minutes or so. Drain well.

In a large deep frying pan warm the olive oil. Flavour it with the sliced garlic and pieces of peperoncino. Now add the drained greens and use a fork to separate them and coat them well with the oil.

Add the torn pieces of dry bread, with a good splash of water, and put a lid onto the frying pan. Steam the escarole for about 10–15 minutes. The bread soaks up all the juices from the greens, giving it a distinctive bitter-sweet flavour. The peperoncino gives a good kick of heat.

I sometimes melt a couple of oiled anchovy fillets into the extra virgin olive oil at the beginning. This adds sweetness to the dish and balances the bitterness of the greens.

The outer leaves are also boiled then added to chicken broth with pastina (see page 92) to give an extra flavour. Try it, it's delicious.

Fennel
FINOCCHIO

I love to eat fennel raw. Its crispy texture and aniseed flavour are addictive. Trim the base and pull off each of the layers. Cut away the coarse stalk; keep any feathery leaves and use as a herb for baked fish. Wash the fennel, cut it into thin slices, and simply dress it with a tasty extra virgin olive oil, a good sprinkling of sea salt and plenty of freshly ground black pepper.

If you are roasting vegetables (see page 292), fennel is worth adding to the roasting dish. Its texture becomes soft and the flavours intensify into a voluptuous sweetness. I also add it to potatoes when I roast them.

Another nice way to prepare fennel is to cook it slowly in a shallow pan just covered with water, chicken or vegetable stock and a blob of butter. The fennel slowly cooks and absorbs the flavour of the stock. Once it is tender, drain it, and season with freshly grated black pepper and a blob of butter. Sprinkle it with grated Parmigiano Reggiano or pecorino and give it a quick blast under the grill. It tastes really good, a tender, juicy vegetable with a crisp, slightly toasted topping.

Mushrooms
FUNGHI

There is such a wide choice of cultivated, wild or dried mushrooms, all with their particular distinctive flavour and texture to choose from. Buy mushrooms fresh and use them within a day or too. Fungi can harbour bacteria, and old, bruised mushrooms can be an unlikely source of an upset stomach. If you are tempted to pick wild mushrooms, then make sure you have an expert to identify them. In Italy it is law that every town has a trained mycologist, usually based in the local pharmacy, to identify wild fungi. Even still, every year there are tragic stories of deaths from poisoning, so don't take the risk.

There's no need to wash or peel mushrooms. Just give them a good wipe with a damp cloth and trim off the base. Throw out any that are contaminated or mouldy.

Never buy mushrooms in plastic or clingfilmed containers. This acts to create a warm microclimate which encourages bacteria to grow more profusely. Charming!

Sautéed Mushrooms
FUNGHI TRIFOLATI

The classic Italian way of preparing mushrooms is 'trifolati'. This means sautéing them gently in extra virgin olive oil, with garlic and flat-leaf parsley. (In Liguria the same technique is called 'al funghetto'.)

225 g chestnut or oyster mushrooms or Scottish chanterelles
2–3 tablespoons extra virgin olive oil
1 clove garlic, peeled and chopped
2 good tablespoons finely chopped flat-leaf parsley
black pepper
lemon juice (optional)

Clean the mushrooms carefully then slice them.

Simply warm the oil in a wide heavy-based saucepan, add the garlic and half the parsley and gently sauté. Add the sliced mushrooms and sauté for about 8–10 minutes. Cook them on a fairly brisk heat. If you let them stew in their juice they become rubbery. Season and dress with the rest of the chopped parsley. You can add a squeeze of lemon juice.

Serve with grilled steak or at room temperature as an antipasto.

Chanterelles with Potatoes
GALLETTI CON PATATE

I adore Scottish chanterelles. They are easy to identify with their distinctive apricot yellow colour and wavy, smooth cap with ridges underneath. Unless it has been raining heavily, they are usually dry and infestation free, easy to brush clean. They have an aromatic, delicate flavour that seduces. They grow prolifically in Scotland in late summer until the first frosts. You can buy them in good food shops, but make sure, as always, that they are identified properly. Cook them as above or with potatoes like this. I also love them in omelettes, with cream and pasta, and in risotto (see page 177).

Cook 4–5 waxy potatoes such as pink fir apple until they are just tender. Allow them to cool, and cut them into bite-sized cubes.

Prepare the mushrooms as above and when they appear to be at their wettest, remove them from the frying pan leaving their juices. Add the potato cubes and a good blob of butter, turning them in the juices of the mushrooms. Cook the potatoes on a high heat until dry, crispy and nicely browned at the edges.

Return the mushrooms and warm them through. Check the seasoning. Sprinkle with a few chopped chives or chopped flat-leaf parsley.

Mushrooms, Dried
FUNGHI SECCHI

Dried porcini (ceps) are perfect for providing an intense mushroom flavour to soup, risotto or stew. The best way to reconstitute them is to soak about 15 g in a cup of warm water for 20 minutes or so. Strain them, keeping the liquid, which has a good, intense flavour. I usually rinse the soaked mushrooms in a little cold water to get rid of any grit that may still be lurking. They can then be chopped and added to any mushroom-based recipe. They can magically enhance the flavour.

Because they grow so quickly, wild mushrooms absorb pollutants from the atmosphere. Wild fungi harvested from the edge of a road or motorway may have a dangerously high lead level. Be very careful where you buy dried mushrooms. If they are from a reputable supplier they will have had a detailed analysis.

Beware of buying dried fungi from market stalls on holiday. Fungi from certain parts of eastern Europe are contaminated with radioactivity and may have been discarded by registered dealers. These often turn up cheap at a market.

Peppers, Sweet
PEPERONI

Don't bother buying green peppers. They're most likely to give you indigestion. Choose red or yellow peppers, if possible those that have been grown south of Watford! Peppers grown in the sun are so much tastier.

In Edinburgh, Maria often prepared peperoni salad for Sunday lunch. Those that were not eaten were packed into panini for Monday morning's lunch box. Oozing with oil and steaming with garlic they were a delicious embarrassment at school for the Crolla children ('peperol' panini', see page 331)!

You need to burn off the skin of the pepper over a naked gas flame, cooking the flesh of the pepper at the same time. I remember Annunziata had a mesh heat-diffuser on which she balanced two peppers at a time. She washed them only, leaving the stalk intact. She used this to hold the peppers as she turned them to blacken every side.

Once they were furiously blackened, she lifted them up, piping hot though they were, and with a twist of the stalk, pulled out the seeds. The juices that oozed out from the peppers were collected on a serving plate as the black skin was deftly whisked away, her fingers moving at speed to avoid them burning.

She then laid them on the plate, cutting the soft flesh into strips and dressed them with some olive oil, slices of garlic and a sprinkling of chopped parsley. They were sometimes adorned with a few pitted black olives and a sprinkling of capers.

Somehow, peppers like these never induced indigestion, just a little antipathy from the garlic in the playground on a Monday morning!

I tend to roast the peppers intact, stalk and all, maybe just drizzled with some olive oil, in a hot oven (230°C/450°F/Gas 8). They'll take 25–30 minutes, and are ready when they are blackened and blistered. You can pop them into a plastic bag so that the skin will come off more easily in the steam, but I like the asbestos finger approach.

Sweet and Sour Peppers
PEPERONATA AGRODOLCE

4 red or yellow peppers (preferably Italian)
2 tablespoons extra virgin olive oil
1 clove garlic, peeled and sliced
1 dessertspoon caster sugar
1 tablespoon red wine vinegar
Maldon sea salt and black pepper
some freshly dried oregano
a handful of black olives, stoned

Wash the peppers, cut them into strips and de-seed them.
Trim off the stalk. Pat them dry. Heat the extra virgin olive
oil in a wide frying pan. Add the garlic and allow it to cook
a little to start to flavour the oil.

Add the peppers and let them cook over a medium heat.
They will take 20 minutes or so to start to soften. When they
are nearly cooked add the sugar, vinegar and some salt, pepper
and oregano.

Continue to cook them until they are soft. Keep the heat
quite gentle so that all the delicious juices don't evaporate. The
peppers should be bathed in their own sweet and sour juices.
Serve cool with a few black olives sprinkled over them.

Neapolitan Peperoni Sugo

Annunziata used to make this sugo for pasta when there was a
glut of peperoni in the summer. It's really fabulous and banishes
forever any misconception that 'vegetarian' or 'healthy' should
be dull, brown or tasteless! You need sweet ripe peppers.

3 red and 2 yellow peppers
2–3 tablespoons extra virgin olive oil
2 cloves garlic, peeled and thinly sliced
50 g unsalted butter (or less)
Maldon sea salt
a bunch of fresh basil leaves
freshly grated Parmigiano Reggiano

Roughly peel the outer skin from the peppers with a potato peeler, de-seed them and cut them into strips, about 3–4 cm thick. Rinse them in cold water.

Warm the oil in a large wide frying pan and add the garlic. Let it infuse and flavour the oil, taking care not to let it burn. Add the peppers, tossing them in the olive oil. Let them cook over a slow heat until they are soft and tender. This will take 20–25 minutes.

Add the butter and a good sprinkling of Maldon sea salt. Taste and check the seasoning. Tear in a good bunch of basil leaves and serve this with plenty of grated Parmigiano with chunky pasta like penne rigate or rigatoni.

Peppers prepared like this can also be eaten as a vegetable or used as a pizza topping.

Potatoes or Tattie Bogles
PATATE

On Sunday evening the immigrant families often visited each other. They would congregate in the 'back shop', which in the early days, served as their living rooms, and exchange gossip and worries. They would sit with a bottle of wine and a pack of cards, as if they were in the piazza in their village.

Invariably the conversation would turn to the price of potatoes. So many of these families made their livings from selling fish and chips that the price they paid for their raw ingredients made a huge difference to whether they could pay their bills and feed their families. Their big worry was the visit from the 'Will's traveller' who supplied them with cigarettes. His was always the biggest bill to pay.

These were shepherds, used to bartering and exchanging services to survive. Bank managers, invoices and debt were new experiences. It worried them intensely. Fear and uncertainty of their future made them work even harder. Shops were open long hours, children and wives helped to serve the customers. Life revolved around the shop counter.

Without realising it, this became their very reason for success. Their small shops and cafés became the focus of life for the community. In towns and villages all over Scotland the local chip shop was the place where gossip was exchanged, youngsters congregated and die-hard drinkers tottered in last thing at night for their 'tea'. The Italians steadily became respected friends and confidants to the locals.

We eat lots of potatoes. Simply mashed with plenty of butter, roasted or boiled, in soups or stews. We are really lucky because there are such a great variety of potatoes these days, home grown and imported. Choose floury, fluffy potatoes for mashing, soups and gnocchi: Maris Piper, King Edward or Wilja. Waxy, yellow-fleshed potatoes such as Charlotte are good for adding to stews or for salads. They hold their shape and eat well when cold.

The first Jersey Royals in May and baby new potatoes – local, Cyprus and Egyptian – that appear in the early summer are most delicious simply boiled and doused in soft, melting butter and a sprinkling of fresh mint. Add new potatoes to boiling salted water to cook them, 10 minutes or so.

New potatoes also make lovely chips. On my daddy's chip-shop window in the early summer he displayed the proud hand-written notice: 'New Potatoes : Frying Tonight.'

The green parts of any potato should always be cut away.

Mash

Add peeled potatoes to cold salted water and bring to the boil. Once they're cooked, I like to dry off the potatoes by draining them then letting them sit in the pot over a low heat for a few minutes. With the heat on, add a good glug of full-fat milk and as big a blob of butter as your conscience allows. Mashed and whisked and piping hot there's nothing simpler or better. Nonna Marietta always put her mashed potatoes into an ovenproof dish and added an extra blob of butter on top. She then popped them into a warm oven until a golden crust formed. Then they were piping hot and fluffy inside but crunchy and toasted on top.

Roast

Cut the potatoes into equal-sized pieces. Put them into a pot of cold salted water and bring them to the boil. Let them cook for no more than 5 or 10 minutes, just enough for them to allow a knife to slip into them easily. Drain and give them a toss in the pot to roughen their edges. This helps them roast well. Now dress them with plenty of olive oil or the fat from a roast. I always add a couple of shallots, whole and unpeeled, or an unpeeled red onion cut into rough quarters. They roast sweetly with the potatoes, adding an extra gooey, caramelised flavour. If you are cooking lamb, add a few sprigs of fresh rosemary; with pork, add some fresh sage. A fennel bulb cut into quarters also roasts well with potatoes.

Di Ciacca's Potato Crisps, c.1950.

You can add a splash of balsamic vinegar towards the end of roasting. This gives the roast potatoes a toffee, sweet flavour that is really tasty.

Roast potatoes in a hot oven (at least 220°C/425°F/Gas 7) for 25–30 minutes until they are golden and crispy at the edges.

Tattie Stovies

Francesca, Margaret Davidson looked after us when we were children. She had come with her mother from Peterhead looking for work. She was initially employed for a few years until the children grew up – but as my mum never stopped having children, eight in all, Margaret looked after us all her life. On Mummy and Daddy's day off, Margaret and Betty who worked in the ice-cream shop under our house, used to spoil us. They gave us too many sweeties and let us stay up too late. Margaret also made us the best tattie stovies.

2 large onions, peeled and finely sliced
2 tablespoons vegetable oil
6 floury potatoes, peeled and cut into chunks
4–5 100% pork sausages
Maldon sea salt and black pepper
1 tablespoon Bovril dissolved in a cup of warm water,
or 2 tablespoons gravy from a roast

Add the onions and the oil to a saucepan and let them cook very slowly until they are transparent and softened. Add the potatoes and a good splash of water and stir everything to coat the potatoes with the onion. Margaret used to put a piece of greaseproof paper over the pot and push the lid down to seal in any moisture. Let the potatoes and onions cook for 20 minutes or so. Add more water if they start to stick.

Add the pork sausages, cut into three pieces each, and season with a good sprinkling of salt and grinding of black pepper. Turn everything round in the pot, add another splash of water and return the lid with the greaseproof paper. The stovies will take another 20 minutes or so to cook. The brown, sticky bits that stick at the bottom of the pot are the best.

You have to eat stovies with lots of HP sauce and a glass of chilled milk.

Potato Salad

It's usually worth cooking more potatoes than you need. Leave them to cool and keep them refrigerated to use the next day. They are perfect to make a potato frittata (see page 329), or you can pan-fry them in olive oil flavoured with garlic and fresh rosemary until they are crispy round the edges and scrumptious. Alternatively, make a quick potato salad. Cut them into bite-sized chunks, not too small, and dress them with extra virgin olive oil, plenty of freshly ground black pepper and either a couple of spring onions finely chopped or a clove of garlic, chopped. Sprinkle the salad with plenty of finely chopped flat-leaf parsley.

Spinach
SPINACI

Spinach is such an easy vegetable to use, especially now you can buy it in ready-prepared bags. I still give it a good rinse in cold water, but it takes seconds.

Unwashed spinach can be very gritty. You will need to wash it in several changes of cold water to make sure that you get rid of it all. Discard any stringy-looking stalks and yellow leaves. Older, larger-leaved spinach definitely tastes stronger and has a more 'irony' flavour. It can leave a slightly rough feeling in the mouth. If you don't like the strong taste, choose young new leaves.

I never use tinned or frozen spinach. I find both slimy and unappealing. Punishment vegetables. Prepare spinach simply, letting its flavour speak for itself.

2–3 tablespoons extra virgin olive oil
1 clove garlic, peeled and cut into slivers
a piece of peperoncino (dried chilli), crumbled
250 g washed spinach
Maldon sea salt
lemon juice

Use a large frying pan. Warm the oil and flavour it with the garlic and peperoncino. Add the spinach, pressing it down to get it all in. Sprinkle it with sea salt and put a lid on top. The spinach takes minutes to cook. It collapses down into a tenth of its size and releases its own lovely juices.

I always serve it with its juices on a plate in the centre of the table at the beginning of the meal. I squeeze lemon juice over just before we eat. (If you add the lemon juice too soon it turns the spinach an unappetising brown colour.) There's plenty of liquid at the bottom of the dish. This is just perfect to dunk crusty bread into.

Use sunflower or vegetable oil and add slices of fresh ginger and garlic to it. Add the spinach and when it is cooked, sprinkle in some sesame seeds and a teaspoonful of sesame oil.

Very young spinach leaves are lovely added to a mixed salad.

Spinach risotto is one of my favourites and very easy (see page 180), and or add spinach to pasta with oil and garlic (see page 138).

Use this spinach cooked in oil and garlic for stuffing the pizza rustica on page 324. Make sure it is very well drained of excess liquid.

I often use spinach as a stuffing for ravioli. Rinse about 200 g of spinach and cook it in a frying pan moistened with a blob of butter. Season it with Maldon sea salt, some freshly ground black pepper and a good grating of nutmeg. Squeeze out any excess liquid, chop it finely and use it instead of the fresh herbs on page 125 to make a filling for home-made ravioli.

Swiss Chard
BIETOLA

Swiss chard is one of those vegetables that have recently become available in this country. Its leaves taste and look like spinach; its flat, pale-ridged stalk more like celery. You may sometimes see Swiss chard with ruby red and yellow stalks, almost like beet-root. (Not so surprising as it is part of the beet family.) It looks very beautiful and has a distinctive bitter-sweet flavour.

Separate the stalks from the leaves and cook them separately, as they take longer to cook. Wash the stalks and cut them into easily handled strips. Cook them in boiling salted water until tender, but still crisp. Drain them.

Rinse the green leaves well. Add a few tablespoons of extra virgin olive oil to a large frying pan and add the cooked stalks. Warm them through then add the leaves. Add a sprinkle of salt, put a lid on and steam them down just like spinach. We eat the Swiss chard simply dressed with lemon juice. The liquid from the leaves coupled with the olive oil is enough to flavour it. Try it. It's really good.

I use chard in vegetable soups (see page 103), and sometimes dress the cooked stalks with butter and grated Parmigiano Reggiano and bake them in the oven for 15 minutes or so.

WHERE'S MUM WHEN I
NEED HER?

*Maria Crolla with her children, Vittorio on her lap, Domenico
and Margherita, c.1920*

Annunziata always knew by looking at you how you were
feeling. She would take a step away from you and give you a
knowing look. She knew if you were tired, if you were hungry,
or if you'd just pulled yourself out of bed. She knew if you had
stomach pains, wobbly tummy or if you were 'incinta', pregnant.

She had a little bottle of 'cognac' to hand at all times, her cure-all.

Francesca, in the 1950s and 1960s the Italian women in Scotland were pretty conservative. They would never say if someone was pregnant. It was almost regarded as an embarrassing condition to be in. Pregnancy implied behaviour that was, for Catholics of that time, unmentionable, even for married couples. If one of their friends was pregnant, the women used humour to cover up their discomfort, saying that she was 'on the road to Morocco', with a knowing look.

According to your bis-nonna Annunziata who, with seventeen pregnancies behind her, was 'on the road to Morocco' most of her life, if you suffer from:

Queasiness, nervousness, shock or morning sickness: take a thimbleful shot of cognac.

Insomnia, nervousness or agitation: take a cup of camomile tea without milk or lemon.

Diarrhoea or gippy-tummy: starve for 24 hours. Drink plenty of water and eat only plain boiled rice the next day to settle the stomach.

Minor cut, burn or scald: spit on it, or Nonna would for you.

If you have a headache you have to investigate the cause: put some water in a saucer and add a teaspoon of olive oil. If the oil separates into little blobs you have been given the evil eye. Throw the water and oil out and your headache will go!

Crying baby: rub cognac on their gums (don't try this at home!).

My mummy, who was also on the road to Morocco fairly often – she had eight children – taught me how to cook from an early age. Francesca, to stop you phoning me up in a panic, here's a checklist of all those recipes that she taught me and that we use all the time in the kitchen. You have made most of them for me over the years, but they're here just in case you've forgotten how. (Phone me anyway to let me know how you got on!)

Béchamel Sauce
SALSA DI BESCIAMELLA

500 ml milk
1 fresh bay leaf
50 g unsalted butter
50 g plain flour
Maldon sea salt and white pepper
freshly grated nutmeg

Heat the milk and the bay leaf together and leave to infuse.

In a separate saucepan, melt the butter. Add the flour, and with a wooden spoon stir them together until they form a ball, a 'roux'. Cook the mixture over a low heat for a few minutes.

Remove the bay leaf, add a little of the warm milk to the roux, and stir everything over a low heat until you have a smooth paste. Keep adding the milk and stirring until the sauce is formed. It does have a tendency to get lumpy but keep stirring. As soon as it gets to simmering point, the lumps disappear and the sauce becomes smooth.

Once you have added all the milk, let the sauce cook on a low heat for 10 minutes or so. Season it with Maldon salt, some ground white (or black) pepper and a grating of nutmeg. It needs quite a bit of seasoning, so taste it to check.

You can add layers of flavour to the milk by infusing a small onion, a clove, some black peppercorns or a sprig of tarragon in the milk before you use it. Strain the milk.

You can add freshly chopped herbs to the sauce once it is cooked: flat-leaf parsley, chives or fresh chervil.

Add grated cheese to make a cheese sauce: strong Cheddar such as Mull or Montgomery's. Gruyère or Roquefort give a delicious sauce. Add grated Parmigiano Reggiano if you want to use the sauce with pasta.

Mayonnaise
MAIONESE

Eggs in mayonnaise are eaten raw and need to be from a salmonella-free source. I use organic eggs from local producers who have very small flocks and limited production. The yolks are wonderfully rich and yellow and the flavour can only be described as 'old-fashioned'. Be aware that organic eggs are not guaranteed to be free of salmonella. Look out for the 'red lion mark' stamped on eggs. This is a guarantee that the eggs have come from a salmonella-free flock.

2 egg yolks
Maldon sea salt and white pepper
300 ml neutral oil such as sunflower, groundnut or refined light olive oil
lemon juice

If you're impatient like me you will curdle the mayonnaise. You need to do this slowly and patiently. Put on the 'Moonlight Sonata' and chill. Don't let the eggs be cool, all the ingredients must be at room temperature. Warm the bowl a little too; the eggs want to feel comfortable.

Put the egg yolks and seasoning into a wide bowl and

whisk them until they start to thicken. Whisk in the oil a single drop at a time. The only way I can control myself is to use a metal skewer to drip the oil in and to use a small hand whisk to beat it in. As the mixture starts to thicken, add more and more oil. Halfway through, add a teaspoon of lemon juice to start to add some flavour. Incorporate the rest of the oil. Taste and adjust seasoning. Towards the end add a tablespoon of warm water to lighten the texture a little.

Keep the mayonnaise covered in the fridge and use it within a few days.

Spoon mayonnaise over hard-boiled eggs.

Chop cold, roast chicken into cubes and mix it together with chopped gherkins, spring onions and a couple of tablespoons of mayonnaise.

Make home-made tartare sauce. Add 2 tablespoons chopped gherkins, 1 tablespoon of capers (those stored in vinegar are fine), a tablespoon of finely chopped parsley and a little more lemon juice. Season to taste. This is a special treat with fried scampi (see page 247).

Add fresh herbs to flavour the mayonnaise, such as finely chopped chives. Chopped dill and a tablespoon of Dijon mustard will give a lovely sweet mustard sauce for gravadlax or smoked fish.

Pound a handful of fresh basil leaves with a sprinkling of Maldon sea salt in a pestle and mortar. Add this to make a lovely basil-flavoured mayonnaise.

Gravy

The best way to make gravy for a roast is to use the juices that come from the meat you are cooking. Once the beef or lamb you have roasted is ready, put it on to a warmed tray and cover it with foil. Leave it to rest in a warm place. The roasting tray is full of tasty juices. Spoon off as much of the fat as you can. Keep it to roast potatoes or Yorkshire puddings with. It's also good for making stovies (see page 216).

Put the roasting tin on a high heat on top of the cooker. Use a wooden spoon to scrape away all the juicy bits on the sides of the tin. Squash down any garlic or onions you have used to flavour the joint. Add a good glass of white wine or water (180–200 ml) and let the juices boil fiercely. I don't add flour, as I prefer thin, smooth gravy. When it has reduced by about a third, and all the alcohol has evaporated, taste it. It usually needs a good amount of seasoning. Strain it into a warm jug, and serve it piping hot.

Green Sauce
SALSA VERDE

I love pungent salsa verde with grilled fish, especially oily, fleshy fish like sea bass or bream. Its kick perfectly complements the richness of the fish. Use this list as a guide. You can substitute the herbs depending on availability and your mood.

2 large handfuls flat-leaf parsley
2 large handfuls fresh basil
2 tablespoons capers (if salted, soaked for a half an hour and rinsed)
3–4 flat anchovy fillets
½ clove garlic, peeled
4 tablespoons red wine vinegar
10–12 tablespoons extra virgin olive oil
Maldon salt to taste

Gertrude, c.1948

Take the herb leaves from the stalks and chop the leaves as finely as you can.

Chop the capers, anchovies and garlic roughly and mix together with the vinegar and herbs. Blend in the olive oil, using enough to make the consistency you want.

Use a pestle and mortar to help mix everything together or you can use a food processor. The salsa should have a rough course texture. Taste and adjust the flavour with some salt, or more anchovies, vinegar or garlic, as you like.

This salsa is best used the day you prepare it, but it will keep a couple of days in the fridge. In which case put it in a sealed jar and cover the surface with a little olive oil.

Traditionally this is served with 'bollito misto', mixed boiled beef, but at home we always got our boiled beef with mashed potatoes and carrots!

Yorkshire Puddings

Remember to bake Yorkshire puddings in a hot oven. They need about 30–35 minutes to cook, which is a pain when you have only one oven. If you are cooking these with roast beef, which I presume you are, take the roast out of the oven as soon as it is cooked the way you like it (see page 270). Cover it well with two sheets of foil. I usually put a clean tea-towel on top of that. Leave it somewhere warm to rest.

As soon as you take it out, whack up the oven temperature and get your Yorkshire puddings and your roast potatoes in.

After about 25 minutes, start to serve the roast. By the time everyone is served, the Yorkshires can be handed round. I love to serve the piping hot, perfectly raised, slightly soggy in the middle Yorkshire puds directly on to everyone's plate.

75 g plain flour, sieved
1 large free-range egg
125 ml semi-skimmed milk
Maldon sea salt and black pepper
some of the melted fat from the roasting, or some flavourless oil

Whizz all the ingredients apart from the fat in a liquidiser and let the batter stand while you organise the tins. I use muffin trays with twelve spaces to make individual puddings. Put a tablespoon or so of the fat or oil into each one. Put the tray into the oven just before you pull the roast out. Put the oven temperature up to high (220°C/425°F/Gas 7).

Take the tray out of the oven and fill each mould half full with the batter. Use up all the batter: this amount makes about ten puddings. Double up the quantity, using another muffin tray, if you want more.

Bake on the second highest shelf for 25–30 minutes. Remember the puddings will rise so don't put them too near the top, or they'll hit the roof – then so will you!

If you want to make one big pudding, use a baking tray about 30 x 19 cm and 6 cm deep. Double the quantity of batter and bake it for 30 minutes or so until it has risen magnificently.

Pancakes
CRESPELLE

Francesca, pancakes were my secret weapon during my courtship. I used to invite your dad home with the excuse that I wanted to make him pancakes. I did this on and off from the age of seventeen until I finally married him at twenty-four. It took some time, but paid off in the end.

Don't let anyone tell you otherwise. The way to a man's heart is through his stomach!

100 g self-raising flour
300 ml semi-skimmed milk
2 large free-range eggs
2 tablespoons caster sugar
some melted butter

Sieve the flour then simply whizz everything together except the butter in a liquidiser. Let the mixture rest for 10 minutes or so.

You really need a decent non-stick frying pan to make pancakes easily. Once you find one you like, call it your pancake pan and keep it just for pancakes.

Melt a little butter in the frying pan. As soon as it starts to sizzle add a ladle of the batter, just enough to coat the bottom of the frying pan. Cook the pancake slowly until it browns underneath and you start to see little bubbles forming on the top. This is when you can flip it over and cook the other side. Flipping is part of the fun but a bit risky. If you've no-one to impress, use a spatula and some nifty wrist action. Practice makes perfect.

Stack the pancakes in a warm place while you cook all the batter. We love these served with whipped cream, maple syrup and fresh berries, or simply butter and lemon juice.

Sweet Shortcrust Pastry
PASTA FROLLA

240 g self-raising flour, sifted
90 g unrefined caster sugar
120 g cold butter, cut into cubes
1 egg yolk
1 tablespoon cold water

Mix the flour and sugar in a large mixing bowl. Add the
cubed butter then, using your fingers, rub the butter into the
flour mixture. Lift the flour up as you rub the butter in to
get plenty of air into the pastry. When the mixture looks like
coarse breadcrumbs, add the egg yolk and the water and mix
it together with a knife. Dust your hands with a little extra
flour and press the dough together. Leave it to rest wrapped
in clingfilm until you are ready to use it.

Miss American Pie

My secret passion is rhubarb pie. Before we were married, your
dad and I fell out and didn't speak for three years. I was broken-
hearted. I ate all day, every day. He was broken-hearted. He went
to the missions. I spent my time sitting curled up in corners,
dreaming, eating and listening to Don McLean.

When we met again we didn't recognise each other. He had
grown a beard, ready to be a priest. I was three stone heavier:
too much American pie!

It's easy to make, but what I really love is when it's two days old and it becomes quite solid and gooey. If I'm in that old nostalgic mood I can eat the whole thing.

> *3–4 big sticks of rhubarb, about 600 g*
> *demerara sugar*
> *1 lemon*
> *1 quantity sweet shortcrust pastry (see page 231)*
> *1 egg yolk*

Preheat the oven to fairly hot (190°C/375°F/Gas 5).

Wash the rhubarb. Trim it and cut it into 5–6 cm pieces. Put it into a saucepan with 3–4 tablespoons of the sugar and let it cook slowly over a low heat. It doesn't need any liquid added and will 'stew in it's own juice'. Keep the heat low so that it doesn't burn dry. I add a squeeze of lemon juice to bring out the flavour. When the rhubarb is soft taste it, adding more sugar if it's too tart.

Now simply grease a 25 cm pie-dish or ovenproof plate, and line it with half the quantity of sweet pastry. If the pastry breaks as you roll it out, just press it together again with your fingers, don't worry. The nicest thing about home baking is that it feels like sitting around with your dressing gown on. Comfortable! Sprinkle the bottom of the pastry with a little sugar.

If the rhubarb is quite moist, strain off some of the juices or it will make the pastry soggy. Pile the cooled rhubarb on top and roll out the rest of the pastry. Play at making sand-pies and do everything you can to press the edges to seal the fruit in. Nip the pastry all the way round to make a pretty pie.

Brush the top of the pastry with some egg yolk and bake the pie on a baking sheet in the preheated oven for 40 minutes or so. The juices inevitably ooze out of the sides and top of the pastry. The smell in the kitchen is delicious, and when you eat a gooey, juicy pie with a big blob of whipped cream you can only feel better!

Fill the pie with any fruit you fancy. Usually 600–800 g fruit is enough. Cook some peeled apples in a little sugar and make a lovely apple pie. Try apricots, plums or gooseberries.

Flaky Pastry

Use ready-made Jus-Rol flaky pastry. It works really well, is light and really saves a lot of hard work.

Custard

I usually use Bird's Custard or Cremola. I make it according to the pack, a tablespoon of powder per 600 ml (or pint), but I make it with single cream instead of milk. It's a good compromise. Dissolve the powder in a little of the liquid first.

If you want to make real custard, make it as you would vanilla ice-cream (see page 348). Crema pasticcera (see page 365) is thickened home-made custard that makes a lovely filling for cakes.

Mascarpone Whip

Instead of whipped cream, flavour some mascarpone and enjoy an indulgent pleasure. Original unpasteurised mascarpone is not easily found here. It is the fullest fat, sweet cream cheese made. The tubs of pasteurised mascarpone that are widely available are very good, but a bit heavy. Lightening it with some cream and flavourings can improve it immensely.

125 g mascarpone
1 tablespoon caster sugar
2 tablespoons Marsala
juice and very finely grated rind of ½ orange
125 ml whipping cream

Use a hand whisk to whip the mascarpone and caster sugar lightly. Fold in the Marsala, the orange juice and the grated rind. (Remember to scrub the orange first. The rind usually has a wax preservative on it like lemons.) Whip the cream lightly and fold it into the mascarpone.

Taste it to check if it's sweet enough.

Meringues
MERINGHE

Francesca, there is always a time in every cook's life when you have egg whites to use up. Make meringues by weighing the egg whites and adding double the quantity of caster sugar. Remember to make sure there is no yolk in the whites and whisk them in a clean, dry bowl until they have doubled in size. Gradually add the sugar and keep whisking until the mixture looks like white peaks.

Space spoonfuls of meringue out on a baking tin lined with greased baking parchment, and bake them in a cool oven (140°C/275°F/Gas 1). They'll take about an hour. I usually switch the oven off and leave them for a couple of hours to dry out.

For a pavlova, do the same thing, but add flavourings and

cornflour to make the meringue fluffy inside. Use 6–8 egg whites, double their weight of caster sugar, a teaspoon of white vinegar, one of cornflour and a couple of drops of vanilla extract. Spread the mixture on to a baking tray lined with greased baking parchment, flatten it into a round and build up the edges making peaks with a skewer. Bake in a cool oven as above for an hour or so.

IN A JAM

I REALLY THINK IT'S WELL WORTH THE EFFORT to make some jam now and then. I don't go in for the massive 10 kg batches I used to, when I had more time. It was such a worry trying to get a big batch of jam to set that I gave up.

These days, I make three or four jars at a time, just if I'm in the mood or see some really nice fruit. I don't mind if it doesn't set exactly right, in fact I prefer to catch the fresh flavour of the fruit by under-boiling slightly. A runny, fruity jam is much tastier than an over-set solid one.

If you're making jam, stick to the same principles: keep it simple and use good ingredients. I really enjoy visiting 'pick-your-own' farms. Children love wandering between the bushes laden with fruit. I defy any child – or adult – to leave without their mouths and hands smeared with tell-tale splashes of juice. We love picking brambles when we go for late summer walks. They make lovely jam.

Unfortunately, because of their perishability, berries are likely suspects for high levels of preservatives. Farmers and suppliers are tempted to spray to prevent spoiling and loss of profit. I remember strawberries used to last a couple of days if you were lucky. These days they can sit in the fridge for up to eight days . . . slightly suspicious? If I can, I use organic berries.

When making jam, make sure the berries you use are as fresh as possible. Don't use pectin or preserving sugar. They both have an artificial flavour and, to my mind, defeat the purpose of making something fresh. I use the flesh and juice from a lemon to add pectin and am prepared to tolerate soft, runny jam. I usually put the jam into sterilised kilner jars. Because I just make a little at a time it doesn't have to last all year, and it saves all the hassle of wax discs and rubber bands.

Best Strawberry Jam
MARMELLATA DI FRAGOLE

Strawberries are low in pectin and the jam is fairly difficult to set. I find using slightly less sugar helps and I add the pulp of the lemons as well as their juice to give an extra shot of acidity.

1.5 kg local strawberries in season, organic if possible
1.3 kg unrefined granulated sugar
juice and pulp of 2 large lemons
a small blob of butter

Mary, three years old, looking up to her sister Anita, aged four

Make sure the strawberries are dry and, if anything, slightly under-ripe. Don't wash them, just hull them and wipe them with a damp cloth. Choose a deep, wide saucepan which will allow the fruit and sugar to double in volume as the jam boils. Put the fruit into the saucepan and slowly bring them to the boil. Let them boil until they are soft and start to break down.

Warm the sugar in a low oven

236

(140°C/275°F/Gas 1) for 10 minutes, then add it to the strawberries with the juice and pulp of the lemons. Stir everything together, and heat the jam through slowly until the sugar has all dissolved. You can tell when it has stopped sounding gritty when you stir it. Check the back of the spoon for signs of granules. Now, bring the jam to the boil and let it bubble fiercely for 10 minutes.

Take the jam off the heat and test a spoonful of jam on a cold plate. As it cools you should be able to push your finger through the jam to form a wrinkle. It will very likely be cooked enough. If you think it's not set enough, boil the jam for another 5 minutes, but, as I say, I prefer to sacrifice solidity for flavour.

Add the blob of butter to dissolve any scum that comes to the surface.

This fills about 5–6 x 450 g jars or 3 x 1 kg kilner jars. Make sure they are sterilised (see overleaf).

Raspberry Jam
MARMELLATA DI LAMPONI

I find raspberry jam the easiest of all. Raspberries are high in pectin and set easily. The addition of some lemon juice just acts as a guarantee of success.

2 kg local raspberries
2 kg granulated sugar
juice and pulp of 1 lemon

Don't wash the raspberries but just check them over for any insects or grit that may be lurking inside. Warm the sugar for 10 minutes in a low oven (140°C/275°F/Gas 1).

Put the sugar and the fruit into a deep, wide saucepan, big enough to allow the jam to boil freely. Add the lemon juice and the pulp. Slowly bring the jam to the boil, stirring to make sure all the sugar is dissolved. Check the back of the spoon for any granules. Once it is dissolved, boil the jam fiercely for 10 minutes.

To test whether the jam is ready to set, put a teaspoonful of the mixture on to a cool plate and check that it wrinkles when you push your finger through it. It sets really easily, so you should have no problems. This makes about 4–5 x 450 g jars of jam.

Make sure you sterilise the jars well. I put them in the glass cycle of the dishwasher or warm them through in a medium oven.

If you want to store the jam for longer than six weeks put a jam-pot wax disc on top of the jam, cover it with a jam-pot cover and elastic and screw a lid on to the jar as well.

When we were kids, we poured hot raspberry jam over ice-cream the minute it was made. Wonderful!

You can use the same quantity of berries to sugar with other tart berries like tayberries, brambles, blackberries or loganberries. They all set well.

Taroccan Orange Marmalade
MARMELLATA DI ARANCE TAROCCO

Marmalade is a bit of a 'faff' and to be perfectly honest, there are very good commercial marmalades around: with pith, without pith, with chopped pith, without chopped pith, with thick pith, with thin pith!

I do love home-made Sicilian Taroccan blood orange marmalade, though. It's really good. You may lose the red colour of the flesh in cooking, but the taste is very sweet and fresh. If you find nice blood oranges have a go. I've adapted Jane Grigson's easy whole orange recipe.

1.5 kg Tarocco oranges
3 litres cold water
3 kg granulated sugar
juice and pulp of 1 lemon

If you can't find organic oranges, you need to scrub the skins of the oranges with soapy water to get rid of any wax. Rinse them well.

Put them into a very large pot with the water and simmer them until the skins are easily pierced. It takes about 1½ hours. Take the oranges out and let them cool. Keep the water.

Once the oranges are cool, cut each one in half, take out the pips and cut the rind into strips. I work with the orange in a bowl because there's lots of water inside each orange. Save this.

Cut the rind into tidy pieces and put it back into the water. This is a bit tedious. The alternative is to chop the rind before you boil the oranges, in which case save the pips and add them to a small muslin bag in the water. The pectin that sets the marmalade is in the pips.

A sharp knife and a bit of patience are all that's required. (I have the first but not the second.)

Warm the sugar in a low oven (140°C/275°F/Gas 1) for 10 minutes. Add it and the lemon juice and orange pulp to the pot. Warm the marmalade slowly, stirring to dissolve the sugar. (If you want a thick set you really should add the pips in a muslin bag. I quite like my marmalade runny.) Boil vigorously for 10 minutes until you get a setting point.

As soon as you see that welcome wrinkle on a cooled teaspoonful of the marmalade, leave the marmalade to cool a little to allow the peel to suspend. Decant it into sterilised jars, up to 6–8 x 450 g jars.

FRYING TONIGHT

Customers and Di Ciacca children outside the Cockenzie Café, c.1930

COCKENZIE, EAST LOTHIAN, SCOTLAND
1950–1970

My father Johnny worked with his father, Cesidio, in the ice-cream and chip shop in Cockenzie. Cesidio taught him to insist on using the best, very freshest ingredients. His philosophy was to 'keep it simple'. He hated what he called 'mucked-up food' and taught me how to respect the ingredients I use in my cooking. Even though he made his livelihood frying fish and chips, he put every effort into making them the very best. There was nothing tastier or more enjoyable than eating his fresh haddock fillets, battered and deep-fried and eaten with dry, crisp chips. He wrapped them in clean white greaseproof paper then

241

in a sheet of old newspaper. Eating them walking along the street was heaven.

His last customer one night, a very drunk man who could hardly stand up and had to be forcibly removed from the shop so that they could close, gave a parting salvo. 'Johnny, you're yin i oo. I could eat yir fish in the dark and I wouldnay hae tae worry.' Johnny took this as a great compliment.

Daddy filleted the fish himself, standing in the fish shed with waders on, a plastic apron covering him from head to toe. He worked with freezing cold water running all the time. He held the fish in his hand and used scissors to clip off the fins. He slashed the belly open, pulling out the guts. A rinse under cold water and the fish was laid on a well-worn wooden board. His knife was thin as a rapier, sharp and deadly. Four flicks of the wrist and the fish was filleted, boned and skinned. The head and guts were unceremoniously tossed into a large bin to his right. The fillets were rinsed again, checked for stray bones and respect-fully pilled up in metal trays, ready for the evening's trade. He had already been up before five to buy the fish at the market in Eyemouth.

I remember watching him work, me no higher than his boots, happy to stand beside him and keep him company.

He was very enterprising and developed a range of crisps fried in vegetable oil. He sold them for threepence a bag, with a free blue sachet of salt to be added as required. Years later we found thousands of little blue packets of salt left over from his frying days.

He was born in Italy, but he had come to Cockenzie before he was three years old. He raised his eight children as strictly as any Italian father would, trying to instil his heritage and ancient traditions. But he was always proud to have been accepted by the locals as 'yin i oo', 'one of us'.

Fish Supper

You can't recreate the flavour and texture of my daddy's fish fried in vast vats of boiling oil at home. Don't try it! But you can shallow-fry fresh haddock, coated in egg and breadcrumbs, and make a delicious supper easily.

2 fresh haddock fillets, bought from a good fishmonger
(or fillets of cod, lemon sole or witch sole)
4–5 tablespoons plain flour
2 eggs, beaten and seasoned
4–5 tablespoons fresh breadcrumbs
corn oil or sunflower oil for frying

First things first, wash the fish. Most people are put off fish because of the taste of stale water that clings to its surface. It seems obvious, but always wash fish (and shellfish) in cold water and pat dry before cooking.

Put the flour, beaten eggs and breadcrumbs in three separate, shallow bowls.

Dip the haddock on both sides firstly in the flour then, shaking off any excess, dip it into the beaten egg, coating each side. Lastly coat the haddock in the breadcrumbs, pressing it down to make sure the breadcrumbs stick.

Heat enough oil to coat the bottom of a large frying pan by at least 3 cm. Check that the oil is hot enough by dipping the end of the fillet into it. When it sizzles really well, it's ready. Lay the fish into the oil. Cook one or two fish at a time only. If you over-crowd the frying pan, the oil will get too cold and the fish will be soggy instead of crisp. Keep the heat on high so that the fish fry briskly.

Let the bottom of the fish crisp and brown before using a spatula and fork to carefully flip the fish over. When it is crisp on both sides lift it with the spatula and drain the oil from it. I usually put it on to some kitchen paper to drain.

I like to sprinkle the fish with a little sea salt and a squeeze of lemon juice before serving it.

You can cut lemon sole into small finger-sized pieces and prepare them the same way: home-made fish fingers. Serve them with tartare sauce (see page 225).

Make a vegetarian version with long slices of aubergine, dipped in flour, egg and breadcrumbs, and fried the same way.

Deep-fried Chips

Oven-baked frozen chips are very good but sometimes, Francesca, you ask me to make home-made chips. There are some rules you need to know in order to deep-fry safely and healthily.

Use good, fresh oil: sunflower or corn oil. Use it once or twice only. After that the chemicals in the oil start to break down and the oil becomes fairly unhealthy.

Fill the fryer no more than half full. Once the food is added and starts to cook, the oil moves nearer the surface and can easily overflow.

Make sure the oil is hot before you start to fry. Add a chip or piece of bread to the oil. When it comes to the surface, sizzles and moves around, the oil is hot enough.

Don't over-crowd the oil. Food needs space to move around, so cook in batches.

Make sure the food you are frying is dry. Water and fat splash dangerously.

Never leave a fryer unattended. Hot oil very easily ignites. If it does lay a damp cloth over the fryer to dampen down the fire. Leave it to cool on the cooker. If you try to move it, the fire can flare up again. Never throw water on an oil- or fat-based fire.

Choose floury potatoes like Maris Piper or King Edward to make the best chips. Peel them and cut them into chips, soaking them in cold water until you're ready to use them. This stops the starch in the potatoes turning black. Before cooking, rinse the chips in fresh cold water to get rid of any starch, then pat them dry.

Heat the oil in a chip pan with a chip basket or in an electric fryer if you have one. Test the temperature of the oil by putting one chip into it. As soon as it rises to the surface and starts to move around and sizzle, the oil is hot enough.

Add just enough chips so that they are well covered with oil. Too many chips and the temperature of the oil will fall and the chips will be soggy and full of oil. Give the chip basket a good shake so that all the chips are free and coated with oil. Keep the heat at a brisk level so that the oil doesn't cool down, keeping an eye on the chips and shaking the basket from time to time.

As the chips cook they will begin to colour. As they get darker and the sizzling slows down they're ready. Lift the chips out of the oil and press one with your fingers (ouch) to check that they're soft inside.

Drain them and put them into a bowl lined with kitchen paper. Whip the paper out and sprinkle them liberally with Maldon sea salt. I love to eat home-made chips with fresh lemon juice squeezed all over them.

DEAR FRANCESCA

Clear-conscience Chips

You don't want to deep-fry but you want chips. Badly! No problem. Peel some floury potatoes and cut them into big chunky chips. Par-boil them in salted water for 10 minutes. Drain well, and shake a little in the pot to roughen their edges. Sprinkle with Maldon sea salt.

Preheat the oven to hot (220°C/425°F/Gas 7).

Put the chips on to a large, greased baking tray in one layer and drizzle them with a splash of extra virgin olive oil. Bake them for 20–25 minutes until they are crispy and golden and would fool a die-hard chip-a-holic.

Fritters

Francesca, if we were very good, your Grandpa Johnny made us fritters, thick slices of potato dipped in a batter and deep-fried.

3 tablespoons plain flour
250 ml cold water
Maldon sea salt and black pepper
corn or sunflower oil for deep-frying
3 large baking potatoes, peeled and sliced into 2 cm thick rounds

Prepare the simple batter in a small bowl by beating together the flour and water with a fork. It should have the consistency of double cream. Season well.

Heat the oil, ready for deep-frying. Rinse the potatoes and pat them dry. Dip them into the batter, slapping them from side to side against the bowl to get rid of excess batter.

Fry the fritters until they are golden brown. They take 3–4

minutes, depending on how thick they are. You just have to eat these with plenty of HP Sauce.

Or, how about onion rings to die for? Soak the onion rings in water for 5 minutes or so to get rid of any milky juices. Drain, dry and dip them in the batter. Fry as above.

Deep-fried Scampi

For a treat, the local fishermen would leave a box of live scampi at the 'back door'. They were in fact wonderful langoustines which, if we were very, very good, Daddy would boil, peel and dip in batter to deep-fry for us. Nothing tastes so good. Perks of the job or what!

Scotland produces some of the best seafood in the world. Most of the catch is sold to European markets, as apparently we don't want to eat them! Langoustines are the most delicious, sweet-flavoured shellfish you could eat, but only if they are fresh. You must buy them when they are still alive. As soon as they die they start to spoil and will quickly smell and take on the flavour of stale ammonia. Not appealing! Use them on the day you buy them. The fishermen used to teach us to crack the back of the shell, twist the tail and pull out the black vein that runs down the back. Or you can clean it out after they're boiled as you shell them. Don't serve them with the vein still inside.

If you go to all the bother of making scampi you should really serve them with real, home-made tartare sauce (see page 225). The business.

about 20 langoustines
1 egg
250 ml cold water
100 g plain flour
50 g cornflour
corn or sunflower oil for deep-frying

Bring a large pot of water to the boil. Hold the langoustine in your left hand, and use your right hand to nip its tail. Twist it, pulling out the black vein that lies down the middle. When you have cleaned them all, drop the langoustines into the boiling water and boil them for 2–3 minutes, just until the shells change colour from bright blue-red to pink.

Let them cool. (They're fabulous to eat just like this dipped in mayonnaise, never mind frying them.) Shell them by squeezing the shell with your fingers, cracking it along the back. Turn the langoustines over and use the length of both your thumbs against the edges of the shell on the underside to pull the shell apart. The beautiful pink flesh comes out in one piece. Check the back to make sure the entire black vein is out. If not, rinse it away with a little water.

Mix the egg and the cold water and sift the flours into the bowl. Mix everything with a fork. The batter should be thin, just enough to coat the fish lightly. If it's too thick, add a little more water.

Prepare the oil for deep-frying as described above.

Dip the langoustines into the batter, shake away any excess and deep-fry them until they are light and golden. They'll cook in 3–4 minutes. Keep the oil hot.

Alternatively use raw tiger prawns, shelled but with the tail still attached so that it sticks temptingly out of the end of the batter.

In the 1960s there was no market for monkfish. The fishermen

Johnny, aged twenty-four. Very smart!

*used to sell it to restaurants to cut into cubes, deep-fry and sell at
vast profits. They called it 'false scampi'. Try deep-fried monkfish.
It's lovely.*

FRITTO

It's not surprising that the Italians opened fish and chip shops
when they came to this country. The bulk of immigrants came
from the south. In the nineteenth century, poverty was extreme.
Few peasants owned their own houses let alone their own land.
Many lived in caves dug out from the side of the hill. They
had no cooking facilities, if anything a fire in a hearth. Those
who became desperate moved in droves into the cities looking
for work. In Naples they called these itinerants 'disgraziati lazza-
roni', 'wretched good for nothings'. They slept in the streets,
worked where they could, and survived on scraps of food
cooked in the streets. Some of them were enterprising and
became street vendors, selling all types of food. Simply grilled
over rough fires or fried in cauldrons of boiling oil, they cooked
everything from courgette strips to calamari, pizza dough and
meatballs. Every morsel of a slaughtered animal was used. The
feet and jowls of slaughtered animals were steamed along with
the lining of the stomach. Literally 'foot and mouth', 'per'e o'
musso', was regarded as a great treat, sold in white conical
paper pokes. In Naples today there are still stalls selling this
delicacy!

'Fritto' is a standard item on all tourist menus in Italy – the
visitors love fried food as much as the locals. When it's done
properly, and the food is fried at the right temperature, it is a
very healthy way to eat. The flavours and vitamins are trapped
inside a protective crust.

If you cook fritto at home, prepare to be standing at the

cooker, handing out food to everyone. Fried food should be eaten quickly, while it is still crisp and hot. As they say in Naples, 'friggendo mangiando', 'fry as you eat'. I make it only for a few at home, never for a crowd. Deep-fat-frying does make a smell. If you find it intolerable, invest in an electric fryer.

4–5 squid, cleaned
the tentacles of the squid
5–6 tablespoons plain flour
Maldon sea salt and black pepper
1.5–2 litres corn or sunflower oil
lemons

Ask the fishmonger to clean the squid for you. You need the tubular body of the squid cut into rings about 1 cm thick. Ask for the tentacles as well. They are the most tender parts. Wash them well in cold water and dry on kitchen paper.

Put the flour into a bowl and season it well with salt and pepper. Heat the oil in a chip pan with a basket until a little bit of bread starts to sizzle. Toss the squid rings in the flour, shake them in a sieve over the sink to get rid of excess flour and cook them in batches, avoiding over-crowding the hot oil. Excess flour makes the oil cloudy, so shake the squid well. Keep the heat fast and as soon as the squid stops moving around in the fat and is a crispy, golden brown, it's cooked. Shake the oil from the squid and drain on kitchen paper. Keep it warm while you fry the rest.

I like to serve this with a sprinkle of salt and a squeeze of lemon juice.

You can deep-fry anything you like. Season it well before you start and make sure that everything is cut in similar-sized pieces. We also sometimes dip the food in egg and then in flour. For added flavour, stir a few teaspoons of fresh pesto into the egg. Try:

Courgettes, sliced into batons

Red peppers, de-seeded and sliced into strips

Aubergine, sliced and cut into batons

SLOW-COOKING

Gertrude and Johnny at Alfredo's

Cooking food on a slow heat is one of the easiest ways to prepare a meal. The ingredients can be quickly put together and the dish is left to cook on its own slowly, in a little liquid. The only bit of patience required is the browning of the meat before everything is added. Work with small batches at a time, keeping the browned pieces in a warmed dish until it's all done. If this is done properly it makes a huge difference to the finished dish. It seals in the flavours of the food and it adds a very tasty, caramelised flavour to the skin, making good eating.

For this type of cooking I prefer a heavy-bottomed oven-proof casserole, something that will transfer directly from the top of the stove to the oven. I tend to cook a stew or casserole only if I'm busy the following day. While I'm cooking the evening's meal, I can quickly put together the next day's dinner at the same time. Most stews actually taste better the next day anyway. The other huge advantage is that vegetables and potatoes can be all cooked in the same pot. In effect a ready-made meal!

Pan-roasted Chicken with Rosemary

This is a classic way to prepare chicken all over Italy. It's very easy and only takes 20 minutes or so. I usually buy free-range legs and breasts of chicken. Their flavour is markedly better than any mass-raised chickens. Look out for French birds tucked away on supermarket shelves. They're more expensive, but I'd rather eat good chicken less often than tasteless birds every day.

If you buy a whole bird, cut off the breasts and legs with a sharp knife, and use the carcass to make a chicken broth (see page 90).

4–6 free-range chicken pieces (legs, breasts, wings), with the skin on
2–3 tablespoons extra virgin olive oil
2 cloves garlic, peeled and cut in two
Maldon sea salt
2 sprigs fresh rosemary
a glass of dry white wine (about 80–100 ml)

Wash and pat dry the chicken. Trim off any excess fat but keep the skin on. Warm the extra virgin olive oil in a heavy-bottomed frying pan. Add the garlic and slowly let it flavour the oil. Put the chicken pieces in one layer into the oil, skin side down. Let them brown well. Keep the heat fairly high so that the skin gets a good chance to brown. As soon as the skin is well browned all over, season the chicken with some sea salt and add the sprigs of rosemary.

Now put the heat up to high and add the white wine. Let it boil rapidly until all the alcohol has evaporated. (The best way to test this is to smell the steam. If there is still alcohol in it, it will sting the back of your throat.) Lower the heat and make sure the chicken is well basted with the wine. Put a lid on and let the chicken cook for 25 minutes or so until the flesh is cooked through. The wine and juices reduce to form really tasty gravy to pour over the juicy chicken.

Puglian food is lighter and more delicate than that in the north of Italy. They tend to use very little garlic, yet when they do, they often let it brown and take on a slightly bitter flavour. They prepare the chicken dish like this with 2 or 3 fresh bay leaves instead of rosemary. It's quite amazing how those two subtle changes make a marked difference to the flavour of the chicken. Try it and see.

You can prepare the chicken in exactly the same way as above, but add a ½ x 400 g tin of tomatoes and 10 g dried porcini mushrooms. Soak the porcini in a cup of warm water for 20 minutes or so first. Drain the liquid through a fine sieve and add it to the chicken as the wine is added. Wash the porcini and chop them finely, adding them with the chopped tomatoes. Add thyme or rosemary. Cook as above.

Calf's Liver with Onions
FEGATO ALLA VENEZIANA

I love calf's liver cooked very quickly like this. Try it with lots of creamy mashed potatoes. I usually make it for myself, as no-one else eats liver, so this serves one.

2 tablespoons extra virgin olive oil
1 clove garlic, peeled
1 piece peperoncino (dried chilli)
1 large red onion, peeled and thinly sliced
2 slices calf's liver, about 180 g
a splash of red wine vinegar or balsamic vinegar
Maldon sea salt and black pepper

Warm the oil in a small saucepan and gently flavour it with the garlic and chilli. Add the onion and cook it slowly until it is very soft and translucent. Be patient. It takes a good 15 minutes.

Slice the liver into strips. Use a sharp knife and trim away any gristle.

Once the onions are soft, put the heat up high and very quickly cook the liver. It takes only a few minutes to sear it in the heat. Add the vinegar and seasoning and cook it on a high heat for a further couple of minutes to reduce the juices. Add a tablespoon of hot water just to loosen the juices from the sides of the pan. Season it and serve it with a rocket and tomato salad (see page 312). The spiciness of the rocket and the sweetness of the tomato are a perfect foil.

Italian Lamb Stew
STUFATO D'AGNELLO

Francesca, as my mother, your Nonna Gertrude, had an Irish father and an Italian mother, she didn't speak Italian. They only spoke English in her house. She was however, bi-lingual in stew! Both this recipe and the following one work equally well with beef or lamb.

This is a really lovely way to cook lamb. I cook a lot of Scottish hill lamb in the spring and summer. It has a mild, sweet flavour and cooks very easily. Buy lamb local to your area from a good butcher. You'll really notice the difference. This recipe is very easy. With the potatoes and red peppers added it is a whole meal in a pot and takes no more than an hour or so to prepare.

Babies love the potatoes mashed with the gravy and a little tender lamb squashed in. It's just the sort of easy food to give them when they're starting to be interested in 'lumps'.

2–3 tablespoons extra virgin olive oil
1 clove garlic, peeled
2 onions, peeled and very finely sliced
1 kg gigot lamb chops (with the bone kept in) or lamb shoulder
Maldon sea salt and black pepper
1 x 400 g tin Italian plum tomatoes, roughly chopped
1 fresh bay leaf
2 sprigs fresh thyme
*6–8 new potatoes, peeled (or 5 King Edwards, peeled and cut
into new-potato-sized chunks)*
1 red pepper, de-seeded and sliced

Warm the extra virgin olive oil in a heavy-bottomed saucepan and flavour it with the garlic. Add the onions and cook them slowly until they start to soften.

Cut the gigot chops into pieces and trim off any excess fat. Season them well with salt and pepper. Take the onions and garlic from the oil. Raise the heat and add the lamb in batches, turning it so that it browns well. Once it is browned return all the lamb, the onions and garlic back into the saucepan.

Stir in the tin of tomatoes and bring the stew up to simmering point. Add the herbs. Cover the saucepan and let the stew cook slowly with the lid on tightly for half an hour or so, depending on the age of the lamb. (Pop it into a medium oven, at 180°C/350°F/Gas 4, if you like.)

After half an hour add the potatoes and the peppers, check the seasoning and add a cup or so of hot water (about 200 ml) if necessary. The peppers will release some juices but the potatoes will soak them up. Put the lid back on and in 25 minutes or so a magical, perfect complete supper will be ready.

You can use exactly the same recipe with best stewing steak or chicken.

Irish Stew

This recipe uses the same principles – seal in the flavour of the meat and cook it over a low heat. As always, buy the best-quality meat you can find. I prefer to use Aberdeen Angus stewing steak in the winter. Buy beef that has been well hung: twenty-one days is recommended by my butcher. It will cook very tender.

2–3 tablespoons sunflower or corn oil
2 onions, peeled and sliced
1 kg stewing steak or lamb gigot chops, cut into pieces
Maldon sea salt and black pepper

a sprig of fresh rosemary
3 carrots, peeled and sliced
3–4 small young turnips or ½ big one, peeled and cubed
5–6 new potatoes (or 4 King Edwards, peeled and cut
into new-potato-sized chunks)

Warm the oil in a heavy-bottomed saucepan and cook the
onions until they are soft and translucent. Trim any excess fat
from the meat and cut it into bite-sized pieces. Season it well
with the salt and pepper.

Take the onions out, raise the heat to high and brown the
seasoned meat in batches until it is well browned. Return the
onions and all the browned meat to the pan, and add the
rosemary. Pour in enough boiling water to cover the stew –
just enough, don't drown it.

Cook slowly in a medium oven (180°C/350°F/Gas 4), or
on top of the cooker with the lid on for 45 minutes or so.
Add the carrots, turnip and potatoes to the stew. Stir everything, adding a little more water if necessary. Check the
seasoning and cook with the lid on for another half-hour
until everything is tender.

Very good to be sure!

Steak and Kidney Pie

I have to include a recipe for my mother's steak and kidney pie.
When her catering business was at its peak she made up to 600
portions of this a week, with the help of Janet and Etta.

From as young as nine or ten, when we came home from
school we had to help at the 'caterings'. We stood like a human
assembly line, passing large white plates to each other, adding
peas, sprouts, mashed potatoes, stew and pastry. The younger

children were given the menial jobs. Promotion meant moving up the assembly line from peas to potatoes to pastry. I don't know why potatoes were considered more responsible than peas. Putting 250 spoonfuls of peas on fast-moving plates without losing half of them on the floor is a very skilled job!

1 kg best stewing steak
100 g ox kidney
1 tablespoon plain flour, well seasoned with salt and pepper
1–2 tablespoons sunflower oil
1 tablespoon Worcestershire sauce
1 dessertspoon Bisto dissolved in cold water (optional)
1 x 500 g pack Jus-Rol pastry, defrosted
a little milk and/or beaten egg

For a really tasty tender stew, make sure you buy well-hung beef. I try to use Aberdeen Angus or highland beef. Cut the beef into 3–4 cm pieces. Trim the kidney, discarding any white fibres, and cut it into small cubes. Toss the beef in the seasoned flour.

Warm the oil in a heavy-bottomed casserole dish and brown the beef in batches. Keep the heat high so that the flavours are sealed in really well. Bits of meat and flour start to stick to the sides of the saucepan. Don't worry, these will dissolve into the gravy as the stew cooks. You can add a little more oil if necessary, but I always try to use as little oil as possible.

Once all the meat is browned return it all to the saucepan. Splash it with an extra flavouring of Worcestershire sauce if you want, and add enough boiling water just to cover the beef. Loosen any bits that are stuck to the sides of the saucepan; these help to thicken and flavour the gravy. Add the kidney. Either cook the stew on a low heat for an hour or so or put the stew in a medium oven (180°C/350°F/Gas 4) for an hour or so until it is tender. Make sure you use a tight-fitting lid so that it doesn't dry out.

Check the seasoning and add a little more water if the

Johnny, far right, and Marietta, second left, and their staff at the Caterings, c.1960

gravy is too thick. Mummy used the Bisto dissolved in cold water to thicken the gravy.

Let the stew cool a little before assembling the pie. Choose a dish that will hold the stew with about 3–4 cm room to spare at the top. Roll out the pastry. Brush the sides of the dish with a little milk and put the pastry on top. I have a little ceramic blackbird that sits in the middle of my pie; its beak pushes through the middle of the pastry to let the steam escape. If you don't have a blackbird, cut a small cross on the top of the pastry to let the steam escape.

Trim the edges of the pastry and press it down around the edges. Nip the pastry with your thumb and forefinger to give a decorated edge. Score triangles on top of the pie, and give it a brush with milk or beaten egg before baking it in a hot oven (220°C/425°F/Gas 7) for 20 minutes. Lower the heat to medium (180°C/350°F/Gas 4) for another 15–20 minutes. Don't forget that you need to make sure the stew is piping hot, especially if you have made the pie the day before. Once the pastry has started to rise and brown, put a piece of foil or greaseproof paper over it to stop it burning.

Slow-cooked Lamb Shank

There is no other slow-cooked food that I enjoy more than lamb shank. The meat becomes so tender and soft it melts in the mouth. The sinews and fat around the bone melt into a creamy, sweet flavour that is surpassed only by the marrow that can be sucked unceremoniously from the bone.

A lamb shank costs no more than a couple of pounds. To make a really good flavour you need half a bottle of good white wine, but even at that, it hardly breaks the bank.

By the way, lamb shank makes lovely broth as well. Follow the beef broth recipe on page 88, or use it in the Scotch barley broth recipe (see page 86). (If the shanks are very long ask the butcher to cut the bone half way through for you otherwise they may not fit in your pot.)

2–3 tablespoons extra virgin olive oil
2 shallots, peeled and very finely diced
1 carrot, peeled and very finely diced
2 sticks celery, peeled and very finely diced
4 lamb shanks
Maldon sea salt and black pepper
500 ml dry white wine

3–4 sprigs thyme
2 fresh bay leaves

Warm the oil in a large, heavy-bottomed ovenproof casserole. Add the shallot, carrot and celery and cook them slowly to soften them. Trim the lamb shanks of any excess fat, wash and dry them. Turn the heat to high and brown the shanks well all over. If they are big you may need to do this in two batches. Be careful not to burn the soffritto of vegetables. Take them out if they are browning too much.

Once all the shanks are browned, season them well and add the wine (and vegetables if you removed them). Let it boil fast to evaporate any alcohol. When the steam no longer catches the back of the throat you know the alcohol has evaporated. Add the herbs and, covered tightly with a lid so that all the juices are trapped inside, let the pot simmer slowly on the lowest heat for 1½ hours or so. I usually put the casserole in a slow oven (160°C/325°F/Gas 3).

Once the shanks are cooked check the seasoning, adding a grinding of black pepper. If you find the gravy very oily just skim some of it off. Sometimes I use kitchen paper to blot any excess fat from the surface.

Serve sprinkled with gremolata, if you like (see overleaf).

I prefer this dish served with simple soft polenta (see page 315) or fluffy mashed potatoes – something to soak up all the lovely juices.

You can add a tablespoon of soaked salted capers and a tablespoon of stoned black olives, whole or chopped, towards the end of cooking to deepen the flavour if you like those ingredients.

Gremolata

Gremolata is a lemon and herb dressing served traditionally with 'osso buco', a stew of shin of veal. It is lovely sprinkled over the lamb shanks above.

½ clove garlic, peeled
2 teaspoons finely grated zest from a washed unwaxed lemon
1 tablespoon finely chopped flat-leaf parsley
1 tablespoon finely chopped mint
Maldon sea salt

Chop the garlic very finely. Add the lemon zest and the chopped herbs and mix everything well. Taste and season with some sea salt. Sprinkle a little over the lamb shank just before serving.

Zampone, Lentils and Mostarda di Frutta

Zampone is in many ways the Italian equivalent of the Scottish haggis. A speciality of Modena, the lean meat of specially reared pigs is flavoured with nutmeg, cinnamon and cloves and seasoned well. The mixture is then cooked after it has been packed into the skin of a trotter, three toes and toenails intact! Its origins go back to ancient times. Rather than being a way to use off-cuts and cheap pork, centuries of experience have ensured that the best cuts of top quality pork are used. As with haggis production, specific recipes are jealously guarded and passed down through generations.

These days zampone, or its simpler relative, cotechino, can be bought from some of the bigger Italian pork manufacturers prepared in an easy-to-boil foil bag. It is simply reheated in boiling water until it is piping hot. The pork is tender and sweet with a distinctive flavour.

In our family zampone is traditionally eaten at New Year with lovely Castelluccio lentils from Norcia. These beautiful grey-green lentils need no pre-soaking and keep their shape beautifully when cooked. It must be served with some spicy mostarda di frutta from Modena (see page 282).

> 1 easy-cook zampone or cotechino
> 225 g Castelluccio or Puy lentils
> 2 tablespoons extra virgin olive oil
> 1 clove garlic, peeled and sliced
> a piece of peperoncino (dried chilli), crumbled
> ½ Fonteluna spicy sausage (150 g), sliced
> ½ x 400 g tin Italian plum tomatoes
> a sprig of rosemary
> Maldon sea salt
> 1 tablespoon chopped flat-leaf parsley
> mostarda di frutta, to serve

Put the lentils into a bowl of cold water and pick out any that float to the surface. Rinse them and put them into a saucepan, covered with plenty of cold water. Bring the water to the boil and simmer the lentils slowly until they are just cooked. Drain off any excess liquid.

Warm the oil in a large frying pan. Gently sauté the garlic, chilli and spicy Fontiluna sausage. Add the tomatoes and the sprig of rosemary. Add the drained lentils and cook them in the sugo for 20 minutes or so. (If you have a piece of Parmigiano skin, wash it and cook it in the sugo to add extra flavour.) Season the lentils with salt and sprinkle the parsley on top.

Warm the zampone or cotechino in boiling water as instructed.

Make some soft polenta (see page 315) or creamy mashed potatoes, and serve the lentils with 2–3 slices of the pork and a few beautiful pieces of the mostarda di frutta.

ROASTING

Marietta and Cesidio just after they arrived in Cockenzie

By all accounts, all my grandparents had to cook with in Italy was a fire in a hearth with a pot suspended over it. They carried their dough for bread and pizza to the communal oven in the village. Deer, wild boar, rabbit or an occasional trout caught in a mountain river would be roasted on an open fire. They would judge by smell, appearance and feel when the food was ready.

Modern ovens are a luxury, but in some ways a hindrance. Written recipes set oven temperatures and cooking times fairly strictly. I sometimes think being given instructions has stunted our natural instinct to think for ourselves. Never forget that there are many variables that a written recipe can't account for: the temperature of the uncooked food, the gauge in any particular oven, the thickness of the food and the material it is being cooked in. A good cook never loses confidence in his or her own common sense in the kitchen. (I'll rephrase that, Francesca. A sober cook never loses confidence. . . . If I join in with the bubbly before lunch is served I do have a habit of losing it!) I would like to encourage you to be independent in the kitchen.

Try to think of oven temperatures in terms of the amount of heat they provide. If I want something to cook very quickly and sear in the flavour, I use a short time in a hot oven. Roasts need to be weighed and a cooking time calculated, but then keep an eye on them and pay attention to how the roasting progresses. They will keep on cooking once they come out of the oven and do benefit from a 'rest' period where the temperature evens out and the fibres get a chance to relax. Rather than drying out, the juices in a roast move back into the centre, making for a tastier flavour.

Slow, steady cooking for stews and casseroles can be achieved in a medium oven.

Gentle, delicate baking as for biscuits, meringues and baked custards do very nicely in a low oven. Baking is a much more exact science, and temperatures and timings should be more carefully adhered to, but still apply your personal experience with your own oven. Remember that cakes and bread especially need to be undisturbed for the first two-thirds of their cooking so that they get a chance to rise.

I have a fan-assisted oven and it will cook food far more efficiently and far faster than a conventional one. Having said that, I know lots of great cooks who hate using their fan-assisted ovens.

Follow the guidelines in a recipe but think about it, watch, smell, prod and pay attention. Most importantly, taste all the time. Flavours develop and change, and seasoning can make or break the flavour of any food. Once you free yourself from the tyranny of recipes and start to cook from gut feeling, you'll enjoy cooking more and I bet you'll cook better food as well.

Think of the oven as very cool, cool or low, moderate or medium, fairly hot, hot and very hot. The temperatures I use most are Gas 4, 6 and 7. Lower the suggested temperature in these recipes by 10 per cent or so if you have a fan-assisted oven.

Heat of Oven	Centigrade	Fahrenheit	Gas Mark
Slow heat, very cool	110°C	225°F	¼
Slow heat, very cool	120°C	250°F	½
Cool	140°C	275°F	1
Cool	150°C	300°F	2
Brisk heat, Moderate	160°C	325°F	3
Brisk heat, Moderate	180°C	350°F	4
Fairly hot	190°C	375°F	5
Fairly hot	200°C	400°F	6
Fast heat, hot	220°C	425°F	7
Roasting heat, very hot	230°C	450°F	8
Extremely hot	250°C	475°F	9

Roast Beef

It can't be stressed enough how important it is to buy well-raised beef from a good breed that has been well hung. I choose Aberdeen Angus or Angus beef, because I live in Scotland. Find a butcher or farmer at the farmers' markets you can trust, and ask him which breed he sells and why. Devon Red, Hereford, Galloway and Longhorn are all traditional breeds. Apart from the breed, a good butcher will hang the beef for two to three weeks. This tenderises it, softening the muscle tissues. The flesh should look a dark, deep red colour and should have a white marbling of fat through it. During the hanging the carcass loses up to 15 per cent of its moisture, and therefore its profitability (one of the reasons that well-hung beef will cost more).

If I am planning a roast beef dinner I usually let my butcher know a week or so ahead. He'll choose a good cut and hang it for me.

I love roast beef when it's caramelised and crispy on the outside but still slightly pink and juicy in the middle. With a large roast, the only way to judge how long a joint will take to cook is to weigh it and work it out. Three-quarters of the way through the roasting it's good to baste the meat and to check how things are progressing. Push a skewer into the fattest part of the joint. Pull it out and press it against the incision. Watch how the juices come out. If they're red and bloody, it's rare. If they're clear, it's definitely cooked. I like to see the juices pink. Remembering that you really should leave the roast covered in a warm place to rest, it will still cook a little as it relaxes and should be perfect when you're ready to carve it.

Remember as well, the meat on the outside will be more cooked than that on the inside. Serve those who like their meat 'well-cooked' first, and save the best for the rest! This roast will serve about eight to ten people.

3–4 kg fore-rib of beef
Maldon salt
1 tablespoon plain flour

I ask the butcher to chine the roast, leave the beef on the
bones but loosen it from the bottom, making carving easier.
Take the meat out of the fridge an hour before you're going
to cook it.

Season the roast well, rubbing a mixture of salt and flour
all over. I like to balance the roast on a rack set above a
roasting tray that will collect all the juices and fat that run
from the meat. I collect the fat a couple of times during the
roasting to make the Yorkshire puddings with. I then use the
tray with its delicious coating of crusts and juices to roast the
potatoes in, and at the end to scrape and scourge to make a
mean gravy (see page 225).

Preheat the oven to very hot (230°C/450°F/Gas 8), and
put the meat in to seal. After 15 minutes' cooking, lower the
temperature to medium hot (190°C/375°F/Gas 5). Allow 15
minutes for each 450 g for rare meat. Allow another 15
minutes if you want the roast medium rare. After this time
keep checking and judge the roast by eye. I really don't think
it's worth roasting the beef until the juices run clear. The
meat stays warm in the middle for up to an hour after you
take it out of the oven. During this time it keeps on cooking
so, if you wait until the juices run clear, you are in danger of
the meat drying out.

Half an hour before I expect the roast to be ready, I
usually give it a basting with the juices from the tray and
check how cooked the beef looks. If it is on schedule, I
throw the par-boiled potatoes, a couple of whole shallots or a
red onion, chopped into six pieces, into the tray and toss
them around in the fat.

As soon as the roast comes out, whack the heat right up to high (220°C/ 425°F/Gas 7), pop the Yorkshires on to the second highest shelf and finish roasting the potatoes. Cover the meat with foil and let it rest on top of the cooker until the potatoes are ready.

Make sure you have a very sharp knife to carve the beef. I use an electric carving knife that my friend Brenda gave me years ago. Whatever you do make sure you serve roast beef on warmed plates. If you don't have room anywhere with all the juggling, pop them into a rinse cycle of the dishwasher. It works a treat.

I love cold roast beef sandwiches with horseradish sauce, so don't mind if I've made extra. If the beef is cooked pink and rare it tastes infinitely better and moister than if it is overcooked.

Roast Leg of Lamb

I prefer hill lamb. It's healthily raised and its flavour is sweet and tender. It's easiest for me to buy Scottish lamb, but choose local lamb wherever you are. Welsh hill lamb is particularly good. I really enjoy spring lamb that comes on to the market from May onwards. We are lucky up here because the Shetland 'spring' lamb doesn't appear until August or September. Their northerly latitude results in later lambing, so good young lamb is in theory available longer.

Prepare the joint by rubbing it all over with Maldon salt and a smear of extra virgin olive oil. Make half a dozen sharp incisions in it and push a little sliver of new garlic and a sprig of fresh rosemary into each. Small pieces of anchovy can be pushed into the flesh. Used sparingly it enhances the delicate flavour of the lamb. Calculate the whole cooking time on an average of 16 minutes per 500 g for medium cooked lamb. Seal the joint first in a very hot oven (230°C/450°F/Gas 8) for 15 minutes before reducing the temperature to fairly hot (200°C/400°F/Gas 6).

As with all cooking times, use these simply as a guide. Keep an eye on the lamb and test it 25 minutes or so before you expect it to be ready. I like lamb fairly pink. Remember that if the juices run completely clear the lamb will be well done. Best to take it out of the oven before this. As with beef, cover it in foil and let it rest for 20 minutes or so in a warm place before carving.

Because the bone runs through the lamb it is a bit tricky to carve. Use a sharp knife and start on the fleshiest side, cutting down towards the bone. Hold the lamb by the ankle and move it round, cutting methodically and logically.

I often roast the lamb on a rack with a tray underneath to collect all the juices. Roast potatoes in these wonderful juices, with plenty of fresh rosemary and some whole shallots. While you are letting the cooked lamb rest, splash the potatoes all over with some balsamic or sherry vinegar, put them on to the highest shelf of the oven, and whack the heat up high. The potatoes will be crisp and crunchy, sweet and delicious, perfect with the juicy lamb.

Baked Herbed Lamb

This method of roasting lamb very quickly with lots of really wonderful flavour couldn't be easier.

1.5 kg leg of spring lamb
3–4 tablespoons extra virgin olive oil
2–3 cloves new garlic, squashed with the back of a knife
(don't bother to peel it)

2–3 sprigs fresh rosemary
4–5 sprigs fresh thyme
Maldon sea salt and black pepper
½ glass white wine (about 100 ml)

Ask the butcher to cut the lamb into pieces of about 4–5 cm, leaving the bone on. Most of the pieces will have some bone. Trim off any excess fat that there is, not much usually. Put the lamb in a bowl and coat it well with the extra virgin olive oil Add the garlic and herbs, and season it well. Cover it and leave it to marinate refrigerated for a few hours or even overnight.

Remove the lamb from the fridge an hour before cooking. Preheat the oven to hot (220°C/425°F/Gas 7).

Put the lamb into a baking tray with all the oil and the herbs. Add the wine and roast it in the oven until it is nicely browned on the outside but still pink inside. It takes only about 20 minutes. Most of the wine evaporates in the oven leaving instant gravy mixed with the juices from the lamb and the flavoured oil. This really is full of gutsy flavour. There's nothing to match sucking the meat off the bones, in a lady-like manner of course!

If the lamb is older it will take a bit longer, about 30 minutes. In which case you can roast potatoes in the same dish. Par-boil in salted water for about 15 minutes. Shake dry and add to the baking tin, coating with the oil before you pour over the wine.

Roast Chicken

Roast chicken is the easiest thing to cook. Make sure you buy a good bird. Free-range is the key, and organic or corn-fed if possible. A free-range bird will have had a life! Its bones and flesh will have built up texture, flavour and character.

An advantage of a chicken is that it is ready-made to be stuffed! The variations are limitless. As usual the simplest combinations work best.

Remove the chicken from the fridge an hour before cooking. Always remember to wash the chicken well, inside and out. Trim off any excess pieces of fat around the tail cavity. Dry it with kitchen paper. Rub the outside with extra virgin olive oil or butter and season it well, with Maldon salt and black pepper. Don't forget to season inside the bird too.

Stuff the cavity with one of the following stuffings. Fold over the flap of neck skin and use a long skewer to push through the left wing tip, twice in and out of the skin flap and through the next wing, to hold all the stuffing intact. I used to really enjoy sewing up the ends of the chicken with a large trussing needle. (I was never taught how to sew a button on a shirt but I'm a dab hand at sewing up the back end of a bird!) These days I use toothpicks, small metal skewers or just the luck of the devil. I don't always bother to tie down the legs, but if you want you can use a long piece of string to tie round the end of each leg and pull the two together.

Roast chicken in a fairly hot oven (200°C/400°F/Gas 6) for about an hour for a 1–1.5 kg bird. (Calculate 18 minutes per 500 g plus 15 minutes or so extra at the end to crisp up the skin.) I confess I never calculate the roasting time of a chicken. I just roast it until its skin is puffed up, brown and crispy, it smells appetisingly juicy, and it is spitting at me to get out of the oven.

Remember that chicken must be cooked right through. Check with a skewer pushed into the thickest part of the flesh, between the leg and the breast. The juices must run clear. If there is any sign of pink then cook the bird for another 10 minutes or so.

Lemon Stuffing

The easiest and one of the most sensational stuffings is two or three whole unwaxed lemons. Wash the lemons well, stab their skin all over with a skewer and push them into the cavity of the bird. Add some unpeeled, squashed cloves of garlic and sprigs of fresh rosemary or thyme. Smear the outside of the bird with plenty of butter and roast the chicken as above. The buttery, lemony juices are wonderful with the moist chicken and crispy skin.

Marietta's Egg and Ricotta Stuffing

250 g fresh ricotta
1 egg, beaten
3 tablespoons chopped smoked pancetta (if you want)
50 g Parmigiano Reggiano, freshly grated
1–2 tablespoons finely chopped flat-leaf parsley
1 tablespoon sultanas (if you want)
a squeeze of lemon juice
1 tablespoon fresh breadcrumbs
Maldon sea salt and black pepper

Beat all the ingredients together in a bowl, adding just enough breadcrumbs to bind. Season it well. The stuffing needs to be firm enough to stay in the cavity of the bird but not too solid, as the egg firms up as the stuffing cooks.

Remember to wash out the cavity of the bird and pat it dry. Season it inside and out and stuff with the egg mixture. Seal the ends well. Rub the chicken with oil, and season it, then roast as above.

The stuffing is sliced and served with the chicken or eaten cold in sandwiches later on.

Fennel and Butter Stuffing

Wash and trim 2 bulbs of fennel, cut the base and cut them into quarters, lengthways. Drizzle with some extra virgin olive oil, sprinkle with Maldon sea salt and roast the fennel pieces in a fairly hot oven (200°C/400°F/Gas 6) until they are softened and caramelised. Let them cool and stuff them, along with plenty of extra butter and a few sprigs of tarragon, into the seasoned cavity of the bird. Smear plenty of butter over the top of the bird and cover it with a couple of rashers of smoked bacon.

Roast it as above, taking the bacon off halfway through to let the skin brown. Enjoy.

POZZUOLI, ITALY 1957

Francesca, your dad was only four the first time he visited his Nonna Annunziata in Naples. As youngsters do, he copied everything he saw. He played with his cousins and before long spoke Neapolitan, gesticulating as wildly as a native. He trotted after Annunziata, fascinated by her slight stature, her long black skirts and the very high-heeled lace-up black shoes that she wore on her tiny feet.

Philip the chicken strangler, aged four, in Italy

Annunziata kept some chickens at the back of her house. There were about a dozen in all, squawking and scratching in a rough wire-run. A proud cockerel strutted up and down, his bad-tempered calls in the mornings wakening all the neighbours.

When Nonna needed eggs, she went down to the chicken-run and took what she needed. The scraggy chickens nipped at her ankles, the cockerel scratched at her feet. Philip was fascinated with the sweet fluffy baby chickens that scattered whenever he went near. Fearless, he quickly learned how to collect the eggs for her.

'Fili'! Prendi due uova per Nonna!'

'Si, Nonna.'

Philip would trot down to the hens and bring back two shiny, brown eggs.

Although Annunziata only cooked a chicken on special occasions – at Easter or Christmas – Carlo visiting with his son was a very special occasion. She'd cook a chicken. She went down to the chicken-run, took the plumpest bird that she'd been fattening for weeks and, without another thought, wrang its neck. She plucked it and gutted it ready for cooking. Philip watched fascinated. She thought she would roast it, stuffed with ricotta and eggs.

'Fili'! Prendi due uova per Nonna!'

'Si, Nonna.'

She waited longer than usual. 'Fili'! Fili' Louder, 'Filippo! Forza!' Where was the boy? Agitated, she rushed down to get the eggs herself.

What a racket. She heard some dreadful squawking, screeching and commotion. What's wrong with that cockerel now? As she went round the corner to the chicken-run she threw up her hands in horror. There was little Philip with half a dozen baby chicks, all ready for the pot. At four years old he showed great initiative. Just like Nonna had shown him, he had wrung all their necks!

Roast Poussin with Orvieto-style Potato and Olive Stuffing

Annunziata would never dream of eating poussin. She would consider it uneconomical to eat a bird so small when you could feed it up for months and have a lovely, plump chicken instead.

I like to use poussins because they cook quickly. Each person can get a whole bird to enjoy, the breast, crispy little legs and all the flavour of the stuffing and chewy bones. Big eaters will eat one each, but I usually share mine with Olivia. You can use this stuffing with guinea fowl or just with a normal-sized chicken.

4 poussins
extra virgin olive oil
2 cloves garlic, unpeeled, lightly bashed with the back of a knife
1 bulb fennel, trimmed and chopped
3 roasting potatoes (King Edward or Maris Piper) , peeled and roughly
chopped
1 tablespoon black olives, stoned
some of the fine herb leaves from the fennel, chopped
Maldon sea salt and black pepper
4 small sprigs fresh rosemary
150 ml dry white wine

Preheat the oven to hot (220°C/425°F/Gas 7).

Prepare the poussin stuffing. Warm 2 tablespoons of the olive oil in a wide frying pan, and gently sauté the garlic to start to flavour the oil. Add the fennel and the potato and cook them for 5–10 minutes until they start to brown, soften and take on some flavour. Remove the garlic and add the olives, the chopped fennel leaves and lots of salt and pepper.

Wash the poussins well inside and out and pat them dry. Stuff each bird with the mixture, pushing a sprig of rosemary in at the end. Close over the cavity of the bird with a couple of toothpicks. Rub some Maldon sea salt over the skin of the bird and a little olive oil. Place the birds in a roasting tin, and roast for 25 minutes. Take them out of the oven and add the wine. Baste the birds with any of the juices and, if you have any stuffing left over, add it to the roasting tin now to crisp and cook.

Cook the birds for another 15 minutes or so until they are crisp and browned. Make sure they are well cooked inside. The stuffing has to be cooked through as well, remember. Push a metal skewer into the fattest part of the bird, between the leg and thigh, to make sure that the juices run clear.

Let the birds rest a little. Serve them warm rather than piping hot. You will want to eat these with your fingers . . . . Allowed!

If you're pushed for time just rub the poussins with plenty of extra virgin olive oil and salt, stuff them with some rosemary and a ½ lemon and roast them for 35–40 minutes.

Poussins usually come wrapped in plastic. As soon as you get them home, remove it and wash the poussins, patting them dry before putting them in a sealed container in the fridge. If you intend keeping them a day or two, cut them in half down the breastbone. Trim off any loose skin or excess fat. Rub them all over with extra virgin olive oil, lemon juice and Maldon salt and store them in a sealed container in the fridge. The oil helps to seal the flesh from the air and bacteria and also acts to flavour and moisten it. Take them out of the fridge a good half-hour before grilling them under a high grill for 15 minutes each side. To make them very spicy add a lot of freshly ground black pepper.

Sticky-finger Chicken for Kids to Make a Mess With

Choose free-range organic chicken pieces. Never compromise your ingredients because you are cooking specifically for kids.

2 packs chicken wings, thighs or drumsticks
3 tablespoons sunflower oil
2 tablespoons clear honey
2 tablespoons soy sauce
1 tablespoon Dijon mustard
black pepper

Make a paste with the oil, honey, soy and mustard, adding a grinding of black pepper. Taste and adjust the seasoning. Rub all the chicken pieces in the sauce and leave refrigerated for a few hours. Remove from the fridge half an hour before roasting.

Preheat the oven to fairly hot (200°C/400°F/Gas 6). Place the chicken pieces in an ovenproof dish and roast for 25–30 minutes. Let them cool a little, then eat with sticky fingers.

Chicken Arms and Legs

If I have only one or two children to feed, I just rub four chicken drumsticks or thighs and a handful of chicken wings with extra virgin olive oil and salt and pop them in a small roasting tin with a sprig of rosemary and a squashed clove of garlic. They will roast in a hot oven in 25 minutes, just enough time to boil some potatoes. Kids love eating the chicken in their hands and always scoff the lot. It really takes no longer than chicken nuggets to heat through, but it's far tastier and, dare I say it, healthier.

Roast Pork and Crackling Crackling

I love this pork with big chunks of 'mostarda di frutta'. Mostarda is one of those fabulous products from Italy that is becoming better known here. Whole fruits, pears, cherries, figs and clementines are preserved in a sugar syrup, which has been highly spiced with mustard. The resulting condiment is sweet, hot and spicy, and the whole gleaming fruits are firm and stunning to look at. It's perfect to eat with spicy roast pork or to use as a stuffing. Serve it with roast turkey at Christmas. This recipe will serve six to eight.

2 kg rolled and boned loin of organic pork, with the rind still on
1 tablespoon extra virgin olive oil to rub on the pork
lemon juice
Maldon sea salt

SAGE PESTO

2–3 cloves fresh garlic, peeled
2 tablespoons coarse Maldon sea salt
2 tablespoons extra virgin olive oil
5 large handfuls fresh sage (don't use dried sage)
1 teaspoon black peppercorns

Ask the butcher to score the pork for you, tracing deep lines through the rind and fat. (If you do this at home, use a small, very sharp knife and make sure you don't cut right through the rind.)

Make the pesto in a pestle and mortar, or in a food processor. Cream the garlic with the sea salt. Add the other ingredients and crush everything together to make a rough paste.

Open out the pork and rub the pesto all over the inside. Roll up the pork and, using some butcher's string, tie the roll together. Start at one end, tying the string in loops spaced about two fingers' width apart. Use a second piece to tie a circle lengthways across the loops, just like sending a parcel in the post. Rub the outside of the pork with some extra virgin olive oil and some more salt. This helps the crackling to crackle! Leave it to marinate for 24 hours in the fridge. Wrap it up well in foil to prevent the fridge reeking of garlic.

Remove the pork from the fridge half an hour before roasting it. Preheat the oven to very hot (230°C/450°F/Gas 8). Roast the pork for 20 minutes to start to crisp up the crackling. Reduce the heat to fairly hot (190°C/375°F/Gas 5) and roast it for 25 minutes per 500 g. Use a skewer to test the pork. Push it into the middle of the roll, away from the crackling for ease, and check the juices that run out. They must run clear. Pork must never be eaten pink.

I usually baste the pork with a little oil or lemon juice while it's cooking to help the crackling crisp up. Check the pork 15 minutes or so before the allotted time. It must be cooked well, but will be dry if it's left in too long. Remember all joints continue to cook during the time they're resting.

Remove the string before slicing it. You need a very good knife. I use a serrated blade to help cut through the crackling.

Serve it with some mostarda di frutta and spoon over some of the juices that ooze into the roasting dish. I really like this on a bed of soft polenta (see page 315), but roast potatoes are good as well. I think roast pork cries out for greens, nice, spicy sautéed spinach or escarole, cooked with a good kick of peperoncino to stand up to the mostarda!

Classic Veal Cutlet
COTOLETTA ALLA MILANESE

It's not easy to find veal, but if you do, this is a classic and perfectly delicious way to prepare them. I serve the cutlets simply with a green dressed salad on the same plate with lots of lemon juice squeezed all over. You can use the same method to prepare pork or lamb chops.

4 veal chops, with the bone in, about 1.5 cm thick
some plain flour
Maldon sea salt and black pepper
2 eggs, lightly beaten
about 2 tablespoons dried fresh breadcrumbs

200 g butter
olive oil
2 lemons

Trim the cutlets, removing any excess fat. Cut into the edges of the fat with a sharp knife every 2 cm or so and it will stay flat while the chops are cooking. Lay each chop between two sheets of greaseproof paper and pound it with a meat tenderiser or the end of a wooden rolling pin.

Prepare three shallow bowls, one with the flour, seasoned with salt and pepper, the second with seasoned egg and the third with the breadcrumbs.

Dip each chop first in the flour, shaking any excess off, then in the egg, and finally press it into the breadcrumbs. Pat it with your hands to make sure the coating sticks. I sometimes leave them in the fridge to let the breadcrumb coating firm up a little.

Heat most of the butter in a large frying pan until it is foaming, and add a little olive oil to stop it burning. Lay the chops in the butter, maybe two at a time, and cook them over a brisk heat until they are golden brown on each side, about 3–4 minutes in all.

Have the oven heated to fairly hot (190°C/375°F/Gas 5).

Lay the browned chops on a baking sheet and put a blob of butter on top. Keep them warm in the oven while you cook the rest. I think the flavour improves if they stay in the oven for 10 minutes or so. Serve them with plenty of lemon juice.

Add 3 or 4 fresh sage leaves to the butter as the cutlets cook. Sage, butter and veal are perfect together.

Instead of bashing the veal, use a very sharp knife to slit the flesh into two. Stuff this pocket with a thin slice of fontina cheese. Breadcrumb as above and cook the same way.

I am more likely to prepare lamb chops this way, only because they are easier to get hold of. Buy double loin chops and trim away a little but not all of the fat. Coat them as above then brown them very lightly before baking them in a medium oven for 25 minutes or so. The fat of the lamb melts into the breadcrumbs and moistens them, making a very tasty supper. When I cook them like this I cover them with foil for the first 15 minutes so that they don't dry out.

You can add chopped herbs to the egg mixture to add a different flavour. Parsley, mint or rosemary will all taste very good with veal or lamb.

I prepare chicken breasts like this for visiting kids. Bash them thin with a rolling pin so that they cook very quickly. Finish them off in the oven as above.

Roasted Monkfish with Tomatoes and Wine

Monkfish is an exceptionally ugly fish and until fairly recently it was most likely tossed back into the sea or sold cheap to unscrupulous restaurateurs who breaded them and sold them as scampi. These days, the tables have turned. It is now respected as an extremely versatile, good-flavoured fish and its price has risen accordingly. It still tastes very good cooked as scampi (see page 247).

1 monkfish tail, about 1 kg
2 cloves garlic, peeled and sliced
extra virgin olive oil
Maldon sea salt and black pepper
about 16 sweet cherry tomatoes
(Pacchino are lovely if you can find them)
a few small sprigs of fresh thyme

a splash of white wine (about 150 ml)
some fresh basil leaves

You need the oven to be really hot (230°C/450°F/Gas 8). Alternatively you can grill or pan-fry the monkfish.

Ask the fishmonger to skin the monkfish for you and take out the central bone. As always, wash the fish well under cold running water to get rid of any stale water. Use a sharp knife to cut the thick flesh into cubes of about 4 cm. Make a slit in each piece of fish and insert a sliver of garlic. Rub it with the extra virgin olive oil and sprinkle with the sea salt.

Lay the cubes in a roasting dish. Add the cherry tomatoes, thyme and a drizzle of extra virgin olive oil. Sprinkle some more salt over and bake in the preheated oven for about 15 minutes until the fish starts to brown.

Add a good splash of white wine to keep the fish moist and finish roasting. This makes a natural sauce mixed with the juices from the fish.

Add a final grinding of black pepper and a few fresh basil leaves. Squash the tomatoes down with the back of a spoon, and serve the fish with all the lovely juices poured over it.

Roast Sole on the Bone

Now, Francesca, I have just one complaint. You have cost Dad and I a fortune in restaurant bills over the years. Not content with fish fingers, or even breaded haddock and chips, you have always had a taste for grilled sole on the bone, the most expensive item on the menu.

Having said that, you now are one of the few young women I know fully skilled in the art of boning a fish. What every twenty-first-century girl needs to know!

Bones are one of the big turn-offs when it comes to fish. If the cooked fish is not boned skilfully the flesh is wasted and the eating spoiled. It's easy to do it properly. It requires logic, patience a sharp knife and a side plate (see opposite).

1 whole sole on the bone (but gutted)

extra virgin olive oil

Maldon sea salt

lemon juice

Preheat the oven to very hot (230°C/450°F/Gas 8).

Wash the fish well in cold water and pat it dry. Use a sharp knife to slash the top dark coloured skin three or four times, just deep enough to open the flesh a little. Lightly oil a baking tin, large enough to hold the fish flat. Rub the fish all over with the extra virgin olive oil and sprinkle with some Maldon sea salt. Roast the fish in the preheated oven for 15–20 minutes until the skin is golden and crisp. Check the flesh in the slits that you made. When it is cooked it should be white and opaque. Use the knife and a fork to open the fish and check near the bone at the thickest part. Make sure there is no sign of blood and that the flesh comes away from the bone naturally. If it sticks to the bone then the fish is not cooked enough. Pop it into the oven for another 5 minutes.

Be careful not to overcook the fish, or it will become dry and dull. Remove the fish with a wide spatula on to a warmed plate. Pour on any juices from the roasting tin. Serve with large wedges of lemon.

BONED MADAM?

To bone the fish, look at the problem logically. Use a small sharp knife and have two plates ready, a side plate to take the debris, and a separate warmed plate for the fish.

Firstly ease away any of the outside fins on each side, pulling gently so that you take away any bones that are attached. Next slide the knife under the top skin and ease it off, revealing two sections of white flesh of the fish. Watch for excess bones. One at a time, ease the knife under the white flesh and gently lift it away from the skeleton. Put this flesh on a separate warmed plate.

Next it should be quite easy to lift away the head and the whole skeleton of the fish. Ease the knife gently under the bones from the tail end first and the whole skeleton will lift away in one piece. This will reveal clearly the bottom fillets of the fish that lie under the skeleton. These can easily be lifted from the bottom skin and on to the warmed plate. As with all things, this takes a bit of practice. Once you've cracked it, you'll enjoy fish on the bone as a real treat.

Practice makes perfect.

Roast Sea Bass

You can roast most whole fish in exactly the same way as the sole above. Try sea bream or sea bass. They are very fleshy and juicy, though a bit more expensive. These are gutted along the side leaving a cavity just crying out to be flavoured. Sprinkle some sea salt and pack some stems of rosemary and thyme into the side. A couple of wedges of lemon can be pushed in as well.

Make a couple of slashes on the surface of the skin and rub it with Maldon sea salt and drizzle it with extra virgin olive oil. You can add a splash of white wine as well.

Roast the sea bass on a greased baking tray in the hot oven as before for 20–25 minutes until its skin is crisp and cooked. Check if the flesh is cooked near the bone in the same way and serve the fish with all its juices.

It is easier to pull out the lemon and herbs and pull away the head before trying to get the flesh off the sea bass. Cut away the bones along the backbone then take the skin off the top fillet. The white flesh is revealed as before. Ease it off, pull away the skeleton and the underside white flesh is clearly seen underneath.

Roast Sardines

If you see fresh sardines or herring ask the fishmonger to gut and de-scale them. Wash them well inside and out and pat them dry with kitchen paper. Season them with salt and pack a punch of fresh thyme or lemon thyme into the cavity at the side. Slide a couple of wedges of lemons into them and lay them on to a baking tray. Drizzle with extra virgin olive oil and roast them in the hot oven as above for 15 minutes or so until they are charred and crisp.

Serve warm with more lemon juice squeezed over them and with a gutsy green salad. Very cheap and easy.

Garlic Butter Langoustines

This has to be the best-ever treat you can make at home. Easy to prepare once you get the knack and a doddle to cook. I'll only buy langoustines or Dublin Bay prawns if they are alive. It's the only way to make sure they're spanking fresh. It goes without saying, eat them the day you buy them. You need at least ten per person; it's no good skimping.

Lay the langoustines on a work surface with the rounded back facing towards you. Put a small sharp pointed knife into the top of the shell, just below the head, and cut through the shell, right down to the end. With the length of your two thumbs along each side of the shell, pull it apart, opening the prawn out like a butterfly.

You will see a black vein running down the back. Wash out the vein and rinse the prawn. They sometimes have deep green sludge behind the head. This can just be washed away. (I usually twist the tail and pull it out before I cut the prawn open, see page 247.) Use which method you feel most comfortable with.

Make garlic butter for 20 prawns with 125 g soft butter, 2 cloves garlic, very finely chopped, and 3 tablespoons very finely chopped flat-leaf parsley. Mix this all together to make a paste. (Double this for 40 prawns.)

Marietta, left, with a Cockenzie fishwife, c.1950

Spread some into the flesh of each prawn. As you work, lay them on a wire rack on a baking tray or on a grill tray, flesh and garlic butter facing up to the heat. The shell acts as natural plate to hold the deliciously buttery juices as they melt.

Roast these in a very hot oven (230°C/450°F/Gas 8), or alternatively grill them under a very hot grill. Depending on how much heat you apply they'll take 10–15 minutes until the flesh is cooked to a glistening white, the shells are slightly charred and they are dripping with sweet, delicious garlic butter.

Serve with lemon wedges and a bib! They can only to be eaten with friends or lovers. You really need to 'sook' out all the juices from the head and the shells to get the best from these stunning shellfish.

Roast Vegetables

The great discovery of the late twentieth century in Britain was that vegetables taste a million times better roasted instead of boiled. How this was such a surprise is a mystery.

You can roast potatoes, parsnips, baby turnips, pumpkin, red onions (very delicious), spring carrots, courgettes, peppers, asparagus, tomatoes, aubergines, beetroots, mushrooms, fennel . . . the list is endless. There is no secret, just a few logical guidelines. Try roasting different vegetables and experiment with flavours and textures.

Wash and prepare the vegetables, cutting them into similar-sized pieces, not more than 3 cm thick.

Peel those that you want, though the skins often taste good roasted.

Par-boil those root vegetables that are very hard: potatoes, turnips, parsnips. This simply means part-cooking them, putting them in boiling salted water and simmering them for 5 minutes or so. Drain them well.

Preheat a very hot oven, for roast means roast (230°C/450°F/ Gas 8).

Coat the vegetables well with full-flavoured oil. I use extra virgin olive oil because it copes well with high temperatures and doesn't burn.

Season them well with sea salt. Add pepper later to keep the flavour.

Add extra layers of flavour as you like: a couple of whole cloves of garlic just squashed with the back of a knife, a couple of whole shallots with their skin still on, sprigs of rosemary or thyme or a couple of bay leaves. Resist the temptation to use everything under the sun. One or two strong flavours is much more effective.

Roasting takes about 20–25 minutes. Well-roasted vegetables are sweet, juicy and slightly charred at the edges.

Roasted vegetables are good served at room temperature. Add any juices from the roasting tin or dress with more extra virgin olive oil.

Add a final dressing of chopped flat-leaf parsley or torn basil leaves to lift the final flavour.

You can add a splash of red wine or balsamic vinegar to the roasting tin towards the end of cooking to add a further layer of sweetness and taste.

GRIDDLING

Cesidio, c.1935

Food seared over the intense heat of a griddle produces a rustic, distinctive flavour. It's a fairly modern fashion, but its roots go back centuries.

If you buy a new griddle, make sure you season it properly. It's not complicated. Washing in hot soapy water and heating it with some oil for 15 minutes or so, allowing it to cool and wiping it with a kitchen towel, is the usual advice. After you've used it, just soak it in warm soapy water and wipe it dry.

Griddling on steady heat gives an almost barbecued flavour to food. It cooks fairly quickly and produces the distinctive diagonal stripes that add contrast in flavour to the food. As it doesn't require much in the way of oil or butter to lubricate it, you could call it healthy cooking.

I have to be honest. There is a major drawback. If you don't have a good flow of air in your kitchen and a strong extractor fan, you run into the possibility of having the fire brigade pop in for supper every time you cook. (Not necessarily a bad thing.) Griddling can produce a horrendous amount of smoke.

A griddle needs a long warm-up, a good 20 minutes on high before using it. After that lower the heat to medium and it will maintain its heat well. Be aware that the griddle will always be hotter at the point where the heat hits it, and cooler at the edges. You can use this to move the food around as it cooks.

Barely oil the surface of the side of the food that is going to be griddled. If I'm griddling meat, lamb or bacon, I don't oil it at all. The fat will quickly melt down and lubricate the griddle naturally. Always griddle fish or chicken skin side down.

Strongly resist the temptation to play around with the food. Leave it until it lifts away naturally from the griddle. This takes longer than you think and you may be tempted to doubt my advice and yank the food up in a panic. Don't. That's what makes the food stick. As it cooks the bottom of the food forms a natural ridged crust that lifts naturally from the griddle in its own time.

The food will cook three-quarters of the way through on the first side. When you turn it, simply sear it on the other side for a few minutes. If the food is cooking too quickly move it to a cooler part of the griddle and turn the heat down. To get a real outdoor taste – and this is the bit that makes the smoke – once it's cooked, I season the food with Maldon salt, splash it with extra virgin olive oil and douse it with a good squeeze of lemon juice just before I take it off the griddle. You can add these flavourings once the food is off the griddle, which makes less smoke and mess!

Big Phil's Steak Sandwich

Francesca, there's nothing in the world that gets more 'brownie points' with the boys than a well-griddled, juicy steak served in half a French baguette, stuffed with plenty of salad and lots of hot mustard.

There's no work or effort to griddling a good steak . . . the only effort is in finding a good butcher to buy it from. Well-reared, well-hung meat is tasty, juicy and good to eat. Price is not a reliable indication of how it will taste. The cut and thickness of the steak will make a difference as well. Experiment. See what you like, but again, speak to the butcher. One day his sirloin may be in the best condition, another he may recommend the rib eye or 'heuk' bone. By the way, I never freeze steak. It loses moisture as it defrosts and inevitably some of its juiciness with it.

The advantage of using the griddle is that you can char and scorch the outside of the meat quickly, sealing the juices and flavour inside.

1 x 200–300 g sirloin, rib-eye or fillet Aberdeen Angus steak
extra virgin olive oil
a few slivers of garlic
Maldon sea salt and black pepper
lemon juice

TO SERVE
½ *baguette*
shredded lettuce
hot English mustard

Preheat the griddle on a high heat for 20 minutes.

Take the steak from the fridge and bring it back to room temperature while the griddle is heating. Barely wipe one side of the steak with extra virgin olive oil. Make a couple of cuts on the other side and push in a couple of slivers of garlic.

Reduce the heat to medium and place the steak on the griddle, oiled side down. The steak needs to hit the griddle where it is well heated. Leave it to griddle for 5–6 minutes. Let the steak form its own crispy barrier to the heat. Don't pull it from the griddle to turn it until it comes away easily. If you try to turn it and it wants to stick, leave it. In a few minutes it will lift away easily.

Turn the steak, add Maldon sea salt and freshly ground pepper to the cooked side, and let the meat just sear on the bottom for a minute before lifting it off on to a warmed plate. I usually judge how the steak is cooked by cutting into it. If you don't want to, you have to judge it by pressing it with your finger.

Very rare: *cook the meat only until it is seared on both sides. When pressed it is very soft. Inside it is 'blue' or, in other words, raw.*

Rare: *the meat should be soft and a little bit springy when pressed and will be well seared on both sides but pink and juicy inside. (That's the way I like it.)*

Medium: *the meat will start to feel firm when pressed and will have a slight resistance to the pressure. Inside it will have started to change to brown, with the middle still showing pink flesh, but no blood. (That's the way Big Phil likes his!)*

Well done: *very firm when pressed and well cooked inside. There should be no sign of pink or blood, but unfortunately this can also mean it will be less juicy. Some people like steak like this and it is probably the hardest to cook without ruining it.*

Absolutely ruined: *I've done that!*

Once you've decided that the steak is cooked the way you want, drizzle a little extra virgin olive oil over it to catch the juices. A good squeeze of lemon juice can add a great lift to its flavour. Leave the steak on a warmed serving dish for a minute or so just to let it rest. Cut it in two lengthways and lay it in the baguette. Add plenty of shredded salad leaves and a good smear of hot mustard. Big Phil's treat.

When I griddle a fillet steak I serve it cut into three or four slices just to show the crispy, blackened skin and the red juicy meat inside.

To taste a shade of heaven, drizzle the steak after it's cooked with a teaspoon of aceto balsamico tradizionale (see page 50). It's indescribably good.

A wonderful alternative to beef is venison. Well-hung farmed Scottish venison is packed with flavour and is incredibly juicy and flavoursome. Cook it in the same way as steak on the griddle.

Burn-your-finger Chops
BRACIOLETTE SCOTTADITTO

In Rome they griddle very tiny chops from baby, milk-fed lamb extremely quickly on a hot griddle. They need so little cooking once they're laid on the heat, and after a few minutes they're quickly turned with the fingers to griddle the other side. Hence the name, 'burn-your finger chops'!

Griddled chops must have the fat crispy and well cooked.

Choose cutlets, where most of the fat has been trimmed away from the bone. I cook them on the griddle but unless the lamb is very young, it's probably just as easy to grill them.

3 new season's lamb cutlets per person
extra virgin olive oil
fresh rosemary
slivers of garlic
Maldon sea salt

It's worth adding a little extra flavour to the lamb. I usually cut a little slit in the flesh and squeeze in a sliver of garlic, a sprig of fresh rosemary and a drizzle of extra virgin olive oil. Make sure the griddle or grill is well heated.

Cook the chops on one side until the fat is nicely crisped. Move them around the heat if they are cooking too fast. Turn and cook on the other side. When crisp on both sides, sprinkle them with Maldon sea salt.

These take only 4–5 minutes to cook, depending on how thick they are. Don't over-do it. The flesh should still be pink and juicy inside.

Griddled Tiger Prawns

All children love the sweet flavour of prawns. They enjoy the deal that comes with prawns when they're brought to the table. You can break all the rules. You can eat with your fingers, you can 'sook' and slurp, you can make a mess and you can cost your parents a fortune . . .Cool!

Heat the griddle for 20 minutes on high, and then reduce the heat to medium.

Offer 8–10 grey tiger prawns per person, and wash them

Margherita and Domenico Crolla, aged two and three

well under cold water. Use a sharp knife to slit round the back from head to tail, just cutting through the shell and into the flesh and no more. Open out the shell a little and pull away the dark intestinal vein. Wash them again and pat them dry.

When the griddle is hot, turn the heat to medium and lay the prawns on in a single layer. They will gradually turn pink as they cook and then the shells take on a wonderful charred, toasted look. At this stage, turn each prawn to char the other side.

We love these just as they are, with no seasoning or added flavours. The pure sweet taste of the prawn is delicious. Or alternatively you can jazz them up.

Sprinkle on some Maldon sea salt and a good squeeze of lemon juice.
    Drizzle them with extra virgin olive oil and lemon juice.
    Serve them with home-made salsa verde (see page 226).
    Make an easy chilli-garlic butter. Chop a clove of garlic really fine. De-seed a fresh red or green chilli and slice it in fine slivers. (Don't rub your eyes.) Heat the garlic and chilli in some butter. Once it starts to smell fantastic take it from the heat and add a couple of table-spoons of chopped coriander leaves. Pour this over the griddled prawns with a squeeze of lemon or lime juice.

Griddled Wild Scottish Salmon

Lots of people prefer to eat fish that is filleted. The fear of being choked to death is a valid one! Fleshy fish like salmon, trout or sea bass can be filleted or cut into steaks but with the skin left on. The skin will char well on the griddle and act as a protection for the delicate fillet. It has a lovely crisp flavour.

I eat salmon very rarely, but if I do I choose wild. Its flavour and texture are far superior to farmed. Ask the fishmonger to cut fillets from the middle cut of the salmon, leaving the skin on.

Check that there are no bones left by pressing over the flesh with your fingers. Any stray bones can be yanked out with some sterilised tweezers.

4 wild salmon fillets, about 175 g each
Maldon sea salt
extra virgin olive oil
lemon juice
fresh dill

Preheat the griddle on high for 20 minutes or so, then turn it down to medium.

As always, wash fish well in cold running water before you cook it. Pat it dry with kitchen paper. Rub a little salt over the fish and a very little oil.

Now the easy part! Put the fish, skin side down on to the griddle. Let the fish cook through from the skin up. The skin will become crispy, charred and tasty, the flesh gently cooking from the bottom up, staying moist and sweet.

Watch the flesh on the side of the fillet. The colour will gradually change from raw bright pink to opaque pink. When it has changed colour two-thirds of the way up the fillet, turn the salmon over, sear the other side, and then take it off the griddle immediately. The salmon is moist and sweet if it is not overcooked. Don't be afraid to stop cooking while the flesh is still a little raw inside. It will still cook after it has left the heat source. The contrast with the crispy skin and the soft flesh is a treat.

Drizzle the fish with extra virgin olive oil. Add another sprinkling of Maldon salt, a good squeeze of lemon juice and some very finely chopped dill.

I like to serve this with home-made dill and lemon flavoured mayonnaise in my dreams, but I usually just have a green salad and new potatoes.

Use lime juice and coriander instead of the lemon and dill, and drizzle with a little soy sauce mixed with some sesame oil and a few strips of ginger.

You can cook fillets of sea bass or sea bream very successfully on the griddle with a bit of practice. Wipe the skin side with a little oil. Don't panic if the skin sticks. The worse thing you could do is to try to scrape the fish off. Wait another minute or so and the skin will eventually become charred and lift off easily. It tastes delicious like this, just as if it has been barbecued. The fish will almost completely cook from the bottom up: you just turn it to sear the top, and make sure it's cooked enough. These are strong-flavoured, slightly oily fish and really go well with salsa verde (see page 226) or just lots of lemon juice.

Trout and sea trout fillets cook easily like this as well. Always apply them skin side down.

Griddled Squid

Squid is one of those fish that we eat by the ton in Europe on holiday but are afraid to cook with at home. Don't be. Once it's cleaned, it's the easiest fish to cook, and better still, it's very cheap. Ask the fishmonger to clean it for you, but really, it's worth trying to clean it at home. It's a culinary adventure.

Marietta, third from right, at a Cockenzie fish market, 1925

When you get the squid home, clean it right away. Don't tuck it at the bottom of the fridge and wish you hadn't bought it. Working at the sink with the cold water running, pull the head and tentacles gently from the tubular body. With a firm yank the whole thing, grunge and all, comes away.

Deal with the pouch first. Inside you will find a strange clear cartilage that looks like a piece of plastic. Just pull this 'pen' away and bin it. Wash the inside of the tube well, pulling out any matter that is left. (I've found the odd sardine in here on occasion!) There may be a marbled grey film on the outside of the pouch. Just ease this away. Trim away the fins. These can be sliced and eaten. Use a sharp knife to cut the tube into rings, rinsing them as you work. Alternatively, you can open out the tube, cut it into four flat pieces and score the outside surface diagonally.

Now deal with the tentacles and the head. Behind the tentacles lies a little black 'beak'. Twist this away, discarding it with the intestines and the head. This is where the black ink is stored. Watch out, if you pierce it it'll splash all over you. You'll now be left with the familiar-looking tentacles. Cut them into easy-sized pieces and finally pull away any loose grey outer skin.

Now you can cook them. The easy part!

Heat the griddle to high for 20 minutes then lower it to medium.

Salt the squid, add a little oil and griddle it on both sides until it is charred and slightly blackened at the edges. It'll take no more than 5 minutes.

Put it on a warm serving plate and dress it with extra virgin olive oil, green fresh chilli, de-seeded and sliced, lots of lemon juice and a good handful of fresh coriander leaves. You can add a few slivers of fresh ginger as well. Lovely.

Scallops with Caper and Herb Butter

We sometimes get fresh scallops that have been harvested by divers on the west coast of Scotland. They come in their shells, the only way I buy scallops, and are so fresh they almost bite your finger off when you try to prize them open.

If the fishmonger doesn't open them for you, simply prize the shell open, by slipping a sharp knife inside the base of the shell and cut the tight muscle, to free the scallop. Rinse away any sand or grit and use a sharp knife to cut away the black tract that runs along the side of the flesh. Keep the glorious pink coral attached.

Scallops need very quick cooking, over-cooking makes them tough.

5–6 shelled scallops per person
a smear of extra virgin olive oil
a blob of unsalted butter
1 clove garlic, peeled and finely chopped
1 tablespoon salted capers, soaked for 20 minutes and rinsed
chopped herbs (parsley, mint and coriander)
Maldon sea salt
lemon juice

Heat a griddle or heavy frying pan until it's very hot. Add a smear of olive oil and lay the scallops on. Add the butter, garlic and capers and cook the scallops for 2 minutes on each side, depending on how thick they are.

At the last minute add the chopped herbs and a sprinkling of Maldon salt. A squeeze of lemon juice finishes it off.

Green Eggs and Ham

Francesca, I remember the first book you learned to read alone was Dr Zeuss's Green Eggs and Ham. It was first published over twenty-five years ago and is still going strong. We used to giggle at the thought of green eggs. They were such a revolting idea.

I think he was anticipating the organic movement. His green eggs were just that – organic, free-range, beautifully flavoured eggs, laid by 'green' hens kept by organic farmers. I am completely converted to organic eggs. They are wonderfully flavoured, rich and sweet with glorious golden yolks. I usually buy them from a farmers' market or a good butcher's shop. Small producers who can't supply the supermarkets have the best eggs.

The nicest way to eat gammon is to griddle it, either on a griddle or under a medium grill. The slightly charred, smoky flavour is delicious with the sweetness of the pork.

1 free-range pork or gammon steak
2 free-range organic eggs
a little sunflower oil

Heat a griddle until it is nice and hot and then lower the heat to medium. Use a sharp knife to cut into the edge of the gammon right round every few centimetres to stop it curling up while cooking.

Griddle the gammon for about 5 minutes on each side so that it is charred at the edges. If you have a flat part to the griddle, add a little oil and cook the eggs on it as well. If not, heat a little oil in a frying pan, break the eggs into it and cook them until they are crisp at the edges but golden yellow and runny on top. Flip the oil a little over the yolk just to set it.

There you go. Green eggs and ham!

SALADS

'Pe' condì bene l'insalata ce vanno quattro persone: un sapiente pe' mettece er sale, un avaro l'aceto, uno sprecone l'ojo, e un matto che la mischi e che la smucini.'

'It takes four people to make a salad properly: a wise man to add the salt, a miser to put in the vinegar, a spendthrift for the oil and a madman to toss it.'

Hugh Hilley kept fit training regularly

For as long as I can remember we've eaten salad every day. It usually was made of the central, paler leaves from a curly endive, leaves of chicory and some chopped celery and carrots. The whole thing was dressed at the last minute, with a ritual that has never changed. A good sprinkling of sea salt, a splash of red wine vinegar and a far longer drizzle of extra virgin olive oil. I don't know who stood in for the madman, but it was always tossed well with a stainless-steel spoon and fork.

There are so many different lettuces and leaves available these days, we're spoiled for choice. I know the bags of mixed salads you can buy are very handy, and I do use them now and then, but really, there's no comparison to fresh leaves snapped from a head of lettuce. (By the way, these salads in the bags should still be washed, even though they claim to be ready to use. They can still harbour nasty bugs.)

If you are going to get into the habit of eating salad every day then it really is worth buying whole heads of lettuce, storing a couple of different varieties at the bottom of the fridge and pulling off leaves as you need them. It's cheaper for a start, but the salad tastes so much crisper and fresher.

You are more likely to find good lettuces and salads away from the supermarket shelves. Local fruit shops, neighbours' allotments and farmers' markets are all good sources. Look out for cos lettuce, little gem, frisée, Belgian endive or chicory, bitter greens and curly endive. I stick to two or three kinds at any time. Tear out the leaves you want to use, a few from each head, wash them and refresh them in iced water for 10 minutes or so. Shake them dry in a salad spinner if you have one, or in a colander.

When I was young, I remember salad leaves having plenty of flies and slugs in them. We used to soak them in salted water. The bugs floated to the top. The water with the bugs was siphoned off and the leaves were then rinsed. These days, salads and lettuces are suspiciously free of bugs. There has been a bit of worry recently about pesticide remains on lettuce, so if you can, choose organic. Always wash them well, the salt trick works a treat.

Herbs add a real lift to salad. A few chives, chopped, some parsley leaves or a few leaves of fresh coriander add character. A few sprigs of peppery wild rocket can bring a salad to life. I don't like raw onions in salad, but if you do, soaking them in a couple of changes of cold water leaves them sweeter.

Basically any mixture of leaves, herbs and raw vegetables constitute a good salad. Be inspired by what you see in the shops and get into the habit of eating salad every day, especially in the winter. I often serve salad with grilled meat or chicken on the same plate. The juices from the dressing mix with the juices from the meat. It's really easy and very appetising.

Salad Dressing

This will dress a bowl of leaves to serve about two people.

Maldon sea salt
1 tablespoon balsamic vinegar or red wine vinegar
3 tablespoons extra virgin olive oil

Make sure the leaves are washed and dry. Put them in a nice big bowl. Sprinkle them with salt, about 2–3 pinches. Add the vinegar, judging a tablespoon rather than measuring it. Add the extra virgin olive oil, and with a large spoon and fork, toss everything together really well.

Taste the salad and adjust the flavour, as you like. Eat the salad as soon as it's dressed otherwise the leaves go flabby and insipid.

Raw Courgette Salad

a handful of rocket leaves
4 small courgettes, chilled, washed, patted dry and sliced into thin
rounds
Maldon sea salt and black pepper
extra virgin olive oil
lemon juice
shavings of Parmigiano Reggiano

Wash the rocket and break off the stalks. Spin dry. Put the courgette rounds and rocket leaves into a serving bowl. Sprinkle with Maldon sea salt. Add 2–3 tablespoons extra virgin olive oil and a good squeeze of lemon juice. Give the salad a good toss so that everything is well coated with the dressing.

Add a generous amount of Parmigiano shavings and a good grinding of black pepper. Eat right away.

Winter Sardinian Camone Tomato Salad

Sardinian Camone tomatoes are unappealingly small, slightly green and thick skinned, but have a startlingly crisp bite and exquisite sweet flavour. They arrive in season at the very end of winter and are a real treat. I serve them with a young Sardinian pecorino, a delicious contrast to the tomatoes.

250 g Camone tomatoes
extra virgin olive oil
Maldon sea salt
young pecorino cheese, Sardinian if possible
fresh basil leaves

Wash the tomatoes and cut them into quarters. Lay them on a plate and toss them in some extra virgin olive oil and sea salt.

Cut the pecorino into thin slices and remove the rind. Arrange on the tomatoes, drizzle some more olive oil on top, and dress with a few basil leaves.

Serve any good flavoured tomatoes like this. I sometimes add some frisée lettuce and a splash of balsamic vinegar.

Summer Tomato Salad of Nerino Tomatoes

In the summer the tastiest tomatoes are kept for salad. The Nerino plum tomatoes from Sardinia have all the qualities a raw tomato should have: crisp and sweet, tart and full of flavour. They are cut into long, thin slices and dressed simply with olive oil and salt. They are not widely available in Britain, but small producers are growing good-flavoured tomatoes. Look out for different varieties and choose the one you like. A sure bet for flavour are tiny cherry tomatoes grown on the vine.

I simply dress tomatoes with Maldon sea salt, extra virgin olive oil and either a sprinkling of oregano or fresh basil.

I leave my tomatoes in my fruit bowl. They ripen nicely and their flavour improves. Don't put them in the fridge.

Rocket and Tomato Salad

a large bunch of wild rocket
Maldon sea salt
balsamic vinegar
extra virgin olive oil
4–5 tasty tomatoes, cut into quarters

Rinse the rocket and trim off any long stalks or discoloured leaves. Spin it or dry it to get rid of any water. Sprinkle with some salt, a splash of vinegar and a good drizzle of extra virgin olive oil. Toss everything so that the leaves are well flavoured. Taste and check.

Add the tomato quarters and gently coat them in the dressing. Serve right away. This salad is very good with grilled meats or griddled liver. Try it too with the liver recipe on page 256.

Shredded Carrot Salad

4–5 organic carrots
2–3 tablespoons extra virgin olive oil
Maldon sea salt
lemon juice

Simplicity is best. Peel and shred the carrots into long thin strands.

Dress them with the extra virgin olive oil, salt and a squeeze of lemon juice.

TRADITIONS, FEASTS
AND FASTS

Francesca, right, and her cousins Daniela and Natascia

Francesca, even after a century, the Italian immigrants living in Scotland today still keep ancient traditions and feasts alive. Second, third and fourth generation Scottish-Italians still prepare the same foods and recipes that were brought from Italy, many that have been prepared the same way for hundreds of years. Many are prepared on high days and feast days, those days that families still congregate together: picnics, parties, birthdays and Christmas.

The recipes can be prepared every more authentically today than when the immigrants first tried to make them in Scotland. With modern transport links to Europe the ingredients are far more widely available. The recipes and flavours are also widely familiar in Britain, not just with those of Italian origins: pizza, frittata and polenta are now part of every-day culture. These were all special fasting and feasting foods that were made on special occasions throughout the year. I wonder if our great-grandparents and grandparents realised that when they came with their thousands of compatriots to another country to start a new life that they would have such an effect on the food culture of that country ...

FAST FOOD

FRANCESCA, I CAN'T REMEMBER EATING POLENTA WHEN WE WERE young. I really think it reminded our families of poverty and hardship and wasn't celebrated in their homes. Maybe I'm right because in the Crolla house it is still the dish traditionally prepared for religious feasts of Fast and Abstinence, 'Il Pranzo del Purgatorio', 'the Purgatorial Lunch'!

Since I have been married, your dad's mum, Olivia, has sent him a bowl of polenta with greens and a plate of baccalà with prunes every Ash Wednesday and Good Friday. This, no doubt, is to help him cope with the strain of fasting. No matter that both dishes are his favourites of all time!

His Purgatory is that his mother doesn't cook them for him every day, and on these two days a year his extra hardship is remembering how well she cooks! Both recipes come directly from the Crolla kitchen in the Fontitune.

Francesca, one day, if you see your poor dad fasting, you're now obliged to cook them for him.

Soft Polenta with Bitter Greens
TORDIGLIONE

Francesca, Roman coins have been found in the Fontitune area, dated the Republic of Rome 509 BC-30 AD. More have been found nearby in the waters of Canneto, near the Monte Meta, where Hannibal and his Carthaginians fought the Roman legions in 216 AD.

The hamlets of I Ciacca and Fontitune may well have dated from these times. For centuries the population of these remote villages lived free from authority and preserved the language of the golden age of Rome with spoken Latin, unaffected by outside influences. The dialect spoken today still has many hundreds of traditional Latin words. In fact at the beginning of the last century many of the women, who rarely left the village, spoke virtually no Italian at all, only the Latin dialect.

Hand in hand with this comes a heritage of dishes with roots in Roman times which has remained unchanged. Local dialect words can be traced back directly to Latin. Words like 'fressora', a frying pan, is 'frixoria' in Latin. In Italian it's 'padella'. 'Sisimegle' is our dialect for a cake. The Latin is 'sesaminus'. The Italian, 'torta'. The Fontitune polenta is called 'tordiglione'. The Latin word, 'tordilion', is mentioned in Plinus Secundus AD 79 as a 'green' polenta. In Italian these days it is called simply 'polenta verde'. There are hundreds of words that have a similar fascinating connection. Your sweet Uncle Dominic and brilliant Uncle Victor Crolla, Maria and Alfonso's sons, have spent many years studying these words and have accumulated evidence firmly linking the dialect and recipes directly to Roman times.

The original method of cooking the tordiglione mixes the polenta with water and salt. When it is soft and smooth, a soffritto of garlic, olive oil, peperoncino and bitter wild greens is stirred in. The polenta was most probably set on the wooden table and left to solidify in a green mound. It would have been taken in slabs cold, by the men folk when they went to tend the sheep.

Today, the men folk, your dad and his brother, 'young' Victor, take it with them when they go to tend their shop!

1.4 litres water
Maldon sea salt
220 g coarse-grained polenta (bramata, not instant polenta)
GREENS
500 g bitter greens (curly endive, cime di rapa, kale or spinach)
4–5 tablespoons extra virgin olive oil
2–3 cloves garlic, peeled and finely chopped
peperoncino (dried chilli), crumbled

For the polenta, bring the water to a steady simmer in a large, heavy-bottomed saucepan. Salt it to taste. 'Rain' the polenta slowly in a very fine stream into the water, using a balloon whisk to stir the water in a steady, anti-clockwise direction. Not unlike making porridge, the idea is to make sure the grains are pretty evenly distributed in the water so that, as they start to swell, the polenta is smooth and not lumpy. If you add the polenta all at once, the temperature of the water falls and all the fine grains solidify into a solid lump.

Keep stirring. As it takes on a smooth porridge-like consistency, you can stop worrying! It almost looks like a volcano as it plops and bubbles violently. Take care. It can scald. Reduce the heat and continue cooking, stirring intermittently until it starts to leave the sides of the saucepan. Don't be afraid to add a little more hot water if it gets too thick.

Wash and trim the greens in plenty of changes of cold water to get rid of any grit. Shred them. If they are very coarse you will need to cook them in boiling salted water for

10 minutes or so. Drain them and squeeze out any excess water. If the leaves are tender, like young curly endive or spinach, you can wash them and cook them straight in the oil.

Warm the extra virgin olive oil in a large frying pan. Add the garlic and peperoncino, 4–5 broken pieces to taste, and warm them through to start to flavour the oil. The smells are very appetising. Add the drained greens and put a lid on. Lower the heat and let the greens soften down. Salt to taste.

When the polenta is cooked, and it should be fairly soft and runny, add this mixture of greens, stirring them and all the flavoured oil into it. This is a very traditional flavour, especially if the greens you use are very bitter. It's an acquired taste, but very delicious.

Not traditional at all, my sister Carina adds 4–5 heaped tablespoons of roughly grated fontina cheese from the Alto Adige, north-east Italy. This adds a creamy, decadent flavour to the dish, maybe more like the rich Romans would have eaten!

The polenta can be served with a tomato sugo (see page 157) or simply with the fontina and some Parmigiano stirred in at the last minute.

You can let the polenta set, whether the greens have been added or not. Spread it out on a flat plate and leave it covered with some clingfilm or a sheet of greaseproof paper to cool. It will set solid. (The Scots folk did exactly the same with porridge. They apparently poured it into a drawer in the kitchen. They then cut slices and gave it to the men to eat for their lunch.)

Cook slices of set polenta on a warmed griddle or under a hot grill. Drizzled with some extra virgin olive oil it takes on a wonderful crustiness on the outside but becomes creamy and fluffy inside. Serve it dressed with the roasted vegetables on page 292, or with the chanterelle trifolati on page 208.

Salt Cod with Prunes
BACCALA CON PRUGNE

This is another traditional fasting dish that is prepared the day before feast days.

Baccalà or salt cod was used in the mountains as a valuable source of protein over the winter. The salt cod was most likely traded for pecorino, ricotta or sheepskins when the shepherds made their yearly pilgrimage to the coast for lambing.

There were strict rules of abstaining from meat on Fridays and during the fast periods before Easter and Christmas set out by the Catholic Church. A cynical person may suggest that this was more likely to do with controlling the food supply and fishing rights than strictly for religious reasons. Records show that the Romans themselves had a practice of restricting the eating of meat on certain days. They had brought salting of cod and other fish to a high degree of perfection using spices and strong herbs. By 200 AD the classical writer Athanaeus could list 200 different ways of preparing and preserving fish. Isolated officials in the far reaches of the Roman Empire sent letters pleading for more stores. 'When you came to Byzantium,' begs one, ' bring a piece of salt swordfish, and choose a slice of the back, nearest the tail.'

Salt cod is also traditional to Norway and, via the Vikings, to the north of Scotland, where they have a long history of salting and preserving fish. They salted and dried cod, hanging it out to dry in the wind, like washing on a line. In the far north and on the islands they still practise this today. The Scots have a great recipe where they cook the steeped salt cod with potatoes to make 'hairy tatties'.

Salt cod must be soaked in several changes of water over at least 48 hours to desalinate it and rehydrate its flesh. The easiest way is to leave it in a bowl of cold water under a dripping tap, changing the water two or three times.

Olivia and Carlo at an Italian dance, c.1953

The flavour of the cod is distinctively changed from that of fresh fish. It is pungent, highly flavoured and also an acquired taste. This is exactly how Maria cooked it when she came to Scotland, probably thrilled to find such a distinctive food particular to her cuisine in her new home.

300 g baccalà (salt cod)
3 tablespoons extra virgin olive oil
1 medium onion, peeled and finely chopped
1 piece peperoncino (dried chilli)
4–5 tinned plum tomatoes
8 pitted prunes (semi-dried ones are juicier and don't have to be soaked)
some chopped flat-leaf parsley

Soak the baccalà over two days in several changes of cold water.

Heat the extra virgin olive oil in a saucepan and gently sauté the onion and chilli slowly until the onion is soft and transparent. Add the tomatoes, squash them down, and gently cook them for about 20 minutes.

Rinse the cod and check it with your fingers, removing any of the bones that you can feel. Leave the skin intact, as this will stop the cod disintegrating as it cooks, but cut the fish into five or six pieces. Lay them on top of the tomato sauce, add the prunes and, with the lid on the saucepan, steam the fish through. It takes barely 15 minutes.

Taste at the end of cooking. It shouldn't need any salt, but add some chopped flat-leaf parsley.

PICNICS AND FERRAGOSTO

PICINISCO AND ALVA GLEN, ITALY AND SCOTLAND 15 AUGUST

Ferragosto is celebrated on the 15 August. It's the feast of the Assumption of the Virgin Mary. It's a national holiday in Italy. It's also Francesca's birthday!

Everyone attends Mass and afterwards street parties are held and 'scampagnata' and picnics organised in every town and village. Long trestle tables are set up in the middle of the road. Huge pots of boiling water are prepared to cook what seems like tons of pasta. Roast chickens are prepared, whole suckling pigs are roasted on spits, and pizzas, 'pastone' (ham and egg pie) and plenty of wine are lavishly enjoyed.

To begin the feast, the Virgin is carried from the church on the backs of pole bearers, paraded around the streets, heralded by the local band. The pumpa-pumpa of the horns and trumpets with the melodic swing of the pipes produces a unique sound with an eclectic selection of traditional hymns, Verdi arias, Fascist Party marches and popular songs of the 1950s.

Immigrants away from their home towns kept the tradition alive in Scotland, holding a 'scampagnata' every year at Alva Glen. Buses and cars drove in from every town and village in Scotland that had a fish and chip or ice-cream shop, bringing three or four generations of immigrants together to celebrate their feast. The vast majority of these families originally came from Picinisco, Fontitune or I Ciacca. The children and grandchildren looked suspiciously like each other, had similar mannerisms and a great camaraderie between them.

From each bus and car great mounds of celebratory food were unpacked, prepared to the same recipes and traditions as in Italy: pizza, pastone, crespelle and frittata, salami, peperoni, chunks of pecorino and plenty of flasks of Chianti. (This was

Margaret with Joanna, and Anita, Kevin, Mary and Cesidio at the local Gala

the only Italian wine easily purchased in Scotland for many years.)

After feasting, races and football matches figured highly, with the children competing against each other, the nonni racing against the clock with trouser legs rolled up, shirt sleeves folded over and their trilby hats balanced jauntily on their heads. In the evening dances were held in local halls and the matchmaking initiated at the last year's picnic was subtly encouraged or formalised.

The only difference between the 'scampagnata' here and in Picinisco was that there the sun was guaranteed to shine.

Ham and Egg Pie
PASTONE

A picnic is not a ''scampagnata' without pastone, a crumbly flaky pastry stuffed with a ricotta and spicy sausage filling.

2 x 250 g packets frozen puff pastry
2 egg whites (left over from the filling), lightly beaten
FILLING
4 organic eggs
250 g ricotta, bought or home-made (see page 122)
50 g pecorino, freshly grated
Maldon sea salt and black pepper
75 g smoked pancetta, chopped
75 g Fonteluna sausage, skinned and chopped
2 egg yolks
2 fresh bay leaves

For the filling, beat the eggs lightly with a fork and crumble the ricotta into them. Lightly cream the two together. Fold in the grated pecorino and season the mixture well with salt and freshly ground black pepper.

Lightly grease a round 23 cm baking tin of about 5 cm deep. (Or an oblong tin, about 31 x 21 cm and 3 cm deep.

Preheat the oven to hot (220°C/425°F/Gas 7).

Roll out one of the sheets of puff pastry and line the tin, rolling it thin enough to fall over the edge slightly. Roll out the other to make a topping for the pie.

Half fill the pie tin with half the ricotta mixture, and sprinkle the chopped pancetta and Fonteluna sausage on top. Put the two egg yolks on to the mixture, one on each side of the pie. Break each bay leaf into two or three pieces and scatter over the pie. Add the rest of the ricotta mixture, spreading it over as evenly as you can.

Brush the edges of the pastry with the beaten egg white and cover the pie with the second pastry sheet. Pinch the pastry all around, sealing it well. Brush the top of the pastry with the rest of the egg white. (You can use a whole egg here if you want a more golden colour.)

Score the top of the pie with a diagonal design, making a couple of holes in the pastry to let the steam escape. Bake the pie in the preheated oven for 35–40 minutes until it is lightly browned.

Use a knife to loosen round the edges, and invert the pie on to a flat plate or a wire rack. Slide the pie back into the tin, so the base is now on top, and return it to the oven for another 15 minutes or so to let the base brown. Cool the pie on a wire rack and eat it warm or cold.

I often double the quantities of this recipe to make a bigger pastone.

PIZZA RUSTICA

All the women made their own versions of this delicious pizza pie with escarole or spinach sautéed in olive oil and garlic, baked between two sheets of pizza dough.

Make the pizza dough as detailed page 332, and leave it to rise.

While you're waiting, prepare the escarole (see page 205) or spinach (see page 218). If you're using spinach, squeeze out some of the juice that is released when it cooks.

Grease a baking tray with a little olive oil. Roll out half the dough into an oblong roughly 25 x 16 cm, just so that it is the thickness of pizza. Press the edges with your fingers to stop it shrinking in. Brush the edges with a little beaten egg. Spread the dough with a layer of the sautéed escarole or spinach. Roll out the rest of the dough to roughly the same shape and lay it on top of the greens. Press the dough down at the edges with your thumbs to seal it. Drizzle some olive oil on top and add a sprinkling of Maldon sea salt.

Bake the pizza on a hot baking tray in a very hot oven (230°C/450°F/Gas 8) for 20–25 minutes until crispy and baked. Turn it over once the top of the pizza is cooked and put it back into the oven for a further 15 minutes to crisp up the underneath dough. Eat it warm or cold, cut into squares.

If you're keeping some for the next day, don't refrigerate it. Just wrap it carefully in some foil.

Mozzarella in a Carriage
MOZZARELLA IN CARROZZA

This is classic genius. Put the mozzarella in a sandwich of tasty bread, flavour it with a little magical anchovy, dip it in beaten egg and fry it until crisp and golden in a fruity olive oil. This, to serve one, can be eaten hot or cold.

3–4 tablespoons milk
2 tablespoons plain flour
1 egg, beaten
Maldon sea salt and black pepper
2 slices mozzarella
2 slices crusty bread
1 anchovy fillet, chopped
sunflower or extra virgin olive oil

Prepare all the ingredients, putting the milk, flour and beaten egg in three different plates ready to coat the mozzarella. Season the egg with salt and pepper.

Lay the mozzarella on a slice of bread, sprinkling a little chopped anchovy over it. Don't worry. It won't taste fishy. It just lifts the delicate flavour of the mozzarella. Make a sandwich with the second slice of bread and press it down.

Warm the oil in a frying pan.

Dip the sandwich in the milk, just giving it a quick wash so that it doesn't get soggy. Now, dust it in the flour then dip it into the egg, coating the bread well on both sides. This is a bit messy but fun.

The oil should be just at sizzling point. Gently fry the sandwich in the oil until it is lightly coloured. Turn it and cook it on the other side. Drain on kitchen paper and serve warm.

Make anything 'in carrozza'. Try boiled ham and Emmenthal or fontina.

Crisply fried courgettes and peppers sandwiched in between crusty bread can be cooked the same way.

Aubergine and Mozzarella in a Carriage
MELANZANE E MOZZARELLA IN CARROZZA

Slice an aubergine into rounds. Smear each slice with some pesto, add a slice of mozzarella and stick another slice of aubergine on top, pesto side down. Press these together and dip them in egg and breadcrumbs as above. Shallow-fry in the same way as described above, and finish melting the cheese by popping it in a moderate oven (180°C/350°F/Gas 4) for 5 minutes or so.

Serve these with some salsa verde (see page 226) and a
crisp green salad. This makes a lovely light supper.

Carlo's Mozzarella without a Carriage
CARLO'S MOZZARELLA SENZA CARROZZA

Carlo is a 'can't cook, won't cook' kind of man. His mother,
Annunziata, cooked his favourite food for him every day. Once
he married, Olivia cooked his favourite food for him every day,
learning from her mother-in-law Neapolitan cooking to complement her Abruzzan style.

Once I married, I had to be on hand to cook his favourite
food for him every day, if needed. Francesca, I hope you're organised. Looks like you're next in line!

When the chips are down, on the five occasions none of us
have been around, due to births, deaths or marriages, Carlo has
made an omelette. He says this is real 'mozzarella in carrozza',
without a carriage at all, as they make it in Naples.

a splash of extra virgin olive oil
5 organic eggs
Maldon sea salt and black pepper
a ball of the freshest buffalo Mozzarella, about 200 g

Just cover the bottom of a small non-stick frying pan with a
smear of olive oil. Break the eggs into a bowl, whisk them
lightly and season them well. Drain the mozzarella well and
slice it with a very sharp knife into fairly thin slices.

Put the whisked eggs into the frying pan and start to cook
them over a medium heat. Add the mozzarella slices on top of
the egg. Move the frying pan around so that the egg cooks
evenly. As the mozzarella melts it fluffs up with the egg.

Carlo in the police force, c.1948

Just before the egg has solidified, flip the omelette over and cook it for a further few minutes.

FRITTATA

Frittata is the perfect picnic food. In fact it's the perfect food. It is easy to make and somehow appeals at any time of the day. We eat it for breakfast, in a panino for elevenses, warm with a light salad for lunch, or with boiled potatoes and greens for supper.

When we go on a picnic, we take a huge twelve-egg frittata, cooked with potatoes and Fonteluna sausage, and slice it cold.

On Good Friday, a day of Fast and Abstinence, Flora always made a thirty-three-egg frittata. Each egg represented a year in Our Lord's Life.

It is the easiest and most versatile dish to cook. Use good eggs, organic if possible, and keep it simple. I usually use only two or three ingredients to flavour the eggs.

You need a good, heavy-bottomed non-stick frying pan. Use enough eggs to fill the frying pan so that the frittata is nice and thick and cooks slowly. I have a great little non-stick frying pan, about 20 cm wide, which is ideal for two. It holds five eggs perfectly. This potato and onion version is a perfect example of the type.

2 tablespoons extra virgin olive oil and a good blob of butter
2 medium onions, peeled and very finely sliced
2–3 cold, cooked potatoes, diced (save them from the day before)
5 organic eggs
Maldon salt and black pepper

Warm the oil and butter and cook the finely sliced onions until they are soft and slightly singed at the edges. Add the diced potatoes, heat them through and turn the heat up a little to let them crisp up a little at the edges.

Beat the eggs and season them well. Turn the heat down to medium and add the eggs, moving them around so that they coat the potatoes and onions. Now let the frittata cook slowly in its own time. As it solidifies at the bottom, tip the frying pan to let the liquid egg seep underneath but other than that let it be.

When it has almost completely solidified and is dry on top, put a large plate over the frying pan. Tip the frittata on to it and slide it, upside down, back into the pan. Let it cook for a further 5 minutes or so on the bottom just to finish the underside, and it's done. Serve warm or cold, not piping hot.

Frittata with courgettes, pecorino and mint: slice 2 medium courgettes finely and cook them in the butter and oil, browning them a little at the edges. Add the eggs, 3–4 tablespoons grated pecorino and a tablespoon of chopped fresh mint.

Frittata with Fonteluna sausage and potato: skin the sausage by running a sharp knife down the side and sliding off the skin. (If the sausage is very dry, run it under warm water and the skin will come off easily.) Cut the sausage thinly and cook it in the butter and oil. Add a couple of chopped cold, cooked potatoes and cook them until they brown a little too. Add the eggs and cook as above.

Fresh herb frittata: add plenty of chopped parsley, mint and basil and 4 tablespoons of freshly grated pecorino or fontina to the beaten eggs. Mix everything and cook as above. You could also use Gruyère or any melting cheese.

Vegetable frittata: this is really good served warm with lots of salad. Use 2 courgettes, 1 red pepper, ½ aubergine and 2 chopped tomatoes. Dice everything quite small and cook in the frying pan until just browning at the edges. Alternatively, drizzle them with some extra virgin olive oil and roast in a hot oven for 15 minutes. Season them well. You can add a finely sliced onion as well to give a little sweetness. Let the cooked vegetables cool a little. Break the eggs into a bowl, beat them and season them well. Add the cooked vegetables and cook the frittata as normal.

Zia Filomena's Peperol' Panini

It was no good going on a picnic if Zia Filomena didn't bring her 'peperol' panini'.

She slowly roasted whole red peppers in a large frying pan with plenty of garlic, olive oil and seasoning. When they were soft and juicy, collapsed and slightly charred at the edges, she let them cool. She removed the stalk with a twist and eased out the core and all the seeds from the inside of the pepper. She saved the sweet juices from the middle. She sliced them roughly and packed them into white, chewy panini. She brought them along to the picnic, carefully wrapped in foil, invariably enough for four each!

Francesca, Zia Filomena was the best. I have to thank her especially for saving your dad for me. Those peppers were a killer. No girl in her right mind would kiss him at the dances!

GLASGOW PIZZA

FRANCESCA, IF YOU VISITED ANY OF MY NONNAS' HOUSES on a Sunday night there would inevitably be large trays of pizza ready to eat, coated with tomato, glistening mozzarella and sprinkled with dried oregano. Slices were cut and eaten with a glass of Chianti Ruffino, a lovely way to while away the evening. Pizza left to cool takes on a more substantial flavour, the dough chewy and satisfying. Perfect as well to take on picnics or for school lunch boxes.

Don't smother pizza with too many flavours. Two or three is more than enough. You know, keep it simple.

You do need a very, very hot oven to get the base of the pizza crispy. Remember that they are traditionally baked in as little as 6 minutes in a wood-fired oven, which builds up a heat far in excess of a domestic oven. A preheated pizza brick goes some of the way to helping the crispiness of the bottom of the pizza, but I hate most gadgets, so I just use an ordinary tin tray.

I find the instant easy-blend yeast the least bother when making pizza. Fresh yeast is really the preferred option but easy-blend yeast is foolproof.

Pizza Dough

700 g organic strong white bread flour
420 ml hand-hot water
2 sachets instant easy-blend yeast
2 teaspoons table salt or Maldon sea salt ground in a pestle and mortar
extra virgin olive oil

Make sure the kitchen is warm and there are no draughts. Bread and pizza doughs like to be kept snug and cosy or they won't rise.

Put the flour in a cool oven (150°C/300°F/Gas 2) to warm for a few minutes.

Measure out the water. Hand-hot is a bit warmer than you would expect. It should be as hot as a really warm bath. The one that leaves your face pink! (Try 30°C/86°F in summer, 40°C/104°F in winter as a guide.)

Mix the yeast and salt into the flour and, using the handle of a wooden spoon, stir in the warm water, mixing to make a dough that leaves the sides of the mixing bowl clean.

Knead the dough either by hand or in a food processor for about 10 minutes until it is silky and smooth. Put it snugly into the bowl, drizzle a little olive oil over the top and cover the bowl with clingfilm. Put a damp tea-towel on top and leave the bowl in a warm draught-free place to let the dough rise and double in size. It is best to put the dough in an airing cupboard or in a cupboard in the kitchen; the dough will rise more successfully if there is no air movement. It should take about an hour.

PIZZA MARINARA

This is the original pizza topping, poor man's bread and tomato.

1 quantity pizza dough (see opposite)
1 x 400 g tin Italian plum tomatoes or 400 g ripe cherry tomatoes,
cut in half
extra virgin olive oil
Maldon sea salt
2 cloves garlic, peeled and sliced
some freshly dried oregano

If you are using tinned tomatoes, chop them roughly, draining off some of the juice. Mix in a tablespoon of extra virgin olive oil and a good seasoning of sea salt. If you are using fresh cherry tomatoes, wash them, put them into a colander, squash them a little with your hands, and drain them, just to get rid of a little of their juice. Put them into a bowl with a little extra virgin olive oil and Maldon sea salt.

When the dough is ready, preheat the oven.

Be brave and set it to the highest setting (230–240°-

Olivia enjoying a pizza

C/450–475°F/Gas 8–9). Give it at least 20 minutes to heat up. Put a baking tray in the oven so that there is a hot surface to put the pizza tray on.

Knock down the dough and flatten it out with your hands, pulling it into the shape you want. The dough will make two round pizzas or one large oblong one.

Drizzle a little olive oil on to the trays you are using and put the dough on top. Use your fingers to press out the edges, easing the dough into submission.

Divide the tomato over the dough, spreading it with the back of a spoon, and leave about 2 cm clear around the edge. Drizzle with some extra virgin olive oil and add a sprinkling of garlic slivers and freshly dried oregano.

The pizza takes about 15 minutes to cook in a domestic oven. When it's cooked it should be crisp on the bottom, speckled brown at the edges and beautifully cooked and moist on top.

PIZZA MARGHERITA

Make the pizza in exactly the same way as above, but substitute the oregano with fresh basil leaves. Add 2–3 thin slices of buffalo mozzarella or 'fior di latte' to each pizza. The mozzarella melts into a delicious oozing moistness. Perfect!

Other Pizza Toppings

You can add any combination of toppings to a pizza that you fancy. The best flavours come from simple combinations, using the very best ingredients. Be inspired by what you see when you are shopping. Use either fresh basil or freshly dried oregano, not both together. Use tomatoes prepared as in the pizza marinara (see page 333).

Add thin slices of Fonteluna or spicy Italian sausage and some mozzarella and fresh basil leaves to the tomato topping.

Pumpkin works very well on pizza. Cut a 500 g pumpkin into slices, just like melon. Cut the flesh from the skin and scrape off the seeds. While the pizza dough is rising, rub the pumpkin with extra virgin olive oil and Maldon sea salt and roast it in a fairly hot oven (200°C/400°F/Gas 6) until soft and cooked through, but not browned. When the dough is ready, add a slight basting of the tomato topping and add 3 or 4 slices of fontina or mozzarella cheese. Top with slices of the roasted pumpkin and some fresh basil leaves and drizzle with a little olive oil. Bake in a hot oven as usual.

Rocket and fontina pizza is really lovely. Drizzle the pizza dough with extra virgin olive oil and add a few squashed cherry tomatoes. Add 3 or 4 slices of fontina and bake the pizza in the usual hot oven. Take the pizza out 5 minutes before it is cooked and add a good handful of washed and dried rocket. Drizzle a little extra virgin olive oil to moisten the rocket and bake for a further 5 minutes.

You don't always have to use tomato. My favourite pizza is dressed simply with onions. Make the dough as usual. Cut a red onion very finely into slices. Fry them in a couple of tablespoons of extra virgin olive oil until they start to become soft, or alternatively toss them in oil and roast them in the oven as it is heating for the pizza. Cut a buffalo mozzarella into thin slices. Spread it between two pizza rounds and add the onions. Sprinkle on some fresh thyme and a seasoning of Maldon salt. Drizzle some more extra virgin olive oil on top and bake in the usual hot oven until crispy at the edges.

Children love to make their own pizza. Give them the dough (or let them make it with you from scratch) and lay out a selection of toppings: tomato, mozzarella, ham, spicy sausage, olives or mushrooms. Let them create their own. It's a fun idea to have a cooking birthday party where the kids make their own dough then create their own lunch. Just try to stop them gobbling it all down after it's cooked. (Mum gets to clean up the mess!)

Fried Pizza
PIZZA FRITT'

Don't tell anyone who is trying to lose weight about this. It's an unadulterated sin! (Is there such a thing?)

1 quantity pizza dough (see page 332)
extra virgin olive oil
2 cloves garlic, peeled and sliced
fresh rosemary
Maldon sea salt

From left, Alex, Anna, Johnny and Carmela, c.1925

In most houses in the villages, there was no oven and pizza dough was often simply fried. It is quick and very tasty. Divide the dough into eight balls. Press each into rounds.

Warm the extra virgin olive oil in a large frying pan, adding a few slivers of garlic and a sprig of rosemary to flavour it. Fry the pizzas for 4–5 minutes on each side.

Drain the oil from the pizzas, sprinkle some Maldon sea salt on, and eat hot in your hands.

FRUIT

Cesidio, left, and his brothers in Picinisco, c. 1915.
They all eventually emigrated

We eat fresh fruit after every meal. I usually put a large bowl of one fruit in season in the middle of the table: cherries, peaches, plums, apricots, grapes and pears or, in the winter, citrus. It's fairly expensive because if the fruit is good we devour it all. We rarely eat puddings except for special occasions. If we're still hungry we eat ripe cheese with the fruit, again what is in season and best quality.

Summer Fruit Salad
INSALATA DI FRUTTA D'ESTATE

You can use any selection of berries you see. Look out for them in local fruit shops and farm shops.

100 g raspberries
100 g blackberries
100 g blueberries
½ ripe melon, cubed, and some watermelon
icing sugar
lemon juice

Pick over the berries, but don't wash them. Peel and cube the melons.

Mix everything together with a sprinkling of sieved icing sugar and a good squeeze of lemon juice. Serve chilled.

Orange Salad
INSALATA D'ARANCE

You'll need about six oranges. Navel oranges are the best, in season in January and February. Squeeze the juice from one of them. Cut the skin and pith from the oranges and, with a sharp knife, cut out each segment. Serve them in a large bowl moistened with the orange juice and a squeeze of lemon juice, well chilled.

If this is too much bother, simply cut the oranges into quarters or sixths and present them in the middle of the table on a large plate. They're especially refreshing after any spicy food.

Flora served slices of orange in her salads dressed with extra virgin olive oil and vinegar as normal.

Winter Fruit Salad
INSALATA DI FRUTTA D'INVERNO

It's easy to eat lots of fresh fruit in the summer. The shops are bursting with choice, and it's refreshing and tempting. In the winter, when we actually need the boost of vitamin C more, we often go without. There are plenty of dried fruits around and intense exotic fruits.

1 ripe mango, peeled and cubed
1 crisp apple, washed, cored and thinly sliced
1 banana, peeled and sliced
1 ripe papaya, peeled and cubed
1 kiwi fruit, peeled and sliced
juice of ½ lemon
juice of 3 oranges

Work on a clean chopping board or plate so that you can save the juices as they run from the fruits. Cut all the fruits into similar-sized pieces. Dress them first of all with the lemon juice to stop them browning, then pour over the orange juice.

These fruits are all very sweet so the salad shouldn't need any more sugar. Taste to check. Eat well chilled.

Roasted Chestnuts
CASTAGNE ARROSTO

Francesca, it's not unreasonable to imagine that your great-great-grandfather, Marietta's father, sold hot chestnuts in London in the 1880s. Who knows? Many immigrants bought chestnuts as they walked through France to sell them when they got to London.

They're easy to prepare. Buy the big 'marrons', which come into the shops in November and December. Part-cook the chestnuts in boiling water for a couple of minutes, just to soften their skin. They can be surprisingly dirty, so I usually give them a quick rinse.

Preheat the oven to fairly hot (200°C/400°F/Gas 6).

Put the chestnuts on a baking tray and roast them for about 15–20 minutes. You really need to be brave and peel them while they're still hot, otherwise they're impossible to release from the papery skin that lies under the shell.

Tipsy Cherries
CILIEGE SOTTO SPIRITO

Francesca, I don't think you'll need any encouragement to try these. Make them in June when the cherries are in season and abundant. Choose the juiciest best cherries you can find.

1 kg ripe cherries in good condition
500 g granulated sugar
3 or 4 cloves
a piece of cinnamon stick
1 x 500 ml bottle 100 per cent pure spirit, or a good vodka

Don't wash the cherries, but wipe them with a damp cloth. Use only the undamaged, juiciest ones. Pack a sterilised 1 litre kilner jar with the cherries, leaving their stalks on. Drizzle in the sugar as you go and add the cloves and cinnamon stick. Top up the jar with the alcohol.

Seal and leave them in a cool dark place for at least two weeks. The cherries absorb the alcohol, so top up the jar with more if necessary. Leave them undisturbed in a dark cupboard. They will taste fabulous by Christmas.

Peaches and Wine
PESCE CON VINO

Towards the end of the meal, when the children have all left the table, and the women are in the kitchen washing the dishes (yes, I know!), the men relax, half-finished tumblers of wine still to enjoy.

A large bowl of ripe peaches is placed in the middle of the table, nestling on a bed of ice. A plastic-handled, serrated knife is used to slice the peach away from the stone. The pieces are shared among the tumblers. They are left to soak up the flavour of the wine and eaten slowly over the rest of the afternoon.

Wild Strawberries
FRAGOLINE DI BOSCO

Tiny, rich red wild strawberries can still be found growing wild in the south of Italy. They are also cultivated and have an extraordinarily intense sweetness. Try eating these, if you ever come across them, or our own cultivated strawberries, sprinkled with lemon juice and sugar. The lemon juice lifts and enhances the elusive strawberry flavour.

Figs
FICHI

Fresh, ripe figs are absolutely wonderful. Don't waste your money on the dry, dull expensive ones offered in a plastic pack of four. In Italy, from August until the autumn, green or purple figs can be eaten ripe from the tree. Peel off their soft skin and reveal the moist, juicy pink fruit. Eat it in one mouthful. The natural sun-warmed temperature of the fruit brings out its intense moist sweetness.

Persimmons
CACHI

A persimmon tree in full fruit is beautiful. It is the most stunning sight, branches weighed down with hundreds of golden-orange globes of fruit. In the late autumn on the edges of the mountains near Picinisco, trees bearing these fruits look like fairy lanterns in the evening light.

Italian 'cachi' (pronounced 'cakee') are much sweeter and far fleshier than the persimmons we can get in Britain – kaki or sharon fruit – and must be eaten when they are fully ripe. Before that they are woolly and rough in the mouth, not entirely pleasant. When they are soft and pulpy, almost over-ripe, they can be eaten with a spoon. Cut the top off and either simply suck out the glorious sweet juicy flesh or use a teaspoon to scoop it out.

Watermelon
COCOMERO/ANGURIA

There's nothing more refreshing than a huge round slice of watermelon, at least 25 cm in diameter and 6 cm thick, as it's presented with a knife and fork in the south of Italy. The middle is by far the sweetest most intensely flavoured part. Eat it cool but not too chilled.

CAKES AND TREATS

Johnny and his ice-cream freezer, c. 1936

COCKENZIE, EAST LOTHIAN, SCOTLAND
1965–1985

We grew up in the higgledy-piggledy house on top of the Cockenzie Café.

Francesca, your Grandpa Johnny made the best ice-cream. He made the 'mix' for ice-cream every day in the summer, twice a week in the winter. The sweet smell of hot milk, vanilla and sugar permeated the whole house. When it was ' boiled', the steaming, creamy liquid ran through sparkling stainless-steel pipes and miraculously appeared at the top of the cooler. It ran down cold wavy, corrugated steel like a milk waterfall to be collected in steel pails and chilled. The mix was then churned in a freezer with huge in-built, sharp steel paddles. These rotated backwards and forwards, cutting through the ice-cream as it got gradually firmer and smoother, until it was ready to sell.

When the sun shone, or had an intention to shine, the ice-cream was 'lifted' into portable freezers attached to tricycles and cycled down the East Lothian coast to sell to eager holiday-makers. One of Carlo's first jobs when he started to work in Edinburgh was to use his woodwork skills to build these trikes. He made two, enterprisingly shaped as boats, for Johnny in Cockenzie.

By the time I was a teenager Johnny had custom-made kiosks on the road. They were attached to his van and driven down the coast. As a youngster my job was to man the kiosk at the 'faraway car park', about three miles from the shop. When the weather was good I had a queue all day, selling gallons of ice-cream, sliders, black men, 99 cones and home-made crisps. Daddy came back every few hours to top up my freezers with more ice-cream. At night he came and pulled the kiosk, the bag of 'takings' and me back to the shop. Needless to say, I had eaten most of the profit.

Di Ciacca's Vanilla Ice-cream

Sadly our family's ice-cream is no longer made. In its heyday it had the reputation as the best ice-cream around.

To make a traditional custard-based ice-cream at home you need an ice-cream maker.

600 ml full-fat milk
1 vanilla pod, split open
8 organic egg yolks
250 g unrefined caster sugar
300 ml whipping cream, lightly whipped

Put the milk in a saucepan and add the vanilla pod. Bring the milk to the boil, turn off the heat, and leave the flavours to infuse for a half an hour or so.

Beat together the egg yolks and sugar until they are light and fluffy. Strain the milk and beat it into the eggs. Scrape out the seeds from the vanilla pod and add them to the 'mix'.

Heat the mix in a bowl suspended over a pot of simmering water, stirring until it is light and creamy and starts to thicken. It's ready when it just coats the back of the wooden spoon.

Fill the sink with iced water and put the custard into it to lower its temperature quickly. Once it's cool, fold in the lightly whipped cream. Transfer it to a ready-chilled ice-cream maker and freeze it according to the manufacturer's instructions.

Make coffee ice-cream by adding 50 ml strong espresso coffee instead of the vanilla.

I have added a dessertspoon of aceto balsamico tradizionale to the mix – sublime.

Make intense chocolate ice-cream. Melt 30 g of a 70 per cent cocoa solids chocolate and add this and 30 g bitter cocoa powder to the milk as it infuses.

Zabaglione Ice-cream

I think this is my favourite ice-cream. The Marsala has a distinctive, evocative flavour.

6 organic egg yolks
120 g unrefined caster sugar
finely grated zest of 1 unwaxed or scrubbed lemon
6 tablespoons Marsala dessert wine
seeds from 1 vanilla pod
250 ml whipping cream

You need to use a double boiler again or balance a heatproof bowl over a pot of simmering water.

Put the egg yolks and sugar together in the bowl, and, while the water is gently simmering, beat the mix with a whisk until it starts to thicken. The mix will become pale and creamy. When it starts to coat the back of a spoon it's ready.

Add the Marsala, lemon zest and the vanilla seeds and stir in. Put the bowl into a sink half filled with cold water to chill it down.

Lightly whip the cream and fold it in. Freeze the mix in an ice-cream maker. Because of the alcohol content, this ice-cream is very soft, and should be eaten immediately.

HOKEY-POKEY MAN

THE 'HOKEY-POKEY' MAN WAS THE NAME given to the first Italians who travelled the streets of London with makeshift ice-cream carts, sometimes pushed but later ingeniously attached to a tricycle. Sometimes they had a monkey to attract passers-by, or they enticed potential customers to taste their ices by offering a lick of their 'licking glass' on which they scraped a little of their wares. With the invitation 'ecco un poco', 'here's a little', they passed the licking glass between people, wiping it on a cloth between licks. Health and Safety Officers quite rightly eventually put a stop to this innocent, but unhygienic practice.

The names of ices have been handed down through the generations. The 'Black Man' probably referred to the Italian ice-cream sellers who were swarthy and dark . . . and apparently very handsome!

'Black Man'

2 chocolate mallow wafers
3 balls vanilla ice-cream

Lay the first chocolate wafer on a small sheet of greaseproof paper. Put the balls of vanilla ice-cream on to it, two at the bottom and the third between the two. Put the second chocolate wafer on top. Press it down lightly.

Cesidio with his horse-drawn ice-cream cart, the Hokey Pokey man, c.1930

'99' Cone

A '99' is a cone with two balls of vanilla ice-cream and a Cadbury's Flake stuck in the top. If you're off sweets for Lent, you hide the flake inside the cone before you add the ice-cream.

Slider

A 'slider' is two balls of ice-cream sandwiched between two ice-cream wafers. Traditionally the lower wafer was slid on to a special stainless-steel holder and the ice-cream was spooned on, edged skilfully with a flat spoon on each side to build up the ice-cream and make the slider look bigger!

Basher

A 'basher' is a slider with a home-made cream snowball squashed on top of the ice-cream.

HUGH HILLEY AND FLORA, GLASGOW, SCOTLAND 1920–1930

'I eat Antipasto twice, just because she is so nice,
Angelina, the waitress at the Pizzeria.
I eat soup and minestrone just to be with her alone,
Angelina, the waitress at the Pizzeria.
If you'll be-a, my cara mia
Then I'll join in matrimony, with the girl who serves spumone,
*   and Angelina will be mine!'*
Louis Prima ©

Hugh Hilley was a hero. Born in the poor slums of the East End of Glasgow in the last year of the nineteenth century, he was one of eleven children. His was a drastic poverty. City squalor is somehow more dispiriting and degrading than country squalor: high-rise tenements spilling over with large families; stinking with poor sanitation; damp with terrible weather. He had no heritage, only his strict southern Irish 'clip across the ear' upbringing, and a devout, honest Catholic faith.

This didn't deter Hugh. He was a scruffy, bandy-legged youth with a brilliant sense of humour and a zest for life. The original hyperactive, he had boundless energy and spent his youth in the streets, climbing, kicking a football and dreaming up fantastic schemes which always ended up getting him into scrapes.

Ten years previously, Glasgow Celtic Football Club had been founded. A group of businessmen and a Marist priest, Brother Walfrid, became concerned about the extreme poverty and deprivation in the East End Catholic communities they worked in. Inspired to tackle the problem, they founded the football club from humble beginnings to offer some hope and opportunity to the young lads in the streets. They scouted around for boys who showed talent and energy and put together the first team in 1888.

Hugh was a wiry, determined youngster and was quickly signed up by Celtic's talent scouts. By the time he was twenty-one he was playing in the defence line-up of the top football team of the country. His team-mates were sporting heroes like Willie McStay and Patsy Gallacher. His refusal to be the underdog and spirited determination made him a great defender. He wanted to win.

When we were kids, he filled our heads with tall tales of his antics on the pitch. He told us of his glory years when Celtic was top of the league and of his brilliant moves and tackles that saved the day. He boasted how his broken, crooked nose was a testimony to a tackle that saved the match. He never told us, and we didn't find out until after he died, about his antics off the pitch!

He took his training seriously, working out in the mornings and, as instructed by his trainer, resting in the afternoons. He was disciplined and conscientious and well respected in his club.

A creature of habit, he fell into the practice of stopping off at a local Italian café for an ice-cream, believing the advertisement in the window, 'ice-cream is good for you'! By then he was a famous footballer and local hero and was used to a fuss being made of him. He looked forward to chatting with Flora, the girl who served behind the counter, and who seemed to be very good at fussing him!

Flora was the daughter of an immigrant family from Settefrati,

Hugh and Flora Hilley in love!

a village over the mountain from Picinisco. Her family was well established in Glasgow and was doing well. Like all the children of immigrant Italian families she worked long and hard hours behind the counter. The small, narrow shop was always busy and always had a queue, sometimes reaching right up the street.

Flora's father watched his youngest daughter's flirtation with the Irish footballer. He was not impressed to say the least. The Italian immigrants kept themselves to themselves and expected their children to marry within the community. They came from isolated mountain villages and were suspicious of outsiders. To remove the temptation posed by this Irish rascal, Flora was packed off back to Settefrati to simmer down.

Absence made their hearts grow fonder and soon the couple were head over heels. Hugh wrote letter after letter to keep in contact with his sweetheart. The letters arriving in a remote Italian village with a Glasgow post-mark were easily intercepted by her family and destroyed. Flora never saw them. She was broken-hearted that Hugh hadn't written. Her father had been right. He was an upstart.

When he didn't get any replies, Hugh became suspicious. He trusted Flora. He knew she loved him. She would have written.

Always the opportunist, he had a brilliant idea. He started sending copies of the *Glasgow Herald* to Flora. Newspapers from Scotland were nothing to worry about. The girl enjoyed reading them. It was good she kept practising her English. Her censors didn't realise that it was Hugh who was sending the newspapers. Secretly, on the sports pages, he marked letters and words so that Flora could decipher message after message. What a thrill. He did still love her. He'd saved a brilliant tackle. He was missing her dreadfully. He was waiting for her. As soon as she got back, they would elope and marry.

A devout Catholic, and ever willing to obey the church, Hugh checked with the priest at St Mungo's and was given the all-clear. It was perfectly acceptable for a successful Irish Celtic footballer with a not insubstantial amount of money in the bank, to bring his bride-to-be to his own family home and to marry her from there! She couldn't have a full white wedding but, by the grace of God, she could have a discreet wedding instead.

So, to the shock of her doting parents, who presumed the Irish upstart had lost interest, as soon as they brought her back to Glasgow, Flora ran away.

'Scandalosa!'

She was married on the 15 June 1925 in a demure, grey silk suit, in the presence of her new Irish relations. The two romantics were head over heels in love and remained so all their married life.

After a year or so Hugh and Flora were reconciled with her parents. He was so charming and such a good Catholic boy, he became their favourite son-in-law. With the luck of the Irish, he eventually bought their business and put Flora back where he had first found her. Right behind the counter of the ice-cream shop!

By the time he finished his career in football, Hugh was a very wealthy man. He opened an ice-cream factory. His pioneering product, Hilley's Choc Bar, was a block of ice-cream covered with chocolate, and frozen in individual packages. It was just the thing to sell to the thousands of new cinema-goers who were anxious to escape reality and dream the American dream at 'the local flea pit'.

Flora and Hugh had three daughters – Mary, Gertrude, my mother, and Pat – and an adopted son, Michael. Hugh retired from business at fifty and spent the rest of his life in his local church serving Mass every morning. He became known as the oldest altar boy in town. In the afternoons he was on the golf course or down at Parkhead cheering on his team. Flora and Hugh led a charmed life, travelling to Ireland, America and Monte Carlo, staying in the best of hotels and glamorously dressed like Hollywood stars. Not a bad life for a youngster from the slums and his 'waitress from the pizzeria'!

Hilley's 'Choc Bar'

*pan di spagna made with 3 eggs, 90 g caster sugar
and 75 g plain flour (see page 363)
500 ml vanilla ice-cream (see page 348) or good bought ice-cream
Strega or Amaretto liqueur
chocolate sauce (see below) and toasted almonds*

You will need six or seven small moulds, about 7 cm in diameter. Line each of the moulds with some clingfilm so that you can unmould them easily. Line the inside of the clingfilm with a layer of sponge, cutting it and pressing it down so that it fits the inside of the mould neatly. Sprinkle the sponge with a generous amount of liqueur. Fill the sponge with vanilla ice-cream, flattening it across the top. You can press a lid of sponge on top of this if you like. Freeze the mould for an hour or so, just enough time to set the ice-cream.

When you are ready to serve, gently unmould the containers. If they have been frozen for more than an hour, leave them in the fridge for 5 minutes or so to soften a little.

Pour a generous amount of hot chocolate sauce over the sponge and sprinkle it with some toasted almonds.

Hot Chocolate Sauce

*225 g 70% cocoa solids dark chocolate or Cadbury's Dairy Milk
1 tablespoon brandy
1 tablespoon espresso coffee
300 ml double cream*

Put all the ingredients in a heatproof bowl over a pot of simmering water. As they melt, stir everything together to make a deadly illegal chocolate sauce.

CAPPUCCINO SEMIFREDDO

This is really easy because it doesn't need an ice-cream machine. The down side is that it has raw eggs in it, so it's not for tinies, oldies and bumpies (i.e. small children, old people and ladies 'on the road to Morocco')! Alternatively use eggs that have the 'lion mark' and have been laid by hens inoculated against salmonella.

2 large eggs, separated
75 g unrefined caster sugar
50 g great chocolate (Valrhona or Green and Black's 70%), melted
2 teaspoons strong espresso coffee
300 ml double cream
some crushed amaretti biscuits, soaked in 2 tablespoons Kahlua

Use a hand-held blender to beat the egg yolks until they are pale and creamy. Add the caster sugar, melted chocolate and espresso coffee.

Whip the egg whites until stiff and fold them into the mixture. Whip the cream until it forms soft swirls and fold it into the mixture.

Line a 450 g tin with clingfilm and oil it. Stick the liqueur-soaked biscuits on to the bottom and sides of the tin. Pour the mixture in, cover with foil and freeze for 4–5 hours.

Serve this cut into slices. Dip a knife into a jug of boiling water and the ice-cream will cut like a dream.

Pick-me-up
TIRAMISU

This is your favourite pudding of all time, Francesca, so just to remind you.

2 large organic, free-range eggs, separated
4–5 tablespoons icing sugar, sifted
4 tablespoons Marsala or Kahlua
400 g mascarpone cheese
100 ml strong espresso coffee
½ packet Savoiardi biscuits
some chocolate to grate on top

Beat the egg yolks to fluff them up and whisk in three-quarters of the icing sugar. Add a tablespoon of the liqueur to give the eggs some flavour. With a hand whisk, start to add this mix to the mascarpone. A little at a time will

Francesca feeding the ducks, aged three

loosen it and start to make it easier to work with. When it is all added, whisk the egg whites in a separate bowl and fold these in. Taste for sweetness and adjust the flavour.

Mix the coffee and remaining liqueur in a shallow plate and dip the biscuits briefly in to moisten them. Lay them in a layer along a shallow dish. Add half the mixture and then repeat with a second layer of biscuits. Spread the rest of the mix over the top. Sprinkle the surface with grated chocolate and refrigerate for 2–3 hours. Eat this the same day.

I've just checked Mummy's original recipe for this. She doesn't use any raw eggs but 250 ml lightly whipped cream instead. This would be better if there are children to eat this, but, don't quote me, I would leave in the liqueur and coffee!

Toffee Apples

Marietta made toffee apples all summer long to sell to the thousands of tourists who poured into Port Seton and Cockenzie for their holidays. They came in droves from as far away as Glasgow and Hamilton! Business was good and the toffee apples went down a treat.

6 crisp, tart, unwaxed apples (Pink Lady, Braeburn, Cox's Orange Pippins etc.)
butter
750 g unrefined granulated sugar
750 ml cold water

Wash and dry the apples. Push a toffee apple stick, a chopstick or even a fork, into each apple, straight down through the stalk.

Prepare a baking tin or tray with a sheet of greaseproof paper, well buttered.

Put the sugar and water into a heavy-bottomed saucepan and stir it over a low heat until the sugar has completely dissolved. Bring the syrup to the boil and allow it to bubble fiercely until the toffee starts to go brown at the edges. Don't

stir the toffee but swirl the pot slightly to make sure the
toffee at the middle of the pan browns as well.

When all the toffee has just started to go brown, take the
pot off the heat and, holding the pot at an angle, dip each
apple into the toffee, swirling it round so that it is well
coated. Put each toffee apple on to the greaseproof paper to
solidify and cool.

*Any spare toffee can be poured into a greased baking tin and left to
solidify. Once it's solid, lay it between two greaseproof sheets of paper
and smash it with a rolling pin. Now you have praline for biscuits or
ice-cream.*

Add crushed pistachio nuts to the toffee to make nut praline.

Roll the toffee apples in dessicated coconut.

Jeannie Herriot's Shortbread Fingers

Jeannie Herriot was a fisherman's wife who worked for my mum.
She taught her to make shortbread and her recipe was prepared
hundreds of times to serve in the café and the 'caterings'.

300 g soft butter
100 g soft margarine
200 g caster sugar, plus extra for sprinkling
480 g plain flour
200 g cornflour

Preheat the oven to moderate (160°C/325°F/Gas 3). Make
sure the butter and margarine are at room temperature. Use
all butter if you prefer a richer flavour.

Using a food processor, mix the butter, margarine and
caster sugar together until light and fluffy. Mix in the sieved

flour and cornflour to form a dough. The flour flies all over the place so be careful. If your processor doesn't have a shield, cover the bowl with a clean tea-towel when you add the flour.

Pack the dough into a greased baking tin, roughly 28 x 18 cm, and 3 cm deep. Pierce the dough all over with a fork in straight lines so that it looks nice. This allows any steam to escape. Bake for 30 minutes in the preheated oven, then lower the temperature to cool (140°C/275°F/Gas 1), and slowly finish baking the shortbread for another hour or so (see note below).

While the shortbread is still warm, score out fingers with a knife. Leave it to cool a little. Before it gets completely cold, sprinkle the shortbread with some extra caster sugar and use a palette knife to ease the fingers out on to a wire rack to cool. Store in an airtight tin.

The most difficult thing about making shortbread is the baking. It needs long, slow baking but it needs to be pale coloured when it is cooked. Pay attention to the smell as it bakes, don't let it darken or it will burn. Every time I bake this in a different oven, I have to experiment. When the shortbread is baked you can press it with your fingers and it feels quite firm, even although it is pale.

Make traditional shortbread rounds using a wooden mould. The shortbread will be thinner and so will cook more quickly. Bake in a moderate oven (160°C/325°F/Gas 3) for 25–30 minutes.

Make half the quantity and roll the dough out to a biscuit thickness. Use a pastry cutter or a small glass to cut out rounds. Bake the thin biscuits in a moderate oven (160°C/325°F/Gas 3) for about 25 minutes until they are crisp but still pale in colour. Sprinkle them with caster sugar.

I use this recipe to make little tartlets, cooking rounds of the dough pressed into paper baking cases in a shallow twelve-portion bun tray. When they are cold fill them with cream and strawberries or raspberries.

Sponge
PAN DI SPAGNA

This is the standard sponge recipe used all over Italy. It is very easy to make and is versatile used in cakes, puddings and sponges. The hidden ingredient that makes this brilliant is a light touch. Whisk everything lightly and add the flour well sifted so that as much air stays in the mixture as possible.

5 large organic eggs, separated
150 g caster sugar, plus extra for sprinkling
1 teaspoon vanilla sugar, or 2–3 drops pure vanilla extract
very finely grated zest of an unwaxed lemon
125 g plain flour
a pinch of fine sea salt

Preheat the oven to medium (180°C/350°F/Gas 4). You'll need a 25 cm round baking tin, lined and greased. (I love Lakeland's ready-cut baking-tin liners. It's such a brilliant idea!)

Beat the egg yolks and the caster sugar until they are light and creamy and have trebled in size. Add the vanilla sugar or vanilla extract and the grated lemon zest.

In a separate bowl, beat the egg whites until they are light and fluffy. Use a large metal spoon to fold them gently into the mixture, keeping as much air as possible.

Use a sieve to sprinkle the flour and salt into the mix, gently folding them in with a large metal spoon. Just take your time and keep folding to make sure all the flour is incorporated.

Pour the mixture into the cake tin and bake in the preheated oven for 25 minutes or until it is springy when pushed with your fingers and it has shrunk slightly from the sides of the tin. Let the cake cool a little then tip it on to a wire rack.

Sprinkle the surface with some caster sugar while it is still warm to give a lovely crunchy effect.

The traditional way to eat it is to cut it into three or four slices horizontally, and layer it with rich crema pasticcera that has been heavily laced with liqueur (opposite).

Cut the cake in half horizontally and sandwich it together with some home-made jam (see pages 235–40). Dust the top with icing sugar.

Try cutting it in half horizontally and filling it with whipped cream and strawberries.

Substitute a quarter of the flour with bitter cocoa powder to make a chocolate cake. Leave out the lemon zest.

You can use this sponge for tiramisu instead of biscuits. Let it dry overnight so that you can cut it and soak it with the flavoured coffee. I use it if I'm making trifle as the sponge base.

Thick Custard
CREMA PASTICCERA

425 ml full-fat milk
1 vanilla pod, split
2–3 strips unwaxed lemon zest
5 egg yolks
100 g caster sugar
2 level tablespoons plain flour
1 level tablespoon cornflour

First infuse the milk with the flavourings. Put the milk, split vanilla pod and lemon zest into a saucepan and bring to the boil. Remove the vanilla pod and the zest. Scrape out the seeds from the vanilla pod and add them to the milk.

Me and my mummy, c.1958

Whisk the egg yolks with the sugar until they are light and fluffy. Sift the flour and cornflour into the mixture and fold in.

Whisk the hot milk into the yolk mixture, and pour it back into a bowl which fits easily into another saucepan. Fill the saucepan half full with boiling water and slowly cook the mixture over the water until it thickens. Just take your time and be careful not to let the custard burn or curdle.

Once the custard has thickened, take it off the heat. Cover it with clingfilm and leave it to set.

Celebration Cake

Traditionally for a christening, birthday or wedding, Holy Communion or Confirmation, successful exam or engagement, in fact any excuse for a celebration, the 'pan di spagna' is prepared. It's doused with extra alcohol and decorated with profiteroles, filled with even more crema pasticcera, and drizzled with melted chocolate sauce. For a big party make two pan di spagna cakes (see page 363), and cut each into two, making four layers of sponge.

Make two quantities of crema pasticcera (see page 365).

Assemble the cake by sprinkling Strega or any liqueur that you prefer, on each layer of sponge. Add some crema pasticcera, layering it between each sponge, building up four layers. Dust the top with cocoa powder. The cake is also very nice served with lightly whipped cream.

Profiteroles

125 ml cold water
50 g cold butter, cut into small pieces
1 teaspoon caster sugar
75 g strong plain flour, sifted
2 organic eggs

Preheat the oven to hot (220°C/425°F/Gas 7).

Put the cold water, butter and sugar into a medium saucepan and heat it until the butter has melted. Take the saucepan off the heat and add the flour all in one go. Stir the mixture briskly until it becomes a soft-looking ball, coming away from the sides of the saucepan.

Beat the eggs and gradually add them to the paste, mixing

them in a little at a time. You may think that this is a disaster as the eggs make the paste look all gloopy. Don't worry. Keep beating and you will get a nice smooth paste.

Grease a baking tray and run it under a cold-water tap. Knock the water off, leaving globules sticking to the tray. This provides a steamy atmosphere to help the profiteroles to rise.

Use two teaspoons to make small walnut-sized blobs of paste on the tray. You'll get about ten from this amount.

Put them on the highest shelf of the oven. After 10 minutes, turn the oven temperature down to fairly hot (190°C/375°F/Gas 5). Bake them for another 15 minutes until they are crisp and golden and puffed up.

Bring them out of the oven and transfer them to a wire cooling rack. Pierce each one with a skewer just to let any steam inside escape. When they are cooled, cut them open and fill them with crema pasticcera or whipped cream. Eat them as they are, or use them to decorate a celebration cake.

Yum Yum Pudding

Flora visited America a lot. Many of her Irish in-laws had settled in America and were more than happy to entertain visitors with undiluted Irish hospitality.

She was a great cake eater and loved to bake. This is her 'yum yum pudding' that we always have on Christmas Day instead of traditional Christmas pudding. It is lighter, with less dense fruit, and after a whopping plate of home-made pasta goes down a treat.

Before you start make sure you have the right-sized pudding bowls, greaseproof paper and string to cover them with. This is enough to make two 600 ml puddings, or one 1.2 litre pudding. You can use plastic pudding bowls for convenience, but I prefer the traditional ceramic ones. Make sure you have a pot with a tight-fitting lid that will hold the bowl comfortably with water a third of the way up. Best test now, before the pudding is made and the water is boiling.

500 ml cold water
250 g caster sugar
125 g unsalted butter
2 tablespoons treacle
2 teaspoons ground cinnamon
1 teaspoon ground cloves
a good grating of nutmeg
750 g dried seedless muscatel raisins (or mixed dried fruit,
but no currants)
450 g plain flour
3 teaspoons bicarbonate of soda
a pinch of fine sea salt
6 silver threepenny bits (or sixpences)
granulated sugar and some brandy to set it alight

Put the water, sugar, butter, treacle, spices and fruit into a saucepan, stir and slowly bring it to the boil. Switch the heat off and allow the mixture to cool. Stir it now and then as it cools. The fruit starts to swell as it absorbs the water and melted butter. This stage is very important. If the fruit doesn't absorb most of the liquid, the pudding may not steam well.

When the fruit is barely lukewarm, sift the flour, bicarbonate of soda and salt into the mixture, and stir in. Add the silver coins, each wrapped in a little foil.

Grease the pudding bowl(s) well and put a circle of foil on the bottom so that the pudding will tip out nicely.

Don't risk the pot boiling dry as you steam the puddings. Set a timer and check the water level every half-hour or so. If you're using a plastic bowl, sit it on an old upturned saucer. Even if it does boil dry, the pudding will just stop steaming. If not, the plastic has a nasty habit of melting on to the base of the pot, ruining the pudding and Christmas lunch.

Divide the mixture between the bowls you are using, and cover each bowl with a double sheet of greaseproof paper. I put a fold in the paper to give a bit of slack as the pudding rises in the bowl. Get help to tie a piece of string round to secure the paper round the rim and tie it over the top to make a handle. Use this to lower the pudding in and out of the boiling water.

Steam the smaller puddings for 2½-3 hours, 3–4 if it's one big one. Let them cool completely and check with a skewer that the mixture is set in the middle, otherwise steam them longer.

Yum yum pudding stays in good condition for two to three months. I'm usually not organised, and make them just a few days before Christmas. They're always lovely. When you reheat them you'll need to steam them for 2 hours at least.

Francesca, you have to complete the ritual and set the pudding alight with brandy. Tip the pudding out of the bowl and sprinkle a good 2 tablespoons of granulated sugar over the top. Warm at least 5–6 tablespoons brandy (at least!) in a small saucepan. Warm a ladle over a flame, spoon out the hot brandy and set it alight as you pour it over the pudding.

'Buon Natale'
CRUSTOLE

Maria and Marietta both made 'crustole', deep-fried pastries, at Christmas. Both made them exactly the same way with a light handedness and skill that comes from a great experience of cooking. Maria drizzled hers with honey, Marietta with caster sugar.

The name for these is another of those words specific to the dialect of our area, with direct Latin roots. 'Crustole' means 'pastry', the Latin for which is 'crustolae'. The Italian for pastries similar to these from other areas is 'chiacchiere'. There is an intriguing reference to 'crustulum' on an ancient inscription in the Villa Silvestri in Arca di Far Sabina. It was removed there from the forum of the vanished Roman-Sabine city of Curi. The 'crustulum' or 'clustrum' was a holiday treat distributed to the Roman people together with 'mulsum', honeyed wine, on important holidays during the December to January holiday period. Waverley Root in his fascinating book, The Food of Italy, says this was a type of bruschetta drizzled with new season's olive oil. I like to think the crustulum may have really been a sweet pastry similar to the one my grandmothers made, drizzled with honey. Who knows?

I used to help my Nonna Marietta make these many years ago. My job was to turn them over in the oil as they fried. I couldn't have been more than nine or ten years old. I'm sure she did everything by hand. I can't remember her having a pasta machine, only a very long, thin pasta pole. If you fancy having a bash at making these, be patient. The pastry has to be very light and so can be a bit tricky to handle. This recipe makes about fifteen to twenty.

1 large free-range egg
1 tablespoon unrefined caster sugar
1 dessertspoon light olive oil (she used lard)
1 dessertspoon Strega liqueur, or Marsala
3–4 large tablespoons plain flour, sieved
light olive oil or sunflower oil to fry
more caster sugar or runny honey to serve

Beat the egg and sugar together, then beat in the olive oil and Strega. Gradually add enough flour to make a mixture just dry enough to handle.

Using a small amount of the pastry at a time, roll it out in a pasta machine in a fine strip. It tends to stick, so dust it with plenty of flour as you go. You can roll it by hand. Roll it out as thin as you dare.

Using a pastry cutter cut long ribbons, 15 cm long, 2–3 cm wide. Fold each strip into a figure-of-eight, pressing the ends together to make a bow.

You need to fry the pastry immediately. It will collapse if you leave it for any length of time. Heat the oil in a wide frying pan – the pastry will double in size as it cooks. Test that the oil is hot enough by adding a little of the pastry. It should sizzle and move, but not burn.

Cook two to three crustole at a time, turning them as soon as they start to become golden coloured. They take only 1–2 minutes to cook. Don't let them burn or darken in the oil.

Drain them, blot them on kitchen paper and pile them on to a large flat dish. As they cool, sprinkle them with caster sugar or drizzle them with runny honey. Magically, they stay crisp over two to three days. We usually nibble them from Christmas Eve through to Boxing Day, picking up a piece every time we pass.

DRINKS

Scopa, the card game played round the kitchen table

Sitting in the piazza, by the fire in winter or in the 'back-shop' waiting for the pubs to come out, the perfect way to end the day is with an espresso, a Sambuca and a game of 'scopa' (a Neapolitan card game). Marietta was a great flirt. She would always sit with the men and hold court over a game of cards . . . quite daring considering the restrictions in her upbringing. She loved every minute of it. She had a reputation as a cunning player and always insisted in sitting at a certain chair at the table. Unbeknown to her companions, she had a secret drawer tucked under the table where she kept a selection of winning cards which she niftily produced then hid again at times of crisis. 'Furba!'

She taught me about playing scopa and flirting. Did she teach me to cheat? I couldn't possibly comment.

Neapolitan Card Game
Scopa

These are the simplified rules Marietta taught me. Francesca, you usually beat me. Do you cheat?

The Game

Scopa is a card game played round kitchen tables and bars all over the south of Italy. The whole charm of the game is the ritual of friendly competition and comradeship that goes with it. A bit of showmanship is needed. The cry of 'scopa' must be made with a superior flourish; losing cards must be tossed on to the table with a flick of the wrist and disinterested grunt!

The Strategy

To be first to reach the score of 11 or 21. The score is agreed at the start of the game. To win the game you should try to collect as many diamonds as possible, hunt for the 'settebello'. Collect as many cards as you can, paying special attention to face cards and 7s and 6s.

Watch what cards have been played and hold on to good cards until you see an opportunity to match them.

If all else fails, cheat!

The Cards

The Neapolitan cards are beautifully decorated with ancient, exotic symbols. There is no 8, 9 or 10 in the pack. If you don't have Neapolitan cards, use a standard pack of cards, taking out the 8, 9 and 10. The Queen, usually a young boy, carries a value of 8. Jack, an elaborate fighter on a horse, has the value of 9, and the King, a value of 10.

The cards with a golden sun symbol are classed as diamonds, the 7 of diamonds, the 'settebello', being the most prized card in the pack.

The object of the game is to use the cards in your hand to buy cards from the table, placing priority to diamonds, 7s and 6s. If the player manages to buy all the cards on the table a point is scored with the cry of 'scopa' causing suitable disappointment and nervousness in the minds of the opponents.

The Rules

For two to four players. A game will take on average four deals of the pack. Scores are checked after each deal is played.

To begin the dealer shuffles the cards well and invites the player to his left to cut the pack. He then deals four cards face up on the table, and gives three cards face down to each player.

Player to the left of the dealer plays first. Each hand of three cards is played, one card at a time, working round the table anti-clockwise.

A player should use the cards in his hand to take cards on the table to the same value, either with the exact same value, i.e. a 7 takes a 7, or the accumulated value, i.e. 7 can take 1 + 6, 2 + 5, 3 +4, etc.

The player must take the card with the face value first, i.e. the 7 if it is on the table.

Cards picked up during the game are kept in a pile, face down, to be added when all the cards have been dealt.

If there is no card to match any of the player's cards then he must lose a card on to the table. If the player can clear all the cards on the table they call 'scopa'. The scopa card is kept on the player's pile, face up.

At the end of the round, when the last player plays his final card, the player who picked up cards last takes all those remaining on the table.

The next dealer is the player who was sitting to the left of the first dealer.

The Points

At the end of the round points are tallied.

A 'scopa' scores a point.
    The player with the most cards scores a point.
    The player with the most diamonds scores a point
    The player with the 'settebello' scores a point
    The 'primiera' scores a point, the player with the most 7s and 6s, 7s taking priority.
    The player with the most face cards scores a point.
    If there is no clear winner for each point then no score is taken.

The 'settebello', 7 of diamonds, and the 6, the most prized cards of the pack

The Winner

The cars are dealt for subsequent games until one player reaches a score of 11 or 21.

'Buona fortuna!'

Water
ACQUA

I suppose it's because they had to walk to 'la fontana' to fill jars of water that my grandparents had such a respect for it. They drank it always at table, drank it during the day and used it as a basis for soups and stocks. Marietta always appreciated the sheer luxury of running water in her kitchen. Hugh had a similar respect for a commodity we take for granted. Every morning he took a freezing cold shower first thing. He then drank a daily tumbler of warm water to keep his insides regular!

Annunziata, on the other hand, distrusted water. 'Water rusts ships at sea. So imagine what it does to your insides'! She categorically refused to drink it, insisting only on drinking wine – or brandy.

Use water with respect. Drink tap water, but always let it run for 2–3 minutes first. Get into the habit of drinking pure water during the day instead of sweet drinks or tea or coffee. I think it's recommended you drink ten thousand million gallons a day, drink whatever's comfortable for you.

Wine
VINO

'Chi mangia senza bere, mura a secco.' 'Who eats without drinking, builds without mortar.'

Our family ate around the table and on Sundays and special occasions, there was wine. As far as I remember, it was always Chianti Ruffino in the straw flask. We always sat around the table, a mixture of ages, at least ten or twelve in all. The dinner would take 2–3 hours and the afternoon would drift away.

As a special treat we children could have Dunbar's lemonade.

We were offered a tumbler of lemonade and, when the wine was being poured for the adults, our lemonade was tinged a glorious pink with a splash of Chianti. As we got older, the colour of our cocktail became redder and more alcoholic. This early experience taught us to respect alcohol as well as food, and to drink wine with our meal.

Coffee
CAFFE

Use a Moka espresso machine to make great Italian coffee at home.

The principle is simple. Fill the bottom of the pot with cold water as far as the safety valve. Fill the filter with good coffee ground freshly for espresso, very fine. Flatten the coffee but don't press it down too much. Put the filter on to the bottom of the pot and screw the top, with the spout, on top.

Put the Moka on to a low gas or electricity, being careful to keep the handle away from the heat. Leave the lid open.

As the water heats and comes to the boil it spurts and bubbles up through the grounds and coffee starts to splutter out of the middle spout. Lower the heat and let all the water spurt up through the coffee making a very intense, good concentrated caffè. This coffee needs a couple of teaspoons of sugar.

CAPPUCCINO

'Cappuccino' is named after the Capuchin monks who wore long white robes with very fetching hoods. It is downed in the morning to break the fast with a brioche or pastry. An Italian would never dream of drinking cappuccino after dinner, never mind with his pizza and chips!

To make cappuccino at home buy a small milk frother, and add some frothed-up hot milk to a piping hot espresso made in the Moka. The proportion of milk to coffee should be about two to one.

If you really are an addict, ask your best friend to buy you a Baby Gaggia. At £200 and £1.50 a cappuccino outside, it'll have paid its way in 133.33 days!

Sambuca with Flies
SAMBUCA CON LE MOSCHE

Sambuca is the colourless viscous liqueur often drunk by the 'ciociarie'. It is often hidden in the espresso, giving the strong black coffee a natural sweetness and aniseed alcoholic kick, an espresso 'corretto'.

Alternatively, give a coffee kick to the liqueur by drinking it with two or three 'flies' – espresso coffee beans – sunk at the bottom, crunching them with the sweet liquid. The restaurant practice of setting light to the Sambuca is good for sales, but does act to burn off some of the alcohol, defeating the purpose, I would think.

Biscuits
CIAMBELLE

Just to keep the party going. a plate of 'ciambelle' would be placed on the table. These are sweet hard biscuits, just perfect to dip into wine or liqueur.

Zia Pierina, Alfonso's daughter-in-law, still makes them today, exactly the same way they have always been made in Picinisco. As with all the cooking we do, the recipes are never written down, they are learned by example and taste. This is exactly how Zia Pierina explained to me how she makes them:

'You need 2 cups of oil, not olive oil, just ordinary oil. 2 cups sugar, ordinary sugar. You need some aniseed, a good lot to get a good taste. Mix in one egg. Now, this is the secret and I don't know how to tell you. You need flour. Self-raising flour. No, not 2 cups, just enough to make a dough, not too stiff, not too sticky. Now, roll out the biscuits, dip one side in sugar and bake them in the oven' . . .

Lemon Liqueur
LIMONCELLO

Annunziata always made home-made limoncello. The thick-skinned sweet Amalfi lemons are so prolific along the Amalfi coast, almost every home has a tree in their backyard groaning with the fruits.

You may not be able to find Amalfi lemons, so substitute organic lemons. These are her granddaughter Carla Silni's notes on how she remembers Nonna made it. You'll need a large sterilised glass or kilner jar, about 1.5 litres, large enough to hold the ingredients and able to be sealed to stop evaporation (Carla is a trained chemist).

the skin of 6 or 8 unwaxed Amalfi lemons
1 litre pure alcohol or Polish Spirit
1 litre water
900 g granulated sugar

Amalfi lemons are unwaxed, but wash the skins well anyway.
Skin the lemons, cutting the skins wafer thin, with no pith, so
that they are yellow on both sides. Put the skins into the sterilised kilner jar and fill it with the alcohol. Leave it for about
seven days in a dark cool place so that the lemon infuses the
alcohol. It will take on a lovely yellow colour.

Dissolve the sugar slowly in the water. Use cold water if
you want the finished liqueur to be dense and thick.
Lukewarm if you want it lighter. Once dissolved, add to the
alcohol and lemon skins. Leave to settle for about an hour.

Filter the contents through a stainless-steel sieve lined with
coarse muslin and then again lined with fine muslin to get rid
of any impurities. The limoncello is now ready to bottle in
sterilised bottles (beer bottles with a flip seal are perfect).
Store it in a cool dark place.

When you start to use it, serve it straight from the freezer,
well chilled.

Dear Francesca

My grandfather's and your dad's grandfather's lives were intertwined.
They knew each other and each other's families in Italy and they helped
one another when they came to live in Scotland.

In 1934, when Nonno Alfonso went into partnership with a conti-
nental food importer in Edinburgh and founded Valvona & Crolla Ltd,
Nonno Cesidio was the first to wish him well. I never knew either of
them, but have learned to love them from stories and images of them we
have cherished over the years.

These great men were your great-grandfathers. I hope you've come to
know and love them in these pages.

All my love
Mummy

*Cockenzie 1 Settembre 1934
anno XII*

*Carissimo Compare
Ho ricevuto il Vostro avviso
al principio di un'altro
Vostro nuovo Negozio.
Io con mia famiglia
vi mandiamo le nostre
Congratulazioni.
E con tutto cuore vi
auguriamo ogni via di
Successo
Insieme Vostra cara famiglia
auguriamo ancora
Salute e prosperità
Saluti affettuosi
Vostro Compare Cesidio*

*The two great grandfathers:
Alfonso Crolla
in uniform, c.1920 (above),
Cesidio Di Ciacca, c.1922 (below)*

Cockenzie 1st September 1934

Dearest Buddy
I have your notice that you are opening another
shop. I and my family send you our congrats
with hearty good wishes that you are on the
road to success together with your family.
Again good wishes for health and prosperity.

Affectionate greetings
Your Pal Cesidio

Our family all together, still enjoying good food!

INDEX

All my love, Mummy

Acknowledgements
Thank you to all who have helped and encouraged me in countless ways. Thanks to everyone at Ebury Press, especially Fiona MacIntyre, Denise Bates and Sarah Bennie. To Susan Fleming for her invaluable advice and editing and Vanessa Courtier for inspired design. To my agent, Giles Gordon, and Nicky Stonehill at Coleman Getty. For advice and for testing recipes, thank you to Gertrude Di Ciacca, Olivia Contini, Carina Contini, Carrie Anne Baxter and Pina Trano. To Cesidio Di Ciacca, Joe Conetta, Mary Conetta, Carlo Contini and also Winnie Tyrrell at the People's Palace Glasgow for use of photographs. To Mitch Jenkins for the pictures of our family party. Love especially to uncle Tricky Vicky who gave me his research and old manuscripts documenting family history. And most of all, thanks to my daughters Francesca and Olivia, and my darling Philip, all my love, always.

Bibliography
Colpi, Terri, *Italians Forward*, Mainstream, 1991; Colpi, Terri, *The Italian Factor*, Mainstream, 1991; Field, Carol, *Celebrating Italy*, Harper Perennial, 1997; Gray, Patience, *Honey From A Weed*, Prospect Books, 1986; Lawrence, DH, *The Lost Girl*, 1921; Root, Waverly, *The Food of Italy*, Vintage, 1971; Shephard, Sue, *Pickled, Potted & Canned*, Headline, 2000

Valvona & Crolla Ltd,
19 Elm Row, Edinburgh EH7 4AA Tel: 0131 556 6066
www.valvonacrolla.com (On-line shopping and mail order)

DH Lawrence letter reproduced by kind permission of Laurence Pollinger Limited and the Estate of Frieda Lawrence Ravagli.
Photograph: Department of Manuscripts and Special Collections, University of Nottingham ref. La C7